CAREER PLANNING in CRIMINAL JUSTICE

3rd Edition

Robert C.
DE LUCIA

John Jay College of Criminal Justice

Thomas J.
DOYLE

John Jay College of Criminal Justice

anderson publishing co.
2035 Reading Road
Cincinnati, OH 45202
800-582-7295

Career Planning in Criminal Justice, Third Edition

Copyright © 1990, 1994, 1998
Anderson Publishing Co.
2035 Reading Rd.
Cincinnati, OH 45202

Phone 800.582.7295 or 513.421.4142
Web Site www.andersonpublishing.com

Library of Congress Cataloging-in-Publication Data

De Lucia, Robert C.
  Career planning in criminal justice / Robert C. De Lucia, Thomas J. Doyle. -- 3rd ed.
      p.   cm.
  Includes bibliographical references.
  ISBN 0-87084-209-9 (paperback)
  1. Criminal justice, Administration of--Vocational guidance--United States.
I. Doyle, Thomas J., M.A.   II. Title.
HV9950.D45   1998
364 ' .023 ' 73--dc21   98-22531
                                                                     CIP

Cover design by Tin Box Studio/Cincinnati, OH

EDITOR Gail Eccleston
ACQUISITIONS EDITOR Michael C. Braswell

ACKNOWLEDGMENTS

We are deeply indebted to those colleagues and individuals who so graciously lent their professional expertise and support to this book.

To Gerald W. Lynch, Ph.D., President, John Jay College of Criminal Justice; to Roger Witherspoon, Ed.D., Vice President for Student Development; George Best, Assistant Dean of Students; Carina Quintian, Administrative Associate for job placement for her help with the research on criminal justice Web sites; and Paul Wyatt, Executive Director of Career Services.

Special thanks to Matt Larko and Elizabeth Defranco for their research assistance; Jessica Usera for her typing support; to Yvonne Purdie for her career counseling expertise; Premwati Sukhan for her internship and cooperative education experience; to Gail Eccleston, our Editor in the Criminal Justice Division at Anderson Publishing Co., for her patience, support, and helpful guidance; and to Ed Latessa, Ph.D., University of Cincinnati, for his initial constructive suggestions in the development of this text.

In loving memory of my mom and dad, Mary and Thomas, with deepest love for my wife Michelle, my son T.J., and my daughter Shayne Nicole.

T.J.D.

To Maria, Benjamin, and Matthew, of course.

R.C.D.

To those criminal justice professionals who put their lives on the line each and every day.

T.J.D. and R.C.D.

CONTENTS

Introduction
A CAREER IN CRIMINAL JUSTICE:
PREPARING FOR DIVERSE EMPLOYMENT OPPORTUNITIES   *xv*

Chapter 1
THE VALUE OF CAREER PLANNING AND EDUCATION   1

The Value of Career Planning and Education 1
    A Job Versus a Career 2
    What is Career Planning? 2
    Why Plan a Career? 3
    The Importance of a College Education 3

Strategies for College Success 4
    Develop a Positive Attitude 4
    Develop Good Study Habits 5
    Know Your Library 5
    Basic Skills Proficiency 5
    Joining Clubs, Activities 6

Learning About Yourself in Relation to a Career Choice 6
    Your Interests 7
    Your Work Values 7
    Your Abilities 7

College Resource Personnel 8
    Counselors 8
    Career Advisers 8
    Faculty Advisers 9

Gathering Information About Criminal Justice Careers 9

Image Versus Reality: Careers in Criminal Justice 10

Women and Minorities in Criminal Justice 12

Summary 13

Career Planning Activities/Questions 14

Chapter 2
CAREERS IN LAW ENFORCEMENT   19

   Federal Law Enforcement 20
      Air Safety Investigator 20
      Alcohol, Tobacco, and Firearms Inspector 20
      Alcohol, Tobacco, and Firearms Special Agent 21
      Customs Aide 23
      Customs Canine Enforcement Officer 24
      Customs Import Specialist 24
      Customs Inspector 25
      Customs Patrol Officer 26
      Customs Pilot 27
      Customs Special Agent 28
      Deputy U.S. Marshal 29
      Diplomatic Security, Special Agent 31
      Drug Enforcement Special Agent 32
      Federal Bureau of Investigation Special Agent 33
      Investigator, U.S. Investigations Services, Inc. 35
      Federal Protective Service Officer/Criminal Investigator 36
      Fish and Wildlife Service, Special Agent 37
      Immigration and Naturalization Service, Border Patrol Agent 38
      Immigration and Naturalization Criminal Investigator 40
      Immigration and Naturalization Deportation Officer 41
      Immigration and Naturalization Inspector 41
      Inspector General Investigator 42
      Internal Revenue Criminal Investigator 43
      Intelligence Support Analyst. 44
      Internal Security Inspector, Internal Revenue Service 44
      Labor and Pension Compliance Investigator, Department of Labor 45
      Naval Investigative Service/Criminal Investigator 46
      Park Police (United States) 47
      Postal Service Inspector 48
      Secret Service Agent 50
      Secret Service Uniformed Officer 51
      Securities Compliance Examiner 52

  State and Municipal Law Enforcement 53
      Deputy Sheriff 53
      Environmental Conservation Officer 54
      Investigator (State, County, Municipal) 55
      State Police Officer/State Trooper 56
      Police Officer (Municipal) 57

Chapter 3
CAREERS IN THE COURTS 59

Attorney/Lawyer 59
Bailiff (Court Officer) 61
Court Administrator 62
Court Clerk 63
Court Liaison Counselor 64
Court Reporter (Short-Hand Reporter) 65
Court Representative 65
Domestic Violence Counselor 66
Judge 66
Paralegal/Legal Assistant 67
Pretrial Services Officer, U.S. District Courts 68
Release-on-Own-Recognizance (ROR) Interviewer 69
Research Analyst/Statistician 70
Support Services Coordinator 71
Site Supervisor 71
Victim Services Personnel 72
    Victim Services Specialist 72
    Child and Youth Counselor 72
    Crisis Counselor 73
    Runaway Counselor 74
    Homicide Victim Counselor 74

Chapter 4
CAREERS IN CORRECTIONS 77

Correctional Treatment Specialist (Federal Prison) 77
Corrections Counselor 78
Corrections Officer 79
Juvenile Justice Counselor 80
Parole Officer 81
Pre-Release Program Correctional Counselor 83
Pre-Release Program Employment Counselor 84
Pre-Release Program Halfway House Manager 84
Probation Officer 85
Juvenile Probation Officer 86
Warden 87

Other Related Corrections Occupations 88

Chapter 5
CAREERS IN FORENSIC SCIENCE/CRIMINALISTICS 91

Criminalistics 91
Ballistics Specialist 92
Toolmark Specialist 92
Serology Specialist 92
Fingerprint Specialist 92

Arson Specialist 93
Document Specialist 93
Polygraph Specialist 93

The Crime Laboratories 93
Federal Bureau of Investigation 93
Bureau of Alcohol, Tobacco, and Firearms 94
U.S. Customs Service 96
Drug Enforcement Administration 96

Qualifications for Employment 97

Chapter 6
CAREERS IN PRIVATE SECURITY   99

Diverse Employment Opportunities 99
Retail Security 100
Commercial Security 100
Institutional Security 100
Industrial Security 101

Job Responsibilities 102
Administrator/Manager 102
Investigator 102
Technician 103
Protective Specialist 103

Qualifications for Employment 104

Chapter 7
HEARING FROM CRIMINAL JUSTICE PROFESSIONALS   105

Assistant District Attorney 106
Civilian Aviation Security Specialist 106
Confidential Investigator 106
Conservation Police Officer 107
Consumer Safety Officer 107
Correctional Officer 107
Criminal Investigator 108
Customs Inspector 108
Deputy U.S. Marshal 109
Evidence Unit Technician 109
General Duty Road Trooper 109
Internal Revenue Agent 110
Loss Prevention Auditor/Investigator 110
Narcotics Agent 110
Personnel Administrator 111
Police Officer 111
Police Officer/Recruiter 112
Principal Court Analyst 112
Probation Officer 112

Probation/Parole Officer 113
Special Agent 113
Special Agent/Defense Investigative Service 114
Special Agent, Secret Service 114

Chapter 8
TESTING THE WATERS: THE VALUE OF INTERNSHIP EXPERIENCE   117

The Importance of Internships 117

Where to Arrange for an Internship 118

How to Make the Most Out of an Internship 119

Chapter 9
GETTING A FOOT IN THE DOOR – COOPERATIVE EDUCATION
PROGRAMS IN CRIMINAL JUSTICE   121

Federal Agency Cooperative Education Programs 123
The Federal Bureau of Investigation Summer Honors
   Internship Program 123
      Qualifications 123
      Application Requirements 124
      Application Time Frame 124
      Selection Process 125
      Things You Should Know 125
U.S. Secret Service Cooperative Education
   Employment Opportunity 126
      Criminal Investigator (Special Agent Co-Op Positions) 126
      General Qualification Requirements 126
      Work Schedule 127
      How to Apply ... 127
U.S. Customs Inspector Cooperative Education Program 128
      Application Procedure and Requirements 128
U.S. Marshals Service Centralized Student
   Career Experience Program 128
      Co-Op Requirements for Deputy U.S. Marshal 129
Drug Enforcement Administration "Q" Appointment Program 130
      Requirements 130
Federal Bureau of Prisons Cooperative Education Case Manager 131
      Requirements 131
      Method of Application 131
U.S. Department of Justice, Office of Inspector General, Cooperative
   Education Investigative Clerk 131
      Requirements 132
      Method of Application 132

Chapter 10
TEST TAKING: AN IMPORTANT ASPECT
OF CRIMINAL JUSTICE EMPLOYMENT   133

   Seeking Out Job Openings and Test Dates.... 133

   Beginning the Test Preparation Process 134
      Tips to Prepare for the Test 134
      Tips to Help You During the Test 135

   Specific Test Preparation for Law Enforcement Careers 136
      Preparation/Practice Books Help 137

   Six Important Skills on Which You Will Be Tested 137
      Memory/Observation Skills 137
         Tips for Answering These Questions 138
      Judgment Skills 139
         Tips for Answering These Questions 139
      Verbal Comprehension/Expression Skills 141
         Tips for Answering These Questions 142
      Map Reading/Spatial Orientation Skills 144
         Tips for Answering These Questions 144
      Interpretation/Reasoning Skills 146
         Tips for Answering These Questions 147
      General Math Skills 149
         Tips for Answering These Questions 150

   Coming to Terms with Test Anxiety 150
      What Are the Sources of Test Anxiety? 150
      How Do I Cope with Test Anxiety? 153
      Tips for Dealing with Test Anxiety 153

Chapter 11
THE JOB HUNT   157

   Contacts: People Who Can Help 157

   The Résumé/Cover Letter Approach 158
      The Résumé 158
         Basic Information 158
         Objective 158
         Education 159
         Experience 159
         Sample Résumé 160
         Sample Résumé 161
         Sample Cover Letter 162
         Extracurricular Activities 163
         Personal 163
         References 163
      The Cover Letter 163

   The Civil Service Approach 163

The U.S. Office of Personnel Management 164

The New Road to Federal Employment 165

Excepted Service Agencies 168

Outstanding Scholar Program 169
What Is the Outstanding Scholar Program? 169
Requirements for the Oustanding Scholar Program 169
How to Apply as an Outstanding Scholar 169

Law Enforcement and Investigative Jobs 170

Professional-Related Administrative Jobs 170

People with Disabilities 170
Job Opportunities for People with Disabilities 170
Competitive Appointments 171
Selective Placement 171
How to Qualify for Selective Placement Opportunities 172
Disabled Veterans and Other Veteran Opportunities 172
Reasonable Workplace Accommodations 172

Federal Job Scams 173
Consumer Alert – Federal Job Fraud 173

Administrative Careers With America (ACWA) 174

The Job Interview 176
Phase I: Preparation 176
Phase II: Initial Meeting 177
Phase III: Information Sharing 178
Phase IV: The Closing 179
Phase V: After the Interview 180

Chapter 12
USING THE INTERNET TO GET A JOB IN THE CRIMINAL JUSTICE FIELD 181

The Internet: What Is It Really? 181

Get Connected! 182

Full Internet Access 183

Crawling Around the Web 184

Cybersleuthing 184

Jump In – The Water's Fine! 185

Sites with Links 185

Other Law Enforcement Web Sites Worth Mentioning 186

Government Job Sites 189

Applying On-Line 189

Border Patrol Agent On-Line Application 190

Chapter 13
PURSUING FURTHER EDUCATION
TO ENHANCE CAREER OPPORTUNITY   193

Considering Graduate or Law School 193
Deciding on Graduate or Law School 194

BIBLIOGRAPHY   197

Career Planning Sources 197

Criminal Justice Sources 198

Periodicals 200

RESOURCES FOR FURTHER CAREER INFORMATION   203

Law Enforcement 203
Federal Law Enforcement Agencies 203
State Police-Highway Agencies 205
County/Local Law Enforcement Agencies 210
Professional Organizations, Societies 210

Courts 210
Federal Level 210
State and Local Levels 210
Professional Organizations, Societies 211

Corrections 211
Federal Level 211
State and Local Levels 212
Departments of Corrections 212

Academic Forensic Science Programs 214
U.S. Forensic Science Labs 215
Professional Organizations, Societies 219

Security 220
Professional Organizations, Societies 220

Federal Job Information Centers 220

About the Authors 225

INTRODUCTION

A Career in Criminal Justice: Preparing for Diverse Employment Opportunities

We are pleased to bring to you this new edition of *Career Planning in Criminal Justice*. The importance of this book is even more apparent today than when it was first published in 1990, as the nature of work in this field continues to evolve, expand, and become more competitive. Students not only need to be informed of the various employment possibilities in this field, they also need to be armed with the information regarding how to assess information using the latest technology in order to be well prepared to obtain employment upon graduation.

Today's criminal justice professional is expected to be well-educated, possessing both strong writing and communication skills. There is also pressure for prospective candidates to be better trained in a variety of specialized areas as the work becomes increasingly complex and technical. Glamorized and lured by what seems to be an endless array of television shows depicting today's criminal justice professionals, there has been an increase in the number of students pursuing these careers. Across the country, criminal justice educational degree programs are being developed to meet student demand. Increased student interest fosters increased job competition, particularly for those positions considered most prestigious (e.g., the Federal Bureau of Investigation, the Secret Service, and the Drug Enforcement Administration). Although employment in this career field can be competitive, diverse opportunities exist – especially for those who are well prepared. Given the unfortunate fact that crime exists and continues to rise, employment opportunities in areas that ensure the safety of our society will continue to be favorable, particularly at the entry level. Recent data provided by the Bureau of Labor Statistics indicate that careers in protective services are expected to rise faster than average, although keen competition for the higher paying careers is noted.

Where will these opportunities exist? Career opportunities in criminal justice generally can be categorized into five major fields: law enforcement, the courts, corrections, forensic science, and private security. In these career fields, criminal justice professionals function to prevent and control crime, shield the public from harm, provide detention and rehabilitation services, and finally, ensure equal justice for all citizens through the judicial system. Job opportunities exist at the federal, state, and local levels of governmental jurisdiction. The private sector has also demonstrated an increasing need to employ criminal justice professionals within its organizations and agencies.

This book introduces the range of employment opportunities that exist, while emphasizing that choosing and attaining employment in the criminal justice system will be largely dependent upon successful planning and preparation. Regardless of whether you are just beginning college or are ready to graduate, you must first actively engage in a career development process that not only includes gaining information about the criminal justice field, but knowledge about yourself as well as your values, interests, and abilities in relation to a career choice.

This book is meant to be a practical guide in that it provides you with the essential information needed for planning a career in criminal justice. Each chapter is designed to help you accomplish this task, although some chapters may be more relevant to you and your individual needs.

Chapter 1 describes why career planning and education are important. Since a college degree is becoming an increasingly important prerequisite for employment in the criminal justice field, several strategies are provided to help you make the best of your college experience.

In Chapters 2 through 6, you will be introduced to a variety of occupations within the law enforcement, corrections, courts, forensic science, and private security fields. While it would be impossible to cover all of the opportunities that exist in these fields, you will find a representative sampling of occupations in this book. Job responsibilities and qualifications for employment will be discussed. Specific salaries have been omitted deliberately because they vary greatly, depending upon education, experience, and geographic region. However, timely, specific wage information is not difficult for you to obtain on your own.

Subsequently, in Chapter 7 you will be provided a chance to hear from some criminal justice professionals. This material is intended to illustrate realistic, accurate descriptions of some of the careers within this field, as seen through the eyes of those who actually perform these jobs. It is hoped that you will find this section interesting and informative.

Chapter 8 strongly urges you to "test the waters." In other words, you are advised to gain relevant work experience in a particular field through volunteering. The concept of enrolling in an internship program is discussed as the best means of learning about criminal justice careers firsthand. Engaging in such a process will increase the likelihood of your attaining a career that is best suited to your interests and abilities.

Chapter 9, a new edition to the text, provides yet another vehicle to obtain valuable work experience in the criminal justice field. In this chapter you will learn about a variety of exciting cooperative educational programs (paid work experiences) that are available for qualified students. These highly sought after programs not only provide students with true on-the-job training and experience, they often serve to insure the likelihood of job placement upon graduation.

Chapter 10, another new edition to our text, covers an extremely important aspect of criminal justice employment – test taking. All too often students miss out on job opportunities because they have not passed the necessary qualifying exams. This important chapter introduces the importance of test taking and provides students with specific strategies and suggestions to enhance their performance on exams. Sample test questions are provided, as well as suggestions on how to locate job announcements, exam dates and times, and information regarding how best to prepare. A college degree, coupled with some hands-on experience in a particular field, will enable you to pursue your first full-time professional position.

Chapter 11, "The Job Hunt," provides the information and tools necessary to meet this challenge. In this chapter you will learn how to write a résumé and prepare for a job interview.

Chapter 12, perhaps the most important new addition to the text, focuses on the utilization of computer technology to assist you with the job search. In this highly sophisticated computer age there are now a variety of job placement strategies that can be employed using the Internet. This simple, easy-to-follow chapter helps students begin the process of learning how to obtain immediate access to job information including job descriptions, what is currently open, and how to apply – in some cases "on-line," using your computer. Important Web sites for criminal justice employment have been identified for you, thus making the job search easy and comprehensive.

Chapter 13 discusses graduate or law school as considerations. Students are encouraged to see the value of advanced educational training in preparation for entry-level job placement as well as advancement while employed.

To further assist you in your job search, "Resources for Further Career Information" at the back of the book provides an extensive list of resources such as agency addresses and a bibliography of books, directories, and other references, so that you can continue to collect information beyond the scope of what has been made available here. You are also provided with the most recent Web sites and E-mail addresses so that you can obtain current information in a fast, simple, and expedient way.

In the final analysis, the *real effort* will be yours, in taking the time to make use of suggestions and going beyond the information provided. While there is never a guarantee that you will end up in the career of your choice, this book is intended to provide a good foundation from which to begin working toward your career aspirations and goals. Keep in mind that what you are doing *today* will, in fact determine what you will become *tomorrow*.

Chapter 1

The Value of Career Planning and Education

If you have built castles in the air, your work need not be lost; that is where they should be . . . Now put the foundations under them.
— Henry David Thoreau

The very first step towards success in any occupation is to become interested in it. To find out what one is fitted to do and to secure an opportunity to do it is the key to happiness.
— John Dewey

The Value of Career Planning and Education

Few jobs in the criminal justice system are the products of good fortune and luck. Individuals who have been successful in attaining employment usually report that their success was the result of a series of preparatory steps that took place over time. You may be asking yourself, "Where or how do I begin?" You may feel confused or uncertain about what the future holds for you. This is a natural feeling for individuals embarking upon a career search. The first step is simple, yet important. It is important to understand the value of career planning and education. Essential to this notion is the idea that you have the ability to influence the course of events in your life. The winds of fate are not going to blow you into an exciting career in criminal justice. There are few, if any, shortcuts to successful career attainment. Your success will depend on the quality and amount of contribution you make to this process, and career planning and education can assist you in reaching your career goals.

A Job Versus a Career

What is a job? What is a career? Most people spend a large part of their lives working, yet rarely take the time to think about what particular job they might want to do or, for that matter, what a particular job means to them.

Generally speaking, work is an activity that we are paid to perform. Although there are important activities performed without pay (school work, housework), for the most part, work is a process through which one earns the resources to support himself or herself financially.

A person's quality of life can be greatly enhanced by work, or a job, which is right for him or her. What is a job and how does it differ from work or a career?

A job refers to the particular position a person holds or the particular work performed for pay in that position. A career, in contrast to a job, is work that an individual chooses to pursue involving a long-term work commitment to a specific occupational field. A career requires a significant level of formal education, training, and background to successfully perform in the work area.

A career is more than the job one performs, or the field in which one works. A career has longer-lasting impact on one's self, one's family, and one's lifestyle. It is important to spend considerable time thinking about your life's work. Your life will be greatly enhanced by choosing a career that you find personally meaningful. The ideal situation is one in which you enjoy and earn money doing a job in the career of your choice, and that requires planning.

What is Career Planning?

Do you ever wonder about how and why people end up in certain careers? Perhaps you feel that people with good career positions are "lucky" or that they must have had a contact (relative, friend, or acquaintance) in the right place. Sometimes, having contacts in the right places can be a key factor in getting a job. However, you are mistaken if you believe this is how most people reach their career objectives. Most often, students who have successfully found employment in the criminal justice field planned carefully and worked hard in order to achieve their career goals.

Career planning is a way of thinking about your future. It starts with the understanding that you should be concerned and involved in your future career goals. Career planning is an active process that takes place over time. It involves self-assessment, setting realistic career goals and, finally, accepting the responsibility to chart a plan of action to make it happen. A career plan must be flexible and will need to be revised and altered as situations arise, or as you change. It is likely that what you want at one point in your life may not be what you want five years later. An important part of career planning is the notion that you must be open and flexible to change as new information and experiences unfold.

Why Plan a Career?

Did you ever take the time to talk with someone who really enjoys their job? This person would proudly tell you that they derive satisfaction and happiness from the work they do. You, too, should be happy with your career choice. Think about the number of years you will spend working. The choice of a career becomes a major decision when you think in these terms. Of course, career planning implies that there is work to be done. It also implies that there are risks to be taken. You can overcome the possibility of failure by understanding what you need to do in order to succeed. A career plan provides reassuring guidance along with step-by-step manageable tasks which lead to successful career attainment.

To begin planning for a career in criminal justice, your first consideration will be to explore the feasibility of earning a college degree. A college degree plays a key role in determining how successful you will be in obtaining a career within the criminal justice field.

The Importance of a College Education

Many people thinking about employment in the criminal justice field ask the question, "Is college really necessary?" All indicators reveal that a college degree has taken on additional value, as many criminal justice agencies are changing and upgrading their educational requirements for entry-level employment. Even the field of "uniformed" law enforcement (traditionally requiring only a high school diploma) is moving toward a trend that seeks to establish a college education as a requirement for employment. In some police departments across the nation, this requirement is already being enforced. It appears that the continued support for higher education for police officers, corrections officers, and other criminal justice professionals will grow. Even individuals who are currently working in the field without a college degree are being encouraged to further their education.

The value of and support for higher education are also documented by the fact that numerous criminal justice educational programs are being offered across the nation. Such college programs provide students with the opportunity to major or specialize in criminal justice and other related disciplines. These programs exist at a variety of levels (associate degrees, bachelor's degrees, master's degrees and doctoral degrees) and can provide the educational requirements necessary for employment. As a general rule, the bachelor's degree is the minimum entry-level requirement for many criminal justice positions.

Strategies for College Success

All wish to possess knowledge but few, comparatively speaking, are willing to pay the price.

—Juvenal

A college education plays a critical role in determining how successful you will be in attaining a career in the criminal justice field. If you want to fulfill your dreams of working in this field, the next step is to understand the challenges and responsibilities of being a good college student. Many college students never make it as far as graduation. These individuals have not successfully adjusted to the many demands of higher education. Subsequently, the career plans for many of these students are short-lived.

Regardless of your college status, you must earn the best possible grades you can. Think of your college education as a job, and as your next step in the career preparation process. Keep in mind that prospective employers in the criminal justice field may be looking very closely at your college records.

Below are some basic suggestions on how to make the most of your college experience.

Develop a Positive Attitude

Your attitude toward learning is a key factor in determining whether you will succeed in college. You must have a strong desire to do well. Attitudes often develop from your past experiences. Students who have had good experiences with school are likely to be highly motivated. What if you have experienced school in a less than positive light? Perhaps you were not a good student in high school or during your first couple of semesters in college. It is quite possible that on some level, conscious or not, you cannot envision yourself as a good student. This kind of attitude must, and can, change. Ask yourself these questions:

- How powerful is my desire to succeed?

- To what extent do I believe I can make it?

Be honest in your responses. If the answers to these questions are negative, it will be difficult, but not impossible, for you to develop strategies to help you overcome the rigorous demands of academic life. Begin carefully to examine your attitudes. With a more positive attitude, you will be more likely to work harder and, subsequently, you will reach your goals. The successes, however small, become the motivation to continue the pattern.

Develop Good Study Habits

Good study habits are the most important characteristic of a successful student. Some good students may tell you that they hardly study at all; however, most good students work very hard to maintain good grades. In an effort to develop good study habits, you must first map out a weekly schedule of how your time is currently being utilized. How much time do you spend studying? Working part-time? Traveling to and from school? When and where do you think you are wasting time? A weekly time chart can serve as a framework to help you organize your daily activities. How much time should be spent studying? This is difficult to answer. It varies with each student and depends on how difficult the subjects are for you, how many classes you are taking, and how you go about studying. On most college campuses there are workshops that address the topics of time management and study skills.

Know Your Library

Visit your library. Start by getting a general impression of its layout and atmosphere. Gain familiarity with the card catalog, circulation desk, reference section, book stacks, periodicals, newspapers and special collections. After you have made an honest attempt to familiarize yourself with the resources, do not hesitate to ask for assistance. One of the most valuable resources may be the librarian. There is much to learn about how your library is organized. You will need to understand how to operate its various audiovisual equipment and how to locate the various books, articles, and other references that are vital to your schoolwork. Learning how to use the library effectively will save you countless hours. It is also a great place to study if you want to avoid distractions.

Basic Skills Proficiency

To be successful in college, you must make an honest and accurate assessment of your academic preparation. Your college will be helpful to you in this respect as it is quite likely that you will be asked to take a variety of proficiency exams (English, math, reading) prior to entrance. Find out the scores and make sure you understand them. If you find that you are in need of tutoring, make it your first order of business to take the classes that are advised. These courses are designed to improve the basic skills needed for college success. Most students make the mistake of placing too little importance on these test scores, particularly when their results are low. Such students deny that they may need help. In order to succeed in college, you must master the basic skills necessary for learning. You must learn the skills of writing a term paper (i.e., choosing a topic, collecting and organizing information and data), reading and understanding college-level texts, improving study habits, note-taking, and test-taking. Consult your school to see if there is a skills or learning center available to you. It is critical to master these basic skills, as every career field requires that you read, speak, and write effectively.

Joining Clubs, Activities

If you have the time, joining or attending the various activities sponsored by student services is an excellent way to make yourself feel more involved, more a part of your college community. Participating in clubs, student government, intramural, and other programs provides a way to build a network of friends and recreational interests that can last a lifetime. Activities outside the classroom can add to your knowledge of a particular academic subject or increase your understanding and exploration of your occupational interests, all in a relaxed social setting. By participating in a leadership capacity you will learn skills that will be helpful in later years. Employers give strong consideration to candidates who have demonstrated commitment and cooperative spirit in campus clubs and activities. However, one important point needs to be emphasized: Never involve yourself in these activities if the time you spend on them causes you to neglect your studies. Remember, maintaining and improving your grades should be your first priority because employers are not interested in students with mediocre or poor grades.

Learning About Yourself in Relation to a Career Choice

Thus far, the value of career planning and the importance of being successful in college have been emphasized. Students who do well in college feel better about themselves, are more confident, and are better able to tackle the job of exploring their interests, values, and abilities in relation to their career goals. If you have experienced academic success early on, you will be more likely to approach the career planning process with an increased sense of confidence and ambition. The desire to become an FBI agent, lawyer, corrections counselor, etc., will seem more realistic to you. With academic successes, your career goals will not seem out of reach.

The best advice for preparing yourself to make wise career decisions is to know yourself. This is the key to career planning. In assessing yourself, you will need to explore your values, interests, and abilities. This self-understanding will help you decide which occupations in criminal justice are best suited for you. This process requires repeatedly asking yourself a variety of questions that may be interesting and enjoyable at times, difficult at others. The better you are at self-exploration, the more likely you will choose an occupation that is personally meaningful. Also, you will be more assured that you will not make the mistake of finding out too late that the career you thought you wanted or could achieve is unrealistic, unattainable, or not what you had in mind. The more you learn about yourself, the more responsibility and control you will have over your career goals. This can be done by taking a close look at what is meant by interests, values, and abilities.

Your Interests

Your interests can be thought of simply as your likes or dislikes, your preference for or rejection of a variety of things. Students, for example, express an interest in a particular field of criminal justice or for a specific group of courses in college. You may like law courses but would not want to choose a career in law. What you like to do in the short run has a major bearing on what you are willing to do in the long run. What are your interests? What kinds of subjects seem interesting to you? What occupations in the criminal justice field seem attractive? Your interests are important in making a career decision. Exploring and understanding them can broaden your perspective regarding your career choice.

Your Work Values

Work values relate to those aspects of a job that are considered meaningful and important. Most people would say that work means more to them than just a paycheck. We believe you have chosen the criminal justice field because of the values you hold. What is it about work in the field of criminal justice that you expect to find rewarding? Is it the status? Money? Perceived excitement? Job security? Helping others? Leadership? What are your values and how do they relate to your career choices? These are difficult questions to answer; however, they are important questions to consider if you want your future career to provide personal satisfaction and meaning to you. Occupations differ in their ability to satisfy your values. Knowing your values provides a framework for selecting specific types of careers. It is essential that you take the time to examine your values, as they are an important part of the career development process.

Your Abilities

Your values and interests are important in your career plans, but you need corresponding abilities to ensure achieving your career goals. Interests often get confused with abilities. Although you may be interested in a career in the CIA and seek to work in a foreign country, you may not be considered if you have never learned to speak a foreign language. You may want to become a police officer, but if you have an eyesight problem you may not be eligible.

Every student has different abilities. Regardless of the experiences you have had, you possess certain strengths and weaknesses. Your job now is to begin to examine your abilities/skills. Many students have a difficult time recognizing the abilities they possess. One way for you to start examining your abilities is to review your past accomplishments. What have you done well? Consider those activities, work and school experiences that you enjoyed and that gave you a sense of accomplishment. Make a list and then think about the skills, knowledge, and personal attributes that enabled you to accomplish these tasks. Once you are able to accurately assess your abilities, you will feel more confident about choosing a career. In addition, you will recognize your weaknesses. You can then plan to build skills in areas that need improvement. Doing a self-assessment is often difficult. You may wish to seek assistance from counselors, career advisors, or faculty advisors.

College Resource Personnel

Counselors

Professional counselors are available on campus to help you if you are curious, confused, or unsure about any aspect of your college experience. Whether you are having difficulty in a course or are in need of career guidance, it is in your best interest to seek out their expertise. Counselors can play a vital role in helping you explore your interests, values, and abilities in relation to your choice of career. Counselors can administer and evaluate career interest inventories so that you will gain information about how your interests are similar or dissimilar to those of professionals working in the criminal justice field. They can help you decide what courses to take, what to major in, and how to plan for your career goals.

Career Advisers

It is vital that you take the opportunity to visit and utilize the services and resources of the career planning office. In addition to helping you find part-time and full-time jobs, this office performs a variety of other important functions. First and foremost, here is where you will find the most timely information on careers, occupational trends, hiring qualifications, and advice on job openings. In addition, recruiters set up interviews with students through the career planning office. It is advisable to make a personal appointment with a career adviser/counselor each semester. You can discuss your career plans and meet on a regular basis to assess how well you are doing. Stop by the career planning office on a regular basis and collect as much information as possible.

Faculty Advisers

Faculty advisers can be a tremendous source of information, guidance, and support. Many of these individuals are experts in their fields and have much to offer in the way of information about the criminal justice system. Seek out instructors in whose fields you have a particular interest. Take the time to get acquainted with them during their office hours or by appointment. Often times, employment in the criminal justice field or further graduate study requires recommendations from these individuals. If your work has been good and you have taken the time to know your professors, it is quite likely that you will be able to secure a recommendation that addresses both your academic and personal qualities in a favorable light.

Gathering Information About Criminal Justice Careers

> *As a general rule, the most successful man in life is the man who has the best information.*
> —Benjamin Disraeli

Up to now, several aspects of career planning have been discussed without talking specifically about criminal justice careers. This was intentional, as the focus was on you, your career values, interests, abilities, and academic achievements. These are the basic items of any successful career plan. You are now ready to begin gathering information on criminal justice careers.

In the following five chapters you will be provided with important and detailed information about prospective careers in the criminal justice system. You will soon learn that there are many challenging and diverse opportunities in this field. You may want to start by reviewing a specific job title or a particular career field. As you do, ask yourself several key questions along the way:

- What is the nature of the work? What does an individual working in the job actually do?

- Does the work sound like something I would want/like to do?

- How would I feel doing the actual work? Will the job satisfy my work interests and values?

- Do I have (or can I develop) the necessary skills/education to qualify for the job?

- If there are physical requirements, do I qualify?

- What are my realistic chances of entering this career?

Image Versus Reality: Careers in Criminal Justice

Developing a clearer understanding of whether your "perceptions and expectations" of work in the criminal justice field are accurate and realistic is vital to career satisfaction. It is not uncommon that students who plan to pursue criminal justice careers harbor erroneous and unrealistic assumptions of what the work is going to be like once employed. This is certainly understandable given the exaggerated television portrayals of these careers. The media is notorious for distorting the image of the criminal justice professional, creating an impression that does not accurately reflect the modern reality of work in this field. Unfortunately, when individuals enter these professions and engage in the actual day-to-day job responsibilities, they can become frustrated that the job is not measuring up to their expectations.

You can avoid setting yourself up for disappointment by taking a candid appraisal of your assumptions and expectations regarding criminal justice work. Below are described some common images/myths associated with criminal justice employment. The information contained in this section was shared with us by those who know best – criminal justice professionals who were asked to discuss the most common misconceptions that students associate with work in this field.

Consider the following:

Image   ***A career in criminal justice will be exciting/adventurous.***

Reality   Most professionals believed that the work of a criminal justice professional would be *more* exciting than they experienced. The so-called "danger quotient" (i.e., use of weapons, constant arrests, military drug busts, and the general adrenaline rushes) associated with fighting crime represents only a minor portion of this work. In fact, most criminal justice professionals were surprised that much of the day is spent with voluminous, tedious, and routine bureaucratic paperwork. It was also commonly reported that a good portion of the job responsibilities for many careers in this field are considered "social work." Knowing how to talk to people is considered an essential function of these careers. It is more accurate to assume that a career as a criminal justice professional is less dangerous/adventurous than it had been in the past. It is not like what is observed on television. However, professionals also agree that it has become more sophisticated, complex, and nonetheless important.

Image   *Criminal justice professionals have prestige/power.*

Reality Many are initially attracted to a criminal justice career because of the power and prestige associated with carrying a gun and badge and being in a position in which they function to protect and help others. However, professionals in the field of criminal justice commonly report feeling a sense of disappointment to learn that many in the general public do not always respect and appreciate law enforcement professionals. You also learn that your power as a criminal justice professional is limited, as extreme caution and restraint must be exercised in the performance of all duties.

Image   *A career in criminal justice is high paying with steady hours/shifts.*

Reality With the exception of municipal uniformed police officers, many working in the field of criminal justice report that starting salaries are often inadequate. However, those who have been working in their positions for some time, particularly at the federal level, report more satisfaction with their earnings. The bottom line – do not expect to make a lot of money initially, although in time, salaries improve substantially. You should also expect that the hours on the job in this field often extend beyond a 9-5 schedule. Criminal justice professionals are often required to work mandatory overtime and in many positions transfers/travel to other locations are part and parcel of accepting employment in this field.

Image   *Earning a college degree means success on the job.*

Reality While education and earning a college degree are essential prerequisites to obtaining employment in most areas of criminal justice, many career professionals caution that a college degree alone may not guarantee your employment eligibility, or, in fact, provide you with necessary training vital to successful job performance. These professionals emphasize the value of "real world work experience" prior to employment as important to success in the field. Obtaining internships in the field while in college will enhance your understanding of the job and will provide you with the practical experience helpful to enter the field.

Women and Minorities in Criminal Justice

According to the Bureau of Labor Statistics projections (1992), women and minority groups are expected to dramatically increase their share of the labor force in America. By the year 2005, it is estimated that African-Americans who in 1990 represented approximately 10 percent of the labor force will increase to approximately 13 percent. Hispanics who comprised 7.7 percent of the work force in 1990 are projected to account for 15 percent of entrants. Asian-Americans and other races who were 3.1 percent of the labor force are expected to double their share. It is further projected that women will comprise more than 50 percent of all those employed.

Women and minorities who traditionally have been underrepresented in the criminal justice fields, particularly in law enforcement, can anticipate being actively recruited at the federal, state, and local levels. Beyond the push resulting from meeting equal employment opportunity guidelines, many high-ranking officials in criminal justice have recognized the importance and value of hiring individuals more reflective of the nation's composition, particularly for employment in large urban areas. An integrated department or agency enhances understanding, prevents conflicts, and increases opportunity for positive working relations with diverse multicultural/racial community groups, many of which harbor negative feelings toward law enforcement professionals. Although some say "not fast enough," there has been a general change in the public perception regarding a woman's ability to perform the job tasks of the criminal justice professional. Job responsibilities once considered "masculine" have been challenged and dispelled by competent professionals who are women. Essentially, it appears that there is a growing confidence and acceptance of women's rights and abilities to engage in all phases of criminal justice work. No longer are women restricted or limited to specific job tasks (i.e., community relations, communications, and other administrative duties). In major cities, the sight of a patrol car with two female police officers teamed up is perhaps symbolic of this change.

According to The Police Foundation, which examined the status and changes in the representation of female police officers around the country from 1978 to 1986, women comprise less than 10 percent of all police officers and their representation in the ranks of upper management is even lower. However, they do note that the percentages have risen considerably. In New York City, approximately 14 percent of police officers are women, more than 11 percent are African-American, and 33 percent of the African-American officers are female. Proportions of women and minorities employed in law enforcement tend to be greater in the larger urban areas. In fact, it should be noted that the police departments in some of our largest cities (e.g., Chicago, Atlanta, Detroit, Philadelphia, Miami, and Los Angeles) are now headed by African-Americans.

Beyond the active recruiting of qualified minorities and women in municipal police departments, opportunities for employment will also be found at the federal level. Of approximately 10,000 FBI agents, it is estimated that 850 are white females, 450 are African-American males, and 70 are African-American females. This agency, along with other federal agencies, wants to actively encourage and recruit more minorities and women into service. Some of these agencies have developed special programs to enhance their recruitment efforts. As mentioned earlier, positions at the federal level will require strong academic credentials and work experience. There is no doubt that there will be opportunities for women and minorities to increase their presence in criminal justice career fields.

These are but a few important questions that you need to consider. Finally, as you read each chapter, you will become more aware of specific career possibilities that may appeal to you. The process of narrowing your choices is an important step in helping clear your mind about which direction you plan to pursue. Based upon the information provided in these chapters, you should then be able to engage in an evaluative discussion of your findings with others such as your college counselor, faculty advisor, placement and career advisement officer, friends, and family. For example, you may want to discuss any possible conflicts between your interests, values, abilities, and the demands of the career. As you go through this process, it might be a good idea to keep some notes that capture the positives and negatives of your findings. Take the time to contact those offices, agencies, or persons who will provide additional information. It would also be wise to contact your college placement office, criminal justice program faculty, or library, because they may have other books, materials, and contacts that can help.

Summary

- Students who systematically plan their careers are more likely to be successful in obtaining a career in the criminal justice field.

- A college education is increasingly becoming an essential prerequisite for many positions within the criminal justice system.

- There are a variety of strategies and activities that can help you become more successful in college. Developing good study habits is the most important ingredient for college success.

- There are a variety of professionals and services on campus to assist you with your educational and career goals. Contacting and utilizing these resources is important to attain a successful career.

- Exploring and assessing your interests, values, and abilities is an essential process in helping you to choose a criminal justice career that is right for you.

- Learning about the many occupations that exist within the criminal justice field increases your knowledge about career options.

Career Planning Activities/Questions

To further promote your thinking about your educational and career goals, we suggest that you complete the following questions and activities.

CAREER

1. Describe why a career in criminal justice is important to you.

    _____

    _____

    _____

2. What occupation(s) within the criminal justice field is (are) appealing to you?

    _____

    _____

    _____

3. Why does this particular career appeal to you?

    _____

    _____

    _____

4. What skills, interests, abilities, or values do you think individuals employed in your prospective career should have?

    _____

    _____

    _____

5. In what areas would you need to develop or further improve to increase the possibility of attaining this career?

    _____

    _____

    _____

6. Describe why you believe this career will satisfy your needs.

_____

_____

_____

7. When did you first become interested in this career?

_____

_____

_____

8. What factors have influenced your choice of career? Think about people (teachers, friends, family, counselors, etc.), your personal or work experiences, your environment (neighborhood, geographic region).

_____

_____

_____

9. Why do you think you would be good at this particular career? Make a list of your strengths and weaknesses.

Strengths	**Weaknesses**
1. _____	1. _____
2. _____	2. _____
3. _____	3. _____
4. _____	4. _____
5. _____	5. _____
6. _____	6. _____
7. _____	7. _____
8. _____	8. _____
9. _____	9. _____
10. _____	10. _____

10. In terms of your career choice, how important are the following work values to you? Prioritize them from 1-11 (1 being most important, 11 being least important). Will the career you are thinking about pursuing satisfy your values?

_____ Prestige/Status

_____ High Income

_____ Job Security

_____ Excitement/Challenge

_____ Public Service (helping others)

_____ Leadership (directing others)

_____ Opportunity for Advancement

_____ Independence

_____ Work Closely with Others

_____ Travel

_____ Variety (not routine)

11. Visit your career counseling/placement office. Make arrangements to take an interest inventory. Interest inventories are a way of finding out the extent to which your interests are similar or dissimilar to those already successfully employed in the criminal justice field.

12. The following list of job skills/abilities is considered important for employment in many criminal justice careers. Describe situations in which you have demonstrated these attributes.

Directs/supervises others:

_____

_____

_____

Uses logical judgment in responding to people in crisis:

_____

_____

_____

Works well under pressure or when in danger:

_____

_____

_____

Sensitive/concerned for others:

_____

_____

_____

Willingness to take action as situations arise:

_____

_____

_____

Flexible in work hours/assignments:

_____

_____

_____

Good oral communication skills:

_____

_____

_____

Strong writing skills:

_____

_____

_____

Can work independently or cooperatively with others:

_____

_____

_____

High degree of respect for the legal system:

_____

_____

_____

EDUCATION

1. How would you rate yourself as a student? (i.e., outstanding, good, average, poor)

    _____

2. What are some academic achievements of which you feel most proud?

    _____

3. In what areas do you need improvement?

    _____

4. Name three benefits of becoming involved in campus activities:

    1. _____

    2. _____

    3. _____

5. What student activities have you been interested in joining? Now, make a commitment and plan to participate if your time permits.

    _____

6. Make a list of the individuals and college services that can assist you with any of your educational or career concerns. Make appointments to visit those offices.

    1. _____

    2. _____

    3. _____

7. Make a weekly time chart describing what you do each day/hour from the time you get up until the time you go to sleep. Review your written observations and determine: How many hours were spent watching television; socializing with friends; doing household chores; attending classes; employed in a job; preparing or studying for school; miscellaneous; etc.? What have you learned about how you spent your time?

    What would you like to spend more time doing? Less time doing?

    Are you satisfied with the amount of time you spend studying? If not, devise a plan to use your time more wisely. Write down specific goals for the week. Make sure that they are realistic.

Chapter 2

Careers in Law Enforcement

Every society gets the kind of criminal it deserves.
What is equally true is that every community gets
the kind of law enforcement it insists on.
                                        —Robert F. Kennedy

Whether law enforcement personnel are engaged in proactive approaches to deter crime (as through highly visible anti-crime and citizen crime education programs) or through reactive processes (such as investigation and subsequent arrest), law enforcement can be viewed as the initial step in the criminal justice system and is the most highly publicized of the career options in this field. While it frequently appears that our uniformed police services receive the most media attention, many students are not aware of the large number of other careers that exist within this branch of the criminal justice system.

On the federal level, for example, you have probably heard of the FBI and Secret Service, but are you aware that the U.S. Fish and Wildlife Service also employs college-educated agents as criminal investigators? Similarly, on the state level, non-uniformed investigators are employed in such areas as narcotics, organized crime, and client fraud. Cities and counties also hire investigative personnel, many of whom work in district attorney's offices, auditing bureaus, consumer affairs departments, and inspectional services units of many city agencies.

In the following law enforcement positions, profiles have been sketched that describe the nature of the work involved, educational and experiential requirements, and some personal characteristics that would be needed for these positions. Federal careers are described first, followed by positions that exist at the state/municipal levels.

Federal Law Enforcement

Air Safety Investigator

- Investigate aircraft accidents
- Prepare factual reports of findings
- Required pilot in command (flight time) hours
- Knowledge of aircraft design and aviation safety practices
- BA/BS degree required

Air safety investigators conduct investigations of aircraft accidents or incidents involving general aviation aircraft not usually investigated by centralized teams. Investigators can expect to compile and prepare comprehensive written factual reports and draw inferences and conclusions based on their findings.

The primary responsibility of these professionals involve on-site inspection and investigation, assembling factual data, and preparing specialized analysis of findings. Investigators are often called upon to work as a part of a team with other agencies. Investigators will be required to interpret and present their findings and/or testify when needed. Investigators are often called upon, on short notice, to work under some difficult and adverse conditions; to work long hours; or spend periods of time away from home. The work can be physically demanding when working in rough terrain or adverse climates.

To be qualified for this position, investigators must demonstrate knowledge of aircraft design, operations, and safety procedures/regulations. They should have knowledge of basic aviation practices, procedures, and techniques. Candidates must be in possession of appropriate pilot certificates/licenses, ratings, and flight hours. In addition, candidates must be skilled in writing technical reports, and possess a BA/BS degree.

Alcohol, Tobacco, and Firearms Inspector

- Provide industrial regulations and assume collection of excise taxes from alcohol and tobacco industries
- Provide information to ATF special agents
- Firearms not required
- Possible relocation
- Hiring based on combination of education and experience
- Appointment at GS-5 level

Inspectors within the U.S. Treasury Department, Bureau of Alcohol, Tobacco, and Firearms, provide for industrial regulation and assist in ensuring the yearly collection of more than $8 billion in excise taxes on distilled spirits, wines, and tobacco products. ATF inspectors may be assigned to distilleries, and make periodic visits to breweries, wineries, and cigar and cigarette plants. These inspectors may also monitor advertising, packaging, and the correct fill and formula of alcoholic beverages to make certain that the interests of consumers are protected. Two other lesser-known responsibilities of the ATF inspection force are the investigation of trade practices that could result in alcohol law violations (a safeguard against criminal infiltration of the alcoholic beverage industry), and administering certain environmental protection programs, such as efforts to curb water pollution by those industries it regulates.

In carrying out their assignments, ATF inspectors might visit businesses alone or as a team. Part of their job entails interviewing company representatives and reviewing their financial data to make sure taxes have been paid. Another aspect includes ascertaining that the proper licenses have been obtained to legally run those industries.

Since ATF inspectors are not criminal investigators, in cases where criminal violations such as fraud, tax evasion, or falsified inventories have been uncovered, they would provide this information to the ATF special agents and assist them in preparing these cases for criminal prosecution.

To become an ATF inspector, one must be a U.S. citizen, possess a valid driver's license, and be at least 18 years old. Further requirements at this time include a bachelor's degree from a four-year college or university, or three years of relevant work experience. Applicants must submit Form OF-612 to the regional office of the Alcohol, Tobacco, and Firearms unit where they wish to be considered for initial employment. If these requirements have been met, your name would be placed on a certified list of eligibles by the U.S. Office of Personnel Management. Candidates selected from this list by the Bureau of Alcohol, Tobacco, and Firearms must take a qualifying medical examination to determine their physical and medical ability and then pass a background investigation.

After being hired, ATF inspectors undergo training for one year through one month of classroom instruction and further on-the-job training by experienced personnel.

Alcohol, Tobacco, and Firearms Special Agent

- Investigate federal laws regarding firearms or explosives
- Enforce laws of liquor and tobacco industries
- Travel required
- Possible relocation
- Assist Secret Service in Presidential protection when needed
- Firearms required
- College degree and passing grade on Treasury Enforcement Agent Examination required

The Bureau of Alcohol, Tobacco, and Firearms (ATF), part of the U.S. Treasury Department, has jurisdiction for administering federal laws regulating the alcohol, tobacco, firearms, and explosives industries. Special agents at the ATF perform two vital functions.

First, special agents are charged with the responsibility of enforcing the federal laws that affect the sale, transfer, manufacture, import, or possession of firearms and explosives. In this role, special agents conduct investigations into unlawful activities, work to ensure compliance with the law, and apprehend those who are in violation of these federal statutes. With their extensive knowledge of firearms and explosives, special agents may probe cases and participate in surveillance operations and raids aimed at criminal organizations or terrorist groups who are in illegal possession of weapons and explosives. Common assignments include the investigation of such activities as bombing schemes for profit and illegal trafficking of firearms across state lines.

The second major responsibility of the special agent is to enforce the laws pertaining to the liquor and tobacco industries. Special agents investigate such activities as interstate smuggling of non-tax paid or contraband cigarettes. Special agents also work to eliminate bootleg liquor operations as well as to make certain that reputable distillers and breweries are in compliance with the laws.

If appointed as a special agent, you can expect a formal classroom instruction program supplemented by on-the-job training. Appointees undergo approximately eight weeks of intensive training at the Criminal Investigator School in general law enforcement techniques, at the Federal Law Enforcement Training Center in Glynco, Georgia. Subjects of study include: rules of evidence, surveillance techniques, undercover assignments, arrest and raid techniques, and the use of firearms. Agents later attend New Agent Training where they receive highly specialized instruction in their duties as ATF special agents. Subjects studied relate to the laws enforced by the ATF, case report writing, firearms and explosives nomenclature, bomb scene search, arson training, and link analysis. Successful completion of both training courses is mandatory for all newly hired ATF special agents.

In either of the above assignments, the special agent can work alone or in teams to gather this information. Special agents interview suspects, witnesses and informants in the course of their investigations; they also maintain a close professional working relationship with their colleagues in other federal, state, and local agencies. These relationships are for the purposes of joint investigations of criminal offenses, training, laboratory work, the tracing of firearms used in crimes, and in the general exchange of related information. ATF special agents are trained in the use of firearms and in self-defense as these might be employed in the course of their work.

Special agent candidates for the Bureau of Alcohol, Tobacco, and Firearms must meet a number of initial requirements, which include U.S. citizenship, 21 to 37 years of age and successful completion of a college degree. Substitution for the college degree may come in the form of one year of general experience and two years of specialized experience in the field of criminal investigation. The applicant must then attain a passing score on the Treasury Enforcement Examination. If the applicant is in excellent physical condition, has distant vision without correction of at least 20/100 in each eye, and passes a comprehensive medical examination by a licensed physician, he or she will then be required to pass a thorough background investigation.

Customs Aide

- Assist with responsibilities of other Customs Service positions
- Excellent entry-level position with possibility of advancement to higher titles
- Two years of experience required
- Appointed at GS-4 level

The customs aide performs semi-technical duties that require the application of a specialized knowledge of certain provisions of customs laws and regulations. The nature of the work of the customs aide can encompass assignments wherever the customs service has jurisdiction. For example, you might be assigned to a small port performing entry receipt and cash processing functions or to airports, where the aide would assist the customs inspectors and other specialized personnel in carrying out a variety of duties, including security functions in some cases. Other responsibilities might include receiving and acting on entries before final liquidation takes place in the regional offices or even being assigned to assist the Patrol and Marine Offices.

Entry-level appointments to customs aide positions are made at the GS-4 level with opportunities for advancement to the GS-7 level. Some positions at the GS-5 and GS-6 levels and most at the GS-7 level include the responsibility of supervising the work of a group of customs aides in lower-graded positions. For qualified individuals, advancement opportunities to higher-grade levels exist in other occupational customs titles, such as patrol officer, special agent, and inspector.

The two main qualifications for this title include establishing eligibility on the appropriate civil service examination register and having at least two years of progressively responsible experience in government, business, or the armed forces, which demonstrates the ability to interpret and apply laws, rules, and regulations. College students should know that education successfully completed above high-school level may be substituted for experience at the rate of one academic year of study for nine months of experience.

Customs Canine Enforcement Officer

- Train and use dogs to enforce rules and regulations pertaining to smuggling of controlled substances
- Possible advancement to other customs titles
- Appointed at GS-5 level
- No written test, but three years of generalized experience required

Customs canine enforcement officers train and use dogs to enforce customs laws and regulations that pertain to the smuggling of controlled substances such as marijuana, narcotics, and dangerous drugs. Uniformed canine enforcement officers work in cooperation with the customs inspectors, patrol officers, and special agents to interdict and seize all types of controlled substances and to apprehend, search, and arrest suspects and smugglers.

These officers are assigned to the Detector Dog Training Center for a 12-week basic training course; upon completion of this course, they are then assigned to the customs ports where they can be best utilized. Presently, most canine enforcement officers are located at ports of entry along the Mexican border.

The entry level for the customs canine enforcement officer is at the GS-5 level with advancement to the GS-9 level, and as in the customs aide position, there is possibility for advancement to other customs titles.

No written test is required, and candidates are rated on the basis of their education and experience, which should show at the minimum, three years of progressively responsible generalized experience in business, government, education, or the armed forces, involving contact with the public. Great emphasis is placed on skill in dealing satisfactorily with others and correctly applying regulations or instructional material. To apply, contact the Area of Personnel Management, 415 St. Paul Boulevard, Norfolk, VA 23510 and ask for information to establish eligibility on the customs canine enforcement officer register.

Customs Import Specialist

- Determine values of incoming merchandise and classify these goods under tariff
- Use schedules to determine correct duty and taxes required
- Can be assigned to seaport, airport, or land-border post
- BA/BS, or three years of general experience required
- Appointment at GS-5 level

The import specialists of the customs service are trained personnel who convert the language of commerce into the legal terms of customs regulation and are a major factor in making customs one of the federal government's major revenue-producing agencies.

One primary responsibility of the import specialist is in determining unit values, an important and difficult task. The import specialist first examines import entry documents, checking to see that the imported merchandise actually agrees with the invoice description, and then classifies the merchandise under the tariff schedules to determine the correct duty and taxes required.

Working as members of a team at a major seaport, international airport, or land-border post, import specialists become technical experts in a particular line of merchandise such as footwear or heavy machinery. International trade experts, importers, and custom house brokers rely on the import specialist's judgment to grant the lowest allowable duty on their products and thereby encourage legitimate trade.

To assure that their commodity expertise remains up-to-date, they physically examine selected shipments at places of arrival or at trade shows or importer's places of business. When they detect problems or violations related to invoicing, value or fraud laws, import specialists may call for a full-fledged investigation by customs special agents. Later, they may be called upon to provide technical assistance to the justice department in defending the government's position in all litigation resulting from these actions.

Basic requirements of applicants for this position include good physical and mental health, successfully completing an oral interview, passing a personal background investigation and establishing an eligible rating on the civil service examination. A bachelor's degree would meet the requirement of three years' experience, which shows skill in dealing with others, and the ability to follow instructional material and apply rules and regulations.

Customs Inspector

- Ensure compliance with tariff laws and prevent smuggling, fraud, and cargo theft
- Detect illegal importation and exportation of narcotics and other contraband
- Can search holds of ships
- Possible long and irregular hours
- Three years of general experience required
- Appointed at GS-5 level

Customs inspectors provide an important component of the customs service defense in detecting illegal importation and exportation of narcotics, dangerous drugs, and contraband.

To ensure compliance with tariff laws and to prevent smuggling, fraud and cargo theft, customs inspectors review the individual baggage declarations of international travelers and oversee the unloading of all types of commercial shipments. Business personnel and captains of ships are the inspectors' daily contacts as they review manifests, examine cargo carried by container on specially designed vessels, and control shipments transferred under bond to ports throughout the United States.

With today's increased emphasis on law enforcement and detection of illegal drug importation, customs inspectors work closely with other members of the U.S. Customs Service, such as special agents, import specialists and patrol officers, as well as with the FBI and the DEA. Inspectors, as part of their job, will perform searches, seize contraband, and apprehend violators, and they may be required to wear side arms.

Job responsibilities of customs inspectors might take them aboard ships, planes or trains, to inspect, search, and determine the exact nature of the cargo. Cargo manifests and baggage declarations are reviewed, cargo containers examined, and unloading activities overseen, to prevent smuggling, fraud, or cargo thefts. They might even seal the holds of ships and compartments containing sea stores used by crew members, as a means of preventing the illegal sale or smuggling of taxable merchandise into the United States.

Extensive on-the-job and formal training prepares customs inspectors for the varied and often strenuous working conditions. The hours of the typical seaport or airport are often long and irregular, and remote locations characterize the many one-person border posts where customs inspectors often must perform immigration and agricultural inspection in addition to their regular duties.

Attaining the position of customs inspector requires that a number of conditions be met. Physical requirements dictate good color vision and accurate hearing of the conversational voice without a hearing aid.

Three years of progressively responsible experience in government, education, business, or the armed forces, involving contact with the public is required, along with the ability to deal effectively with others and follow regulations and instructional material. The applicant must also successfully complete an oral interview and pass a personal background investigation.

Customs Patrol Officer

- Member of a tactical land, sea, and air effort aimed at prevention of smuggling
- Can conduct patrol by foot, car, boat, or aircraft
- Potentially hazardous work
- Frequent overtime, rotating shifts, weekend work
- Hiring after establishing an eligible rating on Border Patrol Agent Examination
- Duty station, when possible, of applicant's choice
- Appointment at GS-5 level

The prevention of smuggling into the United States is one of the primary missions of the U.S. Customs Service. By utilizing a tactical land, sea, and air enforcement effort, the customs patrol officer (CPO) carries out the challenging and often dangerous task of detecting and apprehending violators of the 400 laws enforced by the U.S. Customs Service. The CPO is a uniformed officer proficient in the use of firearms and other techniques of self-defense and is aided by the latest in sophisticated law enforcement equipment, such as two-way communications units, which enable the officer to keep in touch with and report to supervisory personnel.

On the job, the CPO can expect assignments in airports, seaports, land borders and coastlines, and will patrol these areas by foot, car, boat, or aircraft. In this work the CPO is watching individuals, as well as the movements of ships, planes, land vehicles, and cargo for evidence of unusual or questionable activities. Another important aspect of their work involves providing security at entrances and exits of piers, airports, and other points of entry to assure that all incoming baggage is examined by customs officials.

This position is considered potentially hazardous, as the CPO is subject to possible injury in the course of apprehending violators. Other considerations of the position involve frequent overtime, rotating shifts, weekend hours, and exposure to all types of climatic conditions. The CPO's assignment to a duty station can be anywhere in the United States, Puerto Rico, or the U.S. Virgin Islands, depending on personnel needs, but unlike many other federal law enforcement agencies, the CPO is assigned, whenever possible, to the area of his or her choice.

To qualify for this position, applicants must be less than 37 years of age and must be able to pass an appropriate physical examination to determine general good health and uncover any disability that would impair performance during training and work activities. Another requirement is to establish an eligible rating on the Border Patrol Agent Examination from registers established by the regional personnel offices. The required experience must demonstrate the applicant's ability to deal satisfactorily with others, to correctly follow instructions, and to make clear, concise oral and written reports.

However, one scholastic year of education above high school will equal nine months of work experience, and a bachelor's degree fully qualifies as experience for appointment at the GS-5 level.

Customs Pilot

- Highest technical requirements of any career in law enforcement
- Perform flight duties involving air surveillance of illegal traffic
- Can apprehend, arrest, and search violators
- Must have Federal Aviation Administration commercial pilot's license
- Can fly single- and multi-engine planes or helicopters

The requirements for the customs pilot are the most highly technical of any career in law enforcement. To be considered as a customs pilot, one must possess a Federal Aviation Administration commercial pilot's license. The type of aircraft for which applicants are qualified and the type of ratings required depend on the type(s) of aircraft in use at the duty station where the position is located. Time-in-flight experience requirements are as follows for GS-12 and GS-13: Total hours, 1500; pilot in command hours, 250; multi-engine hours, 500; instrument night hours, 500; hours during last 12 months, 100.

Pilots are hired after submitting a résumé or Form OF-612 and establishing a civil service rating high enough to merit appointment.

Customs pilots perform flight duties in support of a program primarily involving air surveillance of illegal traffic crossing U.S. borders by air, land, or sea. Pilots also perform the duties of apprehending, arresting, and searching violators of Customs and related laws, as well as preparing documentation to be used as a basis for prosecution. The customs pilots are employed along the Mexican and Canadian borders, as well as along coastal areas and, depending on the type of aircraft available at their duty station, may fly single-engine and multi-engine planes or helicopters.

Customs Special Agent

- Investigate criminal fraud against the revenue, counter-valuing, and major cargo thefts
- Investigate illegal importation and exportation of contraband
- Must attain a passing grade on the Treasury Enforcement Agent Examination
- Rigorous physical examination
- Firearms required
- Must pass detailed background investigation
- Must successfully complete 11-week training program
- One-year probationary appointment before receiving permanent status

Customs special agents seek to protect the government's tax revenue on incoming merchandise. Special agents in this branch of government service engage in a variety of investigations ranging from criminal fraud against the revenue, countervaluing, and major cargo thefts. They also investigate the illegal importation/exportation of a wide range of contraband material.

Special agents must, in the course of their work, gather information, examine public and private records, maintain surveillance activities, and question suspects. At times the agent is required to assume another identity and work in an undercover capacity to develop evidence of illegal activities. These investigations are aided by a highly complex radio communications system, which provides critical information on suspect activities and allows the agent to follow the journey of contraband from its entry along U.S. borders and coastlines.

All applicants for this position must post a passing grade on the Treasury Enforcement Agent Examination, which is designed to measure an individual's investigative skills. Candidates must be under the age of 37 and possess a college degree in criminal justice, law or business, in addition to having two years of specialized criminal investigative or comparable experience.

The nature of the work of the special agent requires applicants to be in excellent physical condition and to be capable of strenuous physical activity. Applicants are required to pass a rigorous physical examination, have excellent eyesight (uncorrected vision of 20/200), good near vision, color, and depth perception. The customs service also states that persons with hearing aids, noticeable deformities, or disfiguring conditions should not apply. Finally, the applicant must pass a detailed background investigation.

If candidates manage to satisfy these requirements, an 11-week training period at the Treasury Agents School is the next step. Candidates receive instruction in use of firearms, undercover operations, surveillance techniques, rules of evidence and courtroom procedures, customs laws and regulations, and current law enforcement and investigative techniques. Upon successful completion of this training period, a probationary appointment is made for one year, and if work is satisfactory, the new agent receives permanent employment status.

Deputy U.S. Marshal

- Approximately 3,500 members
- Provide federal court security, protection of federal witnesses, investigation of federal fugitives, liaison with INTERPOL, prisoner transport and custody of federal prisoners, special operations group (dealing with national emergencies requiring swift federal investigation)
- Three years of general experience or a college degree plus passing grade on Marshal's exam
- Worldwide travel
- Physical stamina
- Appointment at GS-5/GS-7 levels

Deputy U.S. Marshals are both officers of the federal courts and law enforcement agents of the Attorney General, U.S. Department of Justice. From this dual responsibility emerges several general areas within which the 2,000 members of the Marshal's Service carry out their duties.

One responsibility is to provide for federal court security. Deputy U.S. Marshals function as specialists in advising the judicial system on the latest physical and personal security techniques and devices used at highly sensitive trials throughout the nation. In addition, they provide "around the clock" protection for our federal judges and attorneys.

The second area for which they are responsible is a result of the Organized Crime Control Act of 1970 which, among other things, gave the Marshal's Service a mandate to protect state and federal witnesses having knowledge of matters pertaining to the operation or activity of organized crime. The Witness Protection Security Program encompasses the period of time between the witnesses first appearance before a grand jury and the culmination of the trial. Since its inception, the Witness Protection Security Program has protected, relocated, and even issued new identities to thousands of witnesses. This process is considered an important tool in the government's efforts against major criminal activity and organized crime.

The third role of Deputy U.S. Marshals is the undertaking of investigations that result in the arrest of approximately 17,000 federal fugitives annually. As a result of this duty, the Marshal's Service has become the primary agency responsible for the extradition of fugitives apprehended in foreign countries and wanted for prosecution in the United States. In connection with its work abroad, the Marshal's Service has been designated by INTERPOL as the primary U.S. agency to apprehend fugitives wanted by foreign nations and believed to be in the United States, and thus has representatives coordinating these matters at INTERPOL headquarters in France.

The fourth area of responsibility entails prisoner custody, and transport of those convicted of violating federal statutes, and the subsequent contract administration of governmental monies used to compensate those state and municipal jails that would house federal prisoners.

The last area of responsibility involves a component of the Deputy U.S. Marshals called the Special Operations Group (SOG). This group is an elite, paramilitary reaction force that enables the Attorney General to provide an immediate response to significant national emergencies requiring swift federal law enforcement intervention. This unit is composed of volunteers from within the Marshal's Service who have shown that they meet rigorous standards of physical and mental ability. These Deputy U.S. Marshals are on call 24 hours a day and can be assembled anywhere in the nation – fully equipped and self-supporting – within a matter of hours.

The position of a Deputy U.S. Marshal is one that is composed of many duties and responsibilities. One requirement is to have at least three years of generalized experience. There are many types of experience that qualify in the application process for this career.

Experience in law enforcement, corrections, teaching, personnel work, counseling, military service, sales, or public relations is considered valuable. Candidates should also demonstrate the ability to accept responsibility, deal with a wide variety of people, make sound decisions, prepare clear and concise reports, and examine practical solutions to problems. The value of a college degree is evident when one realizes that successful completion of a full four-year degree course satisfies the three-year general experience rule.

In addition to the education and/or experience, candidates also must pass a civil service examination. The name, current announcement number, time, date, and place of this exam can be obtained from federal job information centers.

Other requirements include being able to travel to any duty station assigned (whether initially or at any point during a career), having a valid driver's license, being between the ages of 21 and 36, and passing an oral interview.

As in other federal law enforcement positions, the physical and medical requirements of the Deputy U.S. Marshal are strenuous because the position requires great physical stamina. Vision must be 20/20 with glasses; uncorrected vision must not test less than 20/200. Further detailed physical and medical requirements may be obtained by contacting the U.S. Civil Service Commission, 1900 East Street, N.W., Washington, DC 20415.

Upon successful completion of the detailed background investigation required of all federal law enforcement applicants, and if appointed, there is a comprehensive 12-week basic training program conducted at the Federal Law Enforcement Training Center in Glynco, Georgia. Training is required regardless of any prior law enforcement experience. Satisfactory completion of this training is mandatory for continuing as a Deputy U.S. Marshal.

Persons appointed as Deputy U.S. Marshals may advance to the GS-9 level, which is considered journeyman. Advancement above this level is filled through service-wide competition, often requiring relocation.

Diplomatic Security, Special Agent

- Provide security of foreign service personnel
- Provide protection for Secretary of State and other Foreign Dignitaries
- BA/BS Degree and some work experience
- Have arrest authority
- Carry and maintain firearm

The men and women of the Diplomatic Security Service are specially trained Foreign Service career security professionals. They are also federal law enforcement professionals. Overseas, they advise ambassadors on all security matters and manage a complex range of security programs designed to protect personnel, facilities, and information. In the United States, they investigate passport and visa fraud, conduct personnel security investigations, and protect the Secretary of State and certain foreign dignitaries.

Special Agents/Security Officers of the Bureau of Diplomatic Security (DS) are responsible for the security of Foreign Service personnel, property, and sensitive information throughout the world. They are also responsible for the protection of the Secretary of State, certain foreign dignitaries during their visits to the United States, and other as designated by the Secretary of State. Major activities include protective services, criminal investigations, background checks, management of security programs for Foreign Service posts, and administrative, training, and liaison functions.

The requirements for a career with this agency are rigorous. Candidates must be 21-36 years old, be a U.S. citizen, have a bachelor's degree from an accredited college, and have at least one year of general work experience. Domestically, Diplomatic Security special agents are armed and have arrest authority. All applicants must be willing to carry and maintain firearms and to qualify in their use during training and throughout their careers. Applicants must possess a valid U.S. driver's license and must pass a defensive driving course during initial training.

Those who meet the basic qualifications for special agent are then eligible to appear before an oral examining panel of the Foreign Service's Board of Examiners. Those who pass this examination are required to undergo an in-depth personal background investigation for a top secret security clearance.

Special agents are most frequently assigned first to a domestic field office for two years, conducting background investigations on personnel, passport and visa fraud investigations, counterintelligence, and other criminal investigations. Domestic assignments also can include protection services for the Secretary of State and certain visiting foreign dignitaries or temporary assignment to an overseas post to perform a specific task.

Drug Enforcement Special Agent

- Attempt to stop flow of illegal drugs
- Possible relocation at appointment
- Long hours
- Potential for extreme danger
- College degree required
- Excellent physical health required
- Firearms required
- Appointment at GS-5/GS-7 levels, depending on experience

Special agents with the DEA are employees of the U.S. Department of Justice and have as their mandate to conduct criminal investigations relating to the enforcement of federal drug abuse prevention and control laws in an attempt to reach all levels of supply and stop the flow of illegal drugs before they reach the user. Special agents can expect to become involved in the following: criminal surveillance, undercover infiltration of drug channels, identifying and apprehending drug traffickers, confiscating illegal drug supplies, and arresting law violators engaged in criminal drug activities.

Additional aspects of this work can require the collection and presentation of evidence, writing highly detailed and technical reports, and presenting sworn testimony in criminal court cases. Drug Enforcement Administration special agents should also possess the ability to effectively communicate and maintain productive relationships with various city, state, and federal law enforcement agencies. For those interested in this type of an investigative career, there are three conditions of which to be aware. First, special agents must be willing to accept assignments to duty stations anywhere in the United States upon appointment and at any time thereafter, including the possibility of a foreign assignment. Prior to appointment, special agents are required to sign a statement to this effect. In applying for this position, candidates submit applications to the field division office in the area in which they reside. Their first assignment would not be in their hometown; they can expect to relocate. The second condition is continued employment based upon successful completion of the special agent training school, a formalized and extremely rigorous 10-week course in Washington, DC. Here, agents receive instruction in self-defense, firearms, law, court procedure, criminology, investigative techniques, physical training, and drug and narcotics identification. The third condition is that agents will be assigned a considerable amount of overtime. Remember that people who deal in narcotics are not typical nine-to-five workers, and prevention of narcotics crime is a 24-hour-a-day operation. However, agents receive overtime pay at the rate of 25 percent of their base pay per year. Not surprisingly, the basic qualifications for the DEA special agent are very demanding. The candidate must be in excellent physical health and must meet a vision requirement of 20/200 in both eyes without correction for distant vision; and 20/20 in one eye and 20/40 in the other with correction. Before appointment, a detailed background investigation is conducted on all selected candidates with any prior unsuitable conduct or infractions of the law that will possibly prevent them from being selected. Definite cause for disqualification would be drug abuse in any form. The age minimum is 21 years, with a maximum of 37, and candidates must have a valid driver's license.

The first step towards becoming a DEA special agent is to submit Form OF-612 and a college transcript to the nearest regional office. These forms are available at any federal job information center. Applicants who meet all the minimum requirements mentioned above are evaluated and ranked on the extent and quality of their experience, education, training, special skills, and the outcome of a panel interview.

All of these requirements are rated according to the following 100-point system: the panel interview rates a maximum of 40 points; the experience top score is 10 points; education rates 40 points; and any special or extraordinary skills are 10 points. From there, the candidate is placed on a register or list, with a position being offered according to federal budgetary capabilities and the DEA's personnel staffing needs.

Federal Bureau of Investigation Special Agent

- Nation's premiere law enforcement agency
- Mandate includes, but is not limited to, kidnapping, bank robbery, organized crime, civil rights violations, fraud, and spying
- College degree and experience required

- Appointments are extremely competitive
- May require relocation
- Will require relocation for career advancement
- Firearms required
- Appointment at GS-10 level

Special agents within the FBI have as their main role that of investigations or fact-gathering, the results of which are then forwarded to the U.S. Attorney General for possible legal action. A brief look at some of the areas of jurisdiction of the FBI includes, but certainly is not limited to, crimes such as kidnapping, bank robbery, bankruptcy, fraud, spying, organized crime, civil rights violations, sabotage, and illegal financial transactions involving the banking industry.

If the primary function of the FBI special agent is the gathering of evidence, the agent will be expected to work effectively in a variety of situations where his skills and training will be of extreme importance.

The nature of this position can be brought out in a number of ways such as performing solitary or team-type investigations; interviewing and interrogating witnesses, informants, or suspects; using sophisticated electronic devices and cameras; and performing undercover assignments or surveillance. Special agents are required to prepare written and oral reports, testify in court proceedings, carry firearms, and they are exposed to potentially hazardous situations.

United States citizenship, availability for assignment anywhere in the Bureau's jurisdiction and being between the ages of 23 and 37 are the initial requirements. All applicants must pass a color vision test and have uncorrected vision not less than 20/200, corrected to 20/20 in one eye and 20/40 in the other eye. Candidates must have their hearing tested and must pass an audiometer hearing standards exam. Finally, candidates must possess a valid driver's license and be in excellent physical condition with no defects that would interfere in firearms use, raids, or defensive tactics.

If candidates meet all of the above requirements, then there are five possible entrance programs under which they may apply in qualifying for appointment as a special agent.

The first program is LAW. Here, ABA-accredited law school graduates with two years of resident undergraduate work at an accredited college or university may submit application.

Another is ACCOUNTING, which requires the applicant to be a graduate of a four-year college, with a degree in accounting or a degree in another discipline such as economics, business or finance, with a major in accounting. For consideration in this program, the applicant also should have passed the Uniform Certified Public Accountant Examination or provide certification from the school at which the accounting degree was earned that he or she is academically eligible to sit for the above exam.

Still another option is the LANGUAGE program, which seeks college graduates who have a fluency in a foreign language for which the Bureau has a
current need.

The fourth option is the MODIFIED program. In this program, the applicant would need the four-year college degree plus three years of full-time
work experience. If the candidate holds an advanced degree, only two years
of full-time experience would be required.

The fifth option is in the SCIENCES. Qualifying scientific disciplines that
require advanced degrees are in electrical engineering, metallurgy, physics,
chemistry, biology, geology, pharmacy, pharmacology, math, engineering,
computer science, computer systems, or related fields. In most of the above
disciplines, three years of work experience and a bachelor's degree can substitute for the advanced degree. Finally, applicants who have expertise in
firearms, explosives, and document and fingerprint examination may qualify
under this program.

The special agent applicant undergoes an initial battery of written examinations that are computer-scored at FBI headquarters in Washington, DC.
Those who rank high enough as a result of this testing are given a formal
interview, which is also computerized. Subsequently, the highest ranking
individuals in each of the entrance programs are given consideration for
employment based on the needs of the Bureau and are thoroughly investigated for employment. At this stage, a polygraph examination may also be
requested.

Newly appointed special agents report to the nearest FBI field division for
oath of office and then proceed to the FBI Academy at Quantico, Virginia,
where they undergo an intensive classroom, physical fitness, and firearms
training program for 15 weeks. The successful applicant will begin employment at the GS-10 level, and is required to serve a one-year probationary period before becoming a permanent employee.

Investigator, U.S. Investigations Services, Inc.

- Private sector position, not Federal
- Will qualify as experience for Federal investigative titles
- Will not require firearms
- College degree (any major), required
- Possible travel

Formerly the Federal Investigations Program for the Office of Personnel
Management, USIS came into existence in July, 1996, a result of a major federal government reorganization.

USIS, Inc. has approximately 700 full-time investigative employees with
federal experience. The primary responsibility of USIS personnel is to conduct investigations for major corporations and federal, state, and local gov-

ernments to determine the suitability and qualifications of individuals to hold positions of trust and responsibility. Professionalism, integrity, and uncompromising dedication to detail are required for employees of this firm.

The USIS Investigator conducts interviews with diverse individuals in a variety of settings. The Investigator is responsible for organizing his or her day-to-day work in order to meet deadlines. Responsibilities may require working and/or driving in adverse weather conditions; driving to unfamiliar locations; "cold calling" to accomplish interviews; and working at many different times of the day, including evenings. Although there are not set hours, the Investigator must meet challenging deadlines and produce, with fairness and impartiality, accurate and thorough investigative reports.

Because USIS is a private corporation, and the USIS Investigator is different from the special agent title in federal law enforcement agencies, the USIS Investigator does not carry firearms or attend training at the Federal Law Enforcement Training Center.

Requirements for this position include a bachelor's degree, written and verbal communication skills, strong logical reasoning skills and time management skills, U.S. citizenship, a valid driver's license, the ability to travel and to be a self-starter. Contact U.S. Investigations Services, 801 Arch Street, Suite 410, Philadelphia, PA 19107-2489.

Federal Protective Service Officer/ Criminal Investigator

- Has wide law enforcement powers over GSA properties
- Bachelor's degree and ACWA exam eligibility required
- Firearms required
- Appointment at GS-5/GS-7 levels

The Federal Protective Service (FPS) is the security arm of the U.S. General Services Administration (GSA), the agency responsible for most civilian work space owned or leased by the federal government. The FPS provides client or tenant federal agencies with a total security package that combines human, electronic, and educational elements. Responsibilities include: the FPS's own law enforcement, physical security, and investigative personnel; contract guards, electronic surveillance, and entry control devices; and facilitating widespread crime prevention awareness programs.

The FPS consists of a mobile police force of approximately 1,000 uniformed federal protective officers. These officers have all the police powers of sheriffs and constables, with the exception of serving civil processes. They are authorized to enforce laws and to make arrests on property under control of the U.S. General Services Administration. An additional force of non-uniformed criminal investigators examines crimes ranging from theft of government property to homicide. Investigators coordinate their efforts with other federal law enforcement agencies and with state and local groups. About 120 security specialists perform security surveys and conduct crime prevention programs at client or tenant federal work sites around the country.

Other responsibilities of the FPS include: providing mobile response to emergency calls through regional and satellite control centers; conducting physical security surveys to assess facility risk and recommend appropriate security measures; monitoring intrusion, duress, and fire alarm systems; advising and reinforcing contract guards at building access points; protecting federal officials and foreign dignitaries when they are on GSA-controlled space; investigating crime; crowd-control efforts – in cooperation with local police – in group demonstrations and riots; cooperating with other federal law enforcement agencies; and providing and maintaining state-of-the-art electronic intrusion detection and security systems for GSA-controlled space.

Federal protective officers take a rigorous basic police training course at the Federal Law Enforcement Training Center, Glynco, Georgia. Continued training is frequent and is designed to keep officers aware of changing security needs, procedures, and developments in security technology.

Applicants to the Federal Protective Service are generally advised to take the Administrative Careers with America Exam for law enforcement/investigative positions. After establishing eligibility on this list, the Office of Personnel Management would then authorize the Federal Protective Service to contact candidates based on position vacancy and budgetary availability. Exceptions to this would be the Outstanding Scholar Program in which students with a 3.5 index or applicants with Veteran's credit could apply directly to the agency.

Fish and Wildlife Service, Special Agent

- Investigate violations of Federal Fish and Wildlife laws
- Protect, maintain, control, and improve national fish and wildlife resources
- Hiring based on education and experience
- Considerable travel and possible time away from duty station
- Formal training in Washington, DC, followed by on-the-job training
- Appointment at GS-5/GS-7 levels, depending on experience

The U.S. Fish and Wildlife Service, an agency of the Department of the Interior, has responsibility for the protection, maintenance, control, and improvement of our country's fish and wildlife resources.

Special agents of the U.S. Fish and Wildlife Service conduct investigations into violations of federal fish and wildlife laws. They carry out surveillance activities, participate in raids, interview witnesses, interrogate suspects, seize contraband, serve search warrants, and perform other law enforcement-related activities. The duties of all special agents involve considerable travel, frequent periods away from regular duty stations, and a considerable amount of overtime for which they are compensated.

To apply for a position as a special agent for this service, applicants must be between 21 and 37 years of age by time of appointment. All applicants must pass a written test that measures memory and powers of observation, vocabulary, arithmetic, reasoning, spatial perception, investigative aptitude, and judgment. Special agents must meet the standards for a comprehensive physical examination. A copy of these standards is available upon request from the office where the announcement of any given position opening is available. Applicants must possess a valid driver's license at the time of appointment and throughout their job tenure, and will undergo a full background investigation. As in most cases with federal job openings, candidates will be rated according to their combination of education and experience. Candidates are hired either at the GS-5 level or the GS-7 level. A combination of general experience and specialized experience is required.

Those appointed to the U.S. Fish and Wildlife Service are sent to Washington, DC, where they undergo orientation that includes a formalized training program. Following this formalized training, candidates are assigned to a designated law enforcement office for on-the-job training. Within a period of 12-18 months, candidates receive a regular assignment in a district within the country. While some consideration is given to a candidate's location preference, the needs of the service will generally dictate the location and subsequent transfers throughout the career.

Immigration and Naturalization Service, Border Patrol Agent

- Detect and prevent illegal entry of persons into the United States
- Work takes place along the 8,000 miles of land and water defining U.S. territory
- Must speak and read Spanish fluently
- First assignment will be southern border states
- Requires firearms, uniforms
- Hiring based on written exam and combination of education and experience
- Appointment at GS-5 level

Students considering becoming a border patrol agent should take into account two very practical considerations of this position. The first consideration is that a border patrol agent's first duty station is in the southern border states of Arizona, California, New Mexico, or Texas and many of these posts are located in small, isolated communities. The second consideration is that all border patrol agents must be able to speak and read Spanish fluently.

The Border Patrol, a trained uniformed officer corps, is a component of the Immigration and Naturalization Service of the U.S. Department of Justice. They are a mobile, well-equipped law enforcement unit whose primary mission is to detect and prevent the illegal entry of persons into the United States.

This work takes place along the 8,000 miles of land and water that define the territory of the United States. The border patrol makes use of such modern equipment as interceptor-type automobiles, jeeps, fixed-wing aircraft, helicopters, and complex communications and electronic sensing devices. The primary responsibilities of this position include conducting investigations, detecting violations of immigration and nationality laws, and determining whether undocumented aliens may enter or remain in the United States. Additionally, border patrol agents assist in presenting the government's case at hearings and often make recommendations to the courts in such matters as petitions for citizenship.

In carrying out their work, agents might employ a number of techniques including traffic stops to determine the citizenship of an occupant, conducting inquiries of the immigration status of farm and ranch employees, and inspecting and searching trains, buses, trucks, aircraft, ships, and passenger and cargo terminals to locate undocumented aliens. When undocumented aliens are discovered, the border patrol agent is authorized to arrest them without warrant, and use firearms or physical force if necessary. Also, these agents are required to make a detailed written report of these incidents and to provide further testimony in court proceedings if needed.

Experience required for this position involves at least one year in which the applicant has shown that he or she can take charge and make sound decisions in stress situations. Applicants must demonstrate their ability to learn law enforcement regulations, methods, and techniques through classroom training and on-the-job instruction. They gather factual information through questioning, observation, and examination of documents and records, and must establish, maintain, and improve interpersonal relationships with a wide variety of people.

Those who have this type of experience are then required to take a written examination that measures their abilities to learn and perform the nature of the border patrol agent's work. Those who are already proficient in Spanish are given additional credit towards appointment. A college degree may be substituted for the experience outlined above.

Other qualifications for this position include U.S. citizenship, possession of a valid driver's license, successfully passing an oral panel interview, and maintaining excellent physical condition. A detailed list of the physical requirements may be obtained from the Immigration and Naturalization Service, SEU, 425 I Street, N.W., Room 602, Washington, DC 20536.

The first step in applying for this position is to take the Border Patrol Agent Examination. Contact the nearest federal Office of Personnel Management or Federal Job Information Center. When appointed, border patrol agents are required to attend an intensive 16-week training session in Glynco, Georgia.

Immigration and Naturalization Criminal Investigator

- Investigate violation of criminal and statutory provisions of Immigration and Nationality laws
- Some undercover assignments
- Possible relocation
- Travel
- BA/BS or equivalent in experience for hiring
- Excellent physical condition
- Firearms required
- Appointment at GS-5/GS-7 levels

Criminal investigators in the Immigration and Naturalization Service are non-uniformed law enforcement officers with the responsibility of examining factual situations within the administration and enforcement scope of the service. Basically, their work entails planning and conducting investigations concerning the criminal and statutory provisions of immigration and nationality laws through use of such investigative techniques as background checks and undercover assignments.

Many of the requirements for immigration inspector, deportation officer, and criminal investigator are similar. An applicant must have U.S. citizenship, possess a valid driver's license, establish an eligible rating on the written examination (for an applicant with competitive civil service status based on present or past federal employment, the examination may be waived), and have a bachelor's degree or three years of responsible experience (or an equivalent combination of education and experience). Qualifying experience includes administrative, professional, investigative, or other responsible work that has prepared the applicant to enter the position. One academic year of full-time undergraduate study is equivalent to nine months of responsible experience.

Since the duties of these positions are physically demanding, excellent physical condition is a specific requirement for these titles. Manual dexterity (comparatively free motion of fingers, wrists, elbows, shoulders, hips, and knee joints) is required. The applicant must also possess good vision in each eye (with or without correction). The ability to hear the conversational voice and whispered speech without the use of a hearing aid is required. Candidates must also possess emotional and mental stability. These physical standards are considered minimum and are not waived in any case.

The age requirement is a minimum of 21 years and a maximum of 37 years at the time of appointment. However, the maximum age may be waived if you are presently in a federal law enforcement position or have served in such a position in the past. All of these positions require the applicant to pass a personal background investigation to determine suitability for employment. The final requirement is the applicant's signing of an affidavit acknowledging that appointment to these positions is contingent upon successful completion of a formalized training period at the Federal Law Enforcement Training Center in Glynco, Georgia.

Immigration and Naturalization Deportation Officer

- Control and removal of persons who have been ordered deported or required to leave the United States
- Travel required
- Firearms required
- Hiring based on education and experience
- Appointment at GS-5 level

The deportation officer is responsible for the control and removal of persons who have been ordered deported or required to leave the United States. This is accomplished by closely monitoring deportation proceedings from the initiation of the proceedings to the removal from the United States. A close liaison with foreign consulates and embassies is required to facilitate the efficient issuance of passports and travel documents required for deportation. The deportation officer must ensure that no avenues of relief have been overlooked for the person being deported, offering every assistance possible, such as the recommendation for release on bond or recognizance. Deportation officers also may be required to compose letters to foreign consulates and other agencies, and may answer formal responses to congressional inquiries and to application for relief. A combination of education and experience, demonstrating ability to interpret and enforce existing agency rules and regulations, is required. The ability to speak a foreign language is also helpful.

Immigration and Naturalization Inspector

- Work is at land ports of entry, airports, seaports, and places where people enter the United States from other countries
- Prevention of illegal entry and permitting those who are admissible
- Uniformed position
- No firearms
- Hiring at GS-5 level

The key responsibilities of the immigration inspector are to prevent the illegal entry of persons into the United States and to properly permit those who are admissible. Their work is performed primarily at land ports of entry, airports, seaports, and other places where people enter the United States from other countries.

Entry-level immigration inspectors perform certain phases of inspection work under fairly close supervision, and they assist higher grade officers in other inspection processes such as administration of the guidelines controlling laws, regulations, policies, court, and administrative decisions. The initial appointment to the inspector title is at the GS-5 level, with progression to levels GS-7 and GS-9 generally following at one-year intervals. Promotions to higher-graded positions are made in-service and depend on the incumbent's satisfactory work performance, along with the personnel needs and budgetary considerations of the agency.

Inspector General Investigator

- Provide internal investigations of waste, fraud, and mismanagement in many federal agencies
- College degree required
- Excellent written and communication skills
- Some agencies require firearms
- Frequent travel
- May require relocation based on agency needs
- Appointment at GS-5/GS-7 levels after submitting Form OF-612 and interviews

The inspector general's role on the federal level is to investigate any alleged fraud, waste, mismanagement, corruption, or inefficiency that might occur in agencies such as the Departments of Agriculture, Labor, or Transportation.

Investigators for the inspector general can expect to participate in case assignments encompassing the following: planning and conducting general inspections and investigations of fraudulent or criminal activities; conducting interviews and preparing reports of the findings; participating in court hearings or proceedings; researching and applying laws, rules and regulations; auditing financial records; working irregular hours; and traveling.

The position requires, at minimum, a college degree or three years of general experience that demonstrates the ability to work with people, collect and analyze data, prepare clear and concise reports, and accept responsibility. The applicant must also demonstrate such personal qualities as poise, tact, initiative, drive, and self-confidence.

Other points that should be known about the inspector general's offices include being prepared to travel a minimum of 50 percent of the time and being willing to transfer throughout the United States based on agency needs.

To receive consideration for this position, a completed copy of Form OF-612 should be submitted to the headquarters address of the agency of interest.

Internal Revenue Criminal Investigator

- Investigate charges of criminal and civil violations of Internal Revenue laws
- Deal with people from all walks of life
- Potential for irregular hours, travel, and personal risks
- BA/BS including 24 hours in accounting
- Must establish eligible rating on Treasury Enforcement Agent Examination
- Firearms required
- Appointment at GS-5/GS-7 levels

The Internal Revenue Service (IRS) is the largest bureau within the U.S. Treasury Department, and its mission is to encourage and achieve the highest possible degree of voluntary compliance with tax laws and regulations. The duties of the special agent require investigation of charges of criminal and civil violations of Internal Revenue laws, generally involving tax fraud. Agents investigate to determine if there is sufficient evidence to recommend prosecution for willful attempts to violate federal tax laws or to recommend the imposition of civil fraud penalties.

The work of the IRS special agent can be difficult, complex, and challenging. Agents contact and deal with people from all walks of life (individual proprietors, executives of large and small business enterprises, corporations, individuals, etc.).

Applicants must be skilled in oral and written communications, including accounting analyses, to interview and question taxpayers and witnesses, and to report their findings. It is necessary to be qualified in the skills of an accountant, attorney, or criminal investigator in pursuing, uncovering, and evaluating the evidence. Special agents also are expected to participate in surveillances, make arrests, and serve as witnesses in civil and criminal trials. These duties frequently require irregular, unscheduled hours, possibly involving personal risks or physical exertion.

The IRS Criminal Investigation Division special agent position requires the completion of a four-year college degree, including at least 24 semester hours in accounting and related subjects. Eligibility must be established by passing the Treasury Enforcement Agent Examination, which is designed to test memory and powers of observation, vocabulary, arithmetic, reasoning, spatial perception, investigative aptitude, and judgment.

The physical requirements are extremely rigorous, and before entrance to duty, all applicants must undergo a pre-employment medical examination to determine their suitability to perform the full duties of this position.

In addition to the educational and physical standards for the IRS special agent, the applicant must have had three years of accounting and business-related experience, including a knowledge and application of commercial accounting and auditing principles and practices. Candidates must demonstrate clearly the ability to analyze accounting and bookkeeping records, financial statements, related reports; conduct interviews; and to comprehend audit and investigative reports pertaining to federal tax returns of individuals, partnerships, and corporations.

As in all federal law enforcement special agent positions, U.S. citizenship, a valid driver's license, and being younger than 37 are mandatory requirements. Finally, all applicants must have a standard interview to evaluate such factors as poise, tact, and ability in oral expression, and then must pass the personal background investigation.

Intelligence Support Analyst

- Gather statistical data for law enforcement agencies
- Prepare and analyze reports, utilize automatic/computer information systems
- BA/BS degree for appointment to GS-5 level
- Strong academic grades (high GPA)

Working for the Department of the Treasury, Intelligence Support Analysts provide intelligence and analytical support to the operational activities of the criminal investigations. Intelligence support analysts develop and analyze financial and other statistical data impacting on law enforcement operations. They research, collect, and disseminate information/data from a variety of federal law enforcement databases and serve as a focal point for ensuring effective communication of investigative and enforcement data. Analysts utilize such automated information retrieval systems such as TECS, NCIC, NLETS, LEXIS, NEXIS, etc. Analysts also have a training function and frequently conduct training sessions for intelligence employees on the capabilities and functions of a variety of highly sensitive and controversial reports.

To qualify at a GS-5 level or higher, applicants must possess a BA/BS degree. They should have received specialized education in computer, database operations, and intelligence data collection.

A college education with a high grade point average enhances acceptability.

Internal Security Inspector, Internal Revenue Service

- Perform investigations to ensure that honesty and integrity are maintained within all levels of the service
- Job can be stressful
- Travel possible
- Firearms required
- College degree and possible Treasury Enforcement Agent Examination
- Appointment at GS-5/GS-7 levels

Internal security inspectors perform an important and essential function within the Internal Revenue Service. For the most part, they are used in an investigative capacity to ensure that high standards of honesty and integrity are maintained within all levels of the service. This will involve conducting background investigations of new and prospective employees, as well as investigation of alleged misconduct or illegal activities involving service employees. These investigations can be varied and complex. Inspectors must move quickly to gather evidence and resolve situations that indicate possible embezzlement, bribery, fraud, conspiracy, extortion, unauthorized disclosure of information, or any act of wrongdoing that interferes with the administration of IRS statutes.

Additionally, IRS inspectors may be assigned to protect the employees who serve as government witnesses during legal proceedings. They also work closely with other law enforcement personnel and at times may assist in providing security for the President of the United States.

Security inspectors can be assigned throughout the United States and may have to travel in order to carry out their responsibilities. The job, at times, can be stressful and subject to personal risk. Security inspectors are expected to be prepared to use firearms or physical force if necessary.

Applicants for the position of security inspector must be U.S. citizens between the ages of 21 and 37. They must have three years of prior work experience that demonstrates investigative expertise, ability to work effectively with people, and to prepare written reports. A college degree is essential, and in some cases, additional educational attributes may be substituted for experience. A degree in accounting or credentials as a certified public accountant is strongly preferred. A law degree is also desirable.

In addition to these standards, all candidates must pass the Treasury Enforcement Agent Examination given by the U.S. Office of Personnel Management. Candidates are interviewed and a background check is made to evaluate a number of personal qualities and characteristics such as honesty, stability and job suitability.

If hired, all new security inspectors participate in an 11-week training program designed to develop investigative skills and law enforcement techniques. In a classroom format, subjects such as rules of evidence, surveillance techniques, courtroom demeanor, and the use of firearms are taught in a seven-week course at the Treasury Enforcement school. For those interested in this type of work, the first step is to contact the nearest IRS office to gather application information.

Labor and Pension Compliance Investigator, Department of Labor

- As a member of a team, investigate compliance with labor law
- Examine union and organizational documents, contracts to issue compliance

- BA/BS degree plus experience of GS-5 level; ability to speak/ write effectively
- Knowledge of investigatory techniques

Labor and pension investigators provide a variety of supportive tasks that facilitate the efforts of civilian or criminal investigations working as a team member for the U.S. Department of Labor. You will conduct extensive searches for information by reviewing financial reports of labor organizations, examining union constitutions and other documents.

You will participate in investigations to ensure union and organizational compliance with regulations that govern labor operations. Investigators monitor union elections to ensure compliance with laws and conduct audits when appropriate.

In the company of higher grade investigators, you would participate in meetings or conferences, consult with union officials and their attorneys/ accountants and work cooperatively with other Federal and State agencies.

To be eligible for this position, candidates must be U.S. Citizens and possess a BA/BS degree to be approved at the GS-5 level.

Applicants should have knowledge of investigative techniques, ability to prepare and present technical reports containing findings. Candidates must demonstrate ability to communicate and write effectively, possess a valid driver's license, and are subject to frequent overtime travel.

Naval Investigative Service/Criminal Investigator

- Conduct criminal investigations/counterintelligence for the Department of the Navy
- Possible tour of duty at sea
- Requires a baccalaureate degree
- Requires proficient use of firearms
- Currently 1,110 NIS Special Agent/Criminal Investigators

As the primary criminal investigative and counterintelligence agency for the Department of the Navy, the mission of the Naval Investigative Service (NIS) is to support all commands in the discharge of that responsibility. The NIS is a centrally directed, largely civilian organization providing such support, both ashore and afloat, consistent with Department of the Navy policy and with full regard for the constitutional rights of individuals.

Naval investigators have primary responsibility for criminal investigations in such crimes as arson, homicide, rape, robbery, narcotics trafficking, larceny, and the destruction or theft of government property. Still other law enforcement duties can entail foreign counterintelligence, bribery, contract and check fraud, weapons theft, and anti-terrorist activities. Finally, NIS special agents can be expected to provide protective services to visiting dignitaries, physical and port security, and function as a liaison with other law enforcement agencies both nationally and abroad. Prospective agents come to the Naval Investigative Service from a wide variety of backgrounds: law enforcement, law, engineering, military, and from other sectors of public and private business and industry. All are college graduates and each is required to complete a rigorous 11-week basic agent course at the Federal Law Enforcement Training Center (FLETC) at Glynco, Georgia.

The agent trainee receives instruction in three primary types of subjects at FLETC: law enforcement, practical exercises, and physical specialties and firearms. Classroom instruction covers such matters as investigative techniques, criminal law and procedure, and the rules of evidence. Practical exercises cover surveillance techniques, fingerprinting, raids and apprehensions, courtroom testimony and demeanor, and crime scene examinations. Physical specialties include conditioning and instruction in unarmed self-defense, while firearms training includes the proficient use of weapons and survival under various tactical conditions.

In addition, agents receive specialized training from the NIS Training Department in the skills and knowledge necessary to perform their job of protecting national interests and the Navy community.

Over a 20-year period the NIS special agent will normally receive at least six permanent duty assignments. Since 30 percent of the agent force is stationed overseas at any given time, the NIS career path usually includes one or more foreign tours. Overseas duty is generally for three years, during which time the special agent lives within the civilian economy or aboard military installations.

There are six regional offices in the United States, located in San Diego, California; San Francisco, California; Washington, DC; Norfolk, Virginia; Charleston, South Carolina; and New York, New York. Applicants may contact the recruiting agent at these locations for further information concerning employment.

Park Police (United States)

- Provide law enforcement services in national parks
- May require relocation
- Will be trained in use of firearms
- Must have at least two years of college course work
- 20/60 vision or better correctable to 20/20 with glasses or contact lenses

The U.S. Park Police is a unit of the Department of the Interior, National Park Service, National Capital Region, with jurisdiction in all National Park Service areas and certain other federal/state lands. The U.S. Park Police has responsibility for providing law enforcement services within the District of Columbia, as well as other federal reservations in the Washington metropolitan areas, New York, and San Francisco. They are also frequently requested to provide protection for dignitaries, such as the President of the United States and visiting foreign heads of state, and to provide assistance to other areas of the National Park Service and other agencies during law enforcement emergencies.

Initial appointments are made to the Washington metropolitan area where the largest contingent of officers is located. Officers may be reassigned to the Gateway National Recreation Area in New York City or to the Golden Gate National Recreation Area in the city of San Francisco, California. Officers may also be detailed to duty in any area of the National Park Service.

Each officer of the U.S. Park Police is charged with the responsibility of providing law enforcement services that include the investigation and detention of persons suspected of committing offenses against the United States. Additionally, law enforcement services are provided for the many notable civic events conducted within the National Park areas.

U.S. Park Police Officers must possess qualities such as initiative, physical strength and endurance, maturity to remain calm in emotionally charged situations, ability to learn a wide variety of subjects quickly and correctly, the desire and ability to adapt to technological and sociological changes, and the social skills that would include the ability to communicate effectively with persons of various cultural, economic, and ethnic backgrounds.

Other qualifications include: U.S. citizenship; minimum 21 years of age and maximum 37 years of age before appointment; high school diploma or the equivalent; two years of progressively responsible experience that has demonstrated the ability to learn and apply detailed and complex regulations and procedures; ability to pass a full personal background investigation; pass all required written, physical, and medical examinations; a valid driver's license; pass an oral interview; complete the prescribed training required for recruits after appointment; and satisfactorily complete a one-year probationary period. Upon employment, recruits receive 17 weeks of training at the Federal Law Enforcement Training Center (FLETC) and additional training under the supervision of an experienced field training officer. Written tests are required periodically.

Interested persons may apply when the test is announced by the Office of Personnel Management (OPM).

Postal Service Inspector

- Criminal and audit investigations of the Postal Service
- Security and administrative duties
- Frequent travel
- Overtime
- Firearms required

- Applicants selected and screened from within the Postal Service
- College degree required

The U.S. Postal Service has an investigative agency relating to postal operations and illegal activities involving the mails. Generally, postal inspectors carry out the security, investigative, audit, and enforcement responsibilities of the postal system.

More specifically, the duties of the postal inspector can be divided into the categories of criminal investigations, audit investigations, and security/administrative duties.

Criminal investigations relate to all types of postal offenses such as criminal acts against the mails, postal facilities, postal personnel, and criminal misuse of the postal system. Such crimes include burglaries, holdups, mail fraud, internal theft, and the sending of prohibited items through the mail such as narcotics, pornography, and explosives. Postal inspectors work closely with other federal agents in efforts to halt such traffic, and in this work they have statutory power of arrest.

In audit investigations, Postal Service inspectors determine whether postal revenues are being properly protected, funds are spent economically and the Postal Service is operating in the best interest of the public. Postal Service inspectors are expected to conduct comprehensive and objective audits that result in recommendations for improvements, cost reduction and maximum managerial effectiveness in such areas as mail handling, data systems, customer services, financial operations, and outside procurements and contracts.

Postal Service inspectors conduct background investigations on their personnel to make certain that Postal Service standards are met. Another responsibility involves the continuous checking and upgrading of all fire, safety, and security systems used by the Postal Service. Finally, a responsibility a bit out of the ordinary is the inspector's readiness to respond to catastrophic situations such as floods, fires, and air or train wrecks to ensure the safety and recovery of postal valuables, property, and personnel.

The nature of an inspector's work requires much traveling and frequent absences from home. Inspectors must be willing to accept assignments wherever their services are needed. Initial assignments will not be to the immediate area of the office from which appointed. Because inspectors may be required to respond to all types of emergencies, they are often subject to calls at all times.

Another major consideration of this type of work is that Postal Service inspectors sometimes work under dangerous or stressful conditions and can be subject to physical injury during the seizure and arrest of suspects.

First and foremost, be aware that candidates for this position are selected and screened from within the Postal Service. Applicants must be U.S. citizens between the ages of 21 and 37. Essential to attaining this position is experience that demonstrates the ability to prepare clear and concise reports, as well as a knowledge of all phases of postal operations, such as personnel management, mail handling, finance, and security. A variety of postal positions within the system lend themselves to this kind of experience, but having a college degree is mandatory. Additionally, all candidates must be able to speak and write clearly, work well with others, and possess a valid driver's license.

All candidates are given a qualifying oral interview, general aptitude test, and a thorough physical and psychological examination. A background investigation is then conducted on each applicant. This investigation will determine if the applicant has an arrest record and will include interviews with neighbors, work associates, and supervisors who will be asked to provide personal references. Those who meet all the requirements will be given a numerical rating and placed on an eligibility roster for possible future openings.

This is perhaps one of the most difficult law enforcement positions to secure. The turnover rate is low, and all future openings are subject to governmental budgetary considerations. Those interested should begin by contacting and inquiring with the Postal Inspection Services to acquire more specific information.

Secret Service Agent

- Executive protection and investigation of crimes against the currency
- Frequent travel
- Stringent physical requirements
- Low turnover, therefore extremely competitive
- Requires college degree and passing grade on Treasury Enforcement Agent Examination
- Much overtime
- Firearms required
- Appointment at GS-5/GS-7 levels

While the U.S. Secret Service is best known for protection of the President, it was originally a bureau within the Treasury Department, set up to eliminate counterfeiting of our currency, as well as to prevent the forging and cashing of government bonds, checks, and securities.

The protective responsibilities of the Secret Service have broadened over the years. They now include the protection of President and Vice-President of the United States and their immediate families, the President-elect and Vice-President-elect and their immediate families, former Presidents and their wives, the widow of a former President until death or remarriage, minor children of a former President until they reach 16 years of age, major Presidential and Vice-Presidential candidates, visiting heads of foreign governments, and at the direction of the President, other distinguished foreign visitors to the United States, and official representatives of the United States performing special missions abroad.

The protection of the President and other designated persons involves a coordinated effort of protective forces, intelligence operations, and the use of high-tech security systems. Agents assigned to protect a particular person must plan, organize, and implement their security arrangements well in advance. The advance arrangements include the designation of emergency sites, routes of evacuation and relocation sites. The cooperation of local enforcement agencies is essential for successful completion of any protective mission.

The primary investigative responsibilities of the U.S. Secret Service involve efforts to suppress counterfeiting of U.S. stamps, coins, and currency, and to conduct investigations regarding the forgery and fraudulent negotiation of redemption of government checks, bonds, or other obligations or securities of the United States.

Special agents of the Secret Service are charged with extremely important and highly complex investigative and protective responsibilities.

Applicants must be under 37 years of age at appointment. They must have, at minimum, a bachelor's degree, three years of experience with at least two years in criminal investigation and must pass a comprehensive medical examination prior to appointment, with weight and vision strongly considered. It is important to mention that the number of positions of special agents are limited because of extremely high competition and a low attrition rate. Consequently, only the most qualified applicants are appointed. To apply, applicants must take the Treasury Enforcement Agent Examination. Information about this exam may be obtained from the Office of Personnel Management or the local Secret Service branch office. Only a limited number of those who attain a passing score on this exam will receive an in-depth interview and background check. Selected applicants must wait an extended period of time for vacancies to occur. Special agents, once selected, may be assigned to any location in the United States, according to the needs of the Service. Frequent travel and reassignment is not uncommon and should be considered when selecting this career. At present, special agents receive general training at the Federal Law Enforcement Training Center in Brunswick, Georgia, and specialized instructions at Secret Service training facilities in Washington, DC. Training includes comprehensive courses in protective techniques, criminal law, criminal investigations, surveillance techniques, undercover operations, first aid, document and handwriting analysis, and the use of firearms.

Secret Service Uniformed Officer

- Provide security through a network of vehicular and foot patrols, fixed posts and canine teams at White House buildings in which Presidential offices are located and at the main Treasury Building and the Treasury Annex in Washington, DC.
- Requires firearms

- Job site is Washington, DC, exclusively
- High school diploma and written test
- Rotating shifts and weekends
- Appointment at GS-4 level

The Executive Protective Service provides security at the White House buildings in which Presidential offices are located, the Vice-Presidential residence and foreign diplomatic missions located in the metropolitan area of the District of Columbia, and in other areas as the President may direct. Secret Service uniformed officers carry out their responsibilities through a network of vehicular and foot patrols, fixed posts, and canine teams.

The Treasury Security Force is responsible for maintaining security at the main Treasury Building and the Treasury Annex located in Washington, DC. This duty encompasses security for the Office of the Secretary of the Treasury. Officers also have special arrest powers in connection with laws violated within the Treasury Building and conduct investigations of crimes committed at the Treasury.

Applicants are required to have a high school diploma or equivalent, or one year of experience as a police officer in a city with a population of more than 500,000. Applicants must pass a written test and will also be rated during a personal interview. In addition, applicants are required to possess a valid driver's license, qualify for top secret clearance (through a thorough background investigation), and exhibit a willingness to work shifts and weekends.

New appointees to the Secret Service Uniformed Division must be U.S. citizens. Their vision must be at least 20/40 in each eye, correctable to 20/20. Weight must be in proportion to height. Each applicant must pass a comprehensive physical examination.

Once appointed, each officer undergoes intensive training in Beltsville, Maryland, and Brunswick, Georgia. Additional periods of instruction and on-the-job training take place in Washington, DC. Training includes classroom instruction in legal procedures in law enforcement, first aid, community relations, physical fitness, and the professional use and care of firearms.

Those interested in this career should contact the Personnel Division of the U.S. Secret Service.

Securities Compliance Examiner

- Top 10 percent of college graduating class or; 3.45 overall GPA
- BA/BS required, any major
- Keen analytical skills, able to plan and organize
- "Wall Street Detectives"

The United States Securities and Exchange Commission is responsible for the overall regulation and oversight of the financial markets (stocks and bonds) and maintaining the integrity therein.

Securities Compliance Examiners help in assignments associated with compliance examinations and participate in conducting preliminary and formal examinations and investigations. They analyze records and reports about registrants being examined to determine their compliance with the rules and regulations of the Securities and Exchange Commission. They will occasionally interview officials of firms or other persons with relevant information about the firm's operations.

Other areas of responsibility involve the review of financial documents filed by broker-dealers, investment companies, investment advisers or transfer agents and the identification of deficiencies and deviations from Federal securities laws. All of the above responsibilities and duties will involve the preparation of written reports and/or the presentation of oral commentaries on the operations of the company being examined.

Contact the U.S. Securities and Exchange Commission for a detailed position announcement describing application procedures and further requirements.

State and Municipal Law Enforcement

Deputy Sheriff

- Uniformed law enforcement position
- Similar to police and troopers, yet also has court and corrections responsibilities
- Firearms required
- Rotating shifts and weekends
- High school degree and usually a civil service examination

Many counties throughout the nation have a sheriff's department that may have broad-based criminal justice responsibilities in the areas of policing, corrections, and the courts. The deputy sheriff is the line officer assigned to carry out these functions.

Concerning the policing function, the deputy sheriff frequently has duties similar to the municipal police officers and state troopers. Deputy sheriffs conduct patrol, apprehend and arrest suspects at crime scenes, transport suspects, perform traffic control duties, assist at accidents, and sometimes conduct criminal investigations.

The duties of the deputy sheriff differ from his or her police counterparts in the municipalities and state police organizations because of the role he or she plays in the courts and corrections. The deputy sheriff's court-related responsibilities include serving civil papers, court orders and warrants, eviction proceedings, confiscating property, and providing courtroom security. His or her role in county corrections can involve providing security in the county jails and transportation of prisoners for court appearances.

While entry-level requirements can differ from county to county, there are some general requirements for employment as a deputy sheriff. Typically, candidates must be U.S. citizens between the ages of 21 and 29 at appointment, possess a valid driver's license, and have at least a high school diploma (some counties also require college credit). The selection process might require a written or oral exam, or perhaps a rating of the candidate's work history. There are physical, medical, and psychological requirements in addition to a thorough background investigation. Training varies greatly, with some counties requiring six months of training, while others are providing on-the-job training with subsequent attendance at a state or municipal academy at a later date. To receive precise requirements for this position, contact the civil service commission, which is usually located in the county seat.

Environmental Conservation Officer

- Outdoor work required
- Often long and irregular hours
- Possibly carry firearms
- Required to work independently
- Requires 60 college credits in some jurisdictions

If you have a strong appreciation and concern for our environment, along with an interest in law enforcement, then this career may be suited to you. Environmental conservation officers (game wardens, fish and wildlife management officers) can be found throughout the country patrolling and enforcing laws and statutes that pertain to protecting the jurisdictions' natural resources and environment. Employed by the state, and less frequently by the county, conservation officers investigate complaints in order to detect and document environmental conservation law felonies, misdemeanors, and violations. They also meet with school groups, service groups, and hunter's and angler's clubs to promote compliance with environmental conservation law. At times, they are required to work long and irregular hours outdoors, frequently alone and usually carrying a firearm. In some jurisdictions an officer could be required to maintain a residence within the geographical limits of their patrol area. Environmental conservation officers are usually supplied with such things as four-wheel-drive vehicles, power boats, snowmobiles, snowshoes, cameras, binoculars, and two-way radios by their hiring jurisdiction.

Applicants for this position must take a written exam to test their ability to memorize facts and information, prepare written material, read, understand, and interpret written information, and apply written information such as rules, regulations, policies, procedures, and directives in police situations.

Training can entail either a formal, structured residential program or on-the-job training, depending upon the jurisdiction. A driver's license, a good driving record, and the ability to secure a firearm license along with satisfactorily meeting the physical and medical requirements of the jurisdiction are also usually required. To apply, contact the agency that would be responsible for environmental concerns in your area.

Investigator (State, County, Municipal)

- Provide criminal or civil investigative support to agencies with specific responsibilities
- Generally requires a college degree and some related experience
- Degree may be waived on account of experience
- Some investigators will be required to carry firearms
- Valid driver's license required
- Excellent vehicle for developing experience required for investigative counterparts on federal level

Many states, counties, and cities will have criminal and civil investigators who are not assigned to the state police, municipal police, or sheriff's department, but rather, are employed by a public agency with specialized responsibilities such as the district attorney's office, alcoholic beverage license and control, state professional licensing commission, gambling and wagering commission, bureau of taxation and finance, special state prosecutor for narcotics, organized crime and corruption. Others may be employed as municipal inspectors general for agencies such as transportation, environmental protection, sanitation, and public assistance. As employees of such agencies, investigators assure that the role of the agency is carried out according to the guidelines established by the state, county, or municipality.

The nature of the work may involve the investigation and apprehension of persons involved in corrupt activities whether as agency employees, as persons doing business with the agency, or as those over whom the agency has licensing control. These investigators compile information on suspects, maintain surveillance, conduct court-ordered wiretaps, execute search warrants, participate in raids, and operate as undercover agents. As in any level of investigation, report writing is an integral part of the position, as is the ability to work around the clock. Investigators must have excellent communication and research skills, as they will be called upon to interview suspects and provide courtroom testimony.

Requirements will vary depending on the location and the specific nature of an agency's role. Some investigative positions will require a college degree and related experience, in addition to passing a civil service examination. Others might omit the exam but require a résumé and a series of interviews. Any person interested in this field should contact the agency of interest to see if it employs investigators, and ask what the requirements are for the position. Training requirements will vary with each agency, as will the need for use of firearms.

State Police Officer/State Trooper

- Ensure public safety and patrol state and interstate highways
- Enforce motor vehicle and criminal laws
- Traffic enforcement
- Other responsibilities similar to municipal police officer
- Rotating shifts
- Usually alone on patrol
- Firearms required
- Will deal with emergencies and catastrophes
- Excellent physical condition required
- High school diploma and passage of Civil Service Examination
- Extremely rigorous training

State police officers have responsibilities to patrol the state and interstate highways, turnpikes, and freeways in efforts to enforce motor vehicle and criminal laws that ensure public safety. Traffic enforcement can be highlighted as one of their major responsibilities. State police officers on traffic duty perform such tasks as providing assistance to motorists, identifying vehicles that are being operated illegally, using speed detection devices such as radar to apprehend those in violation of speed limit laws and generally watching for other traffic violations. State police officers issue warnings or citations and, where justified, arrest those in violation of motor vehicle regulations and safe driving practices. Common to such traffic work is the day-to-day task of providing information to motorists such as road conditions and directions. When vehicles become disabled or accidents occur, state police officers radio for emergency equipment such as tow trucks and ambulances, and if required, provide first aid to injured parties until help arrives. All accidents are thoroughly investigated and detailed reports are written. In many cases, these reports become the legal evidence which the officer may be called upon to present in court.

One of the most common misconceptions about state police officers is that their work is solely limited to traffic enforcement. In many states, in addition to their highway function, state police officers have responsibilities similar to their counterparts in the municipal setting. Some of these responsibilities include responding to emergency calls involving armed robberies and homicides, investigating felonies and misdemeanors, conducting searches and seizures, making arrests, helping city and county police in riot control and domestic disturbances, and providing public relations services such as educational talks and presentations. With the exception of Hawaii, every state has a state police force.

State police must maintain good physical condition and be prepared to handle a variety of situations. They may be called out at any hour for emergency situations and may work weekends, holidays, and rotating shifts. Finally, the state police officer will undoubtedly encounter tragic accident scenes where emergency care to help preserve life will be needed.

Candidates must have good oral and written communication skills; hold a valid driver's license; have mathematical knowledge of algebra and geometry; and meet hearing, vision, and other physical requirements. Typically, applicants must be U.S. citizens and residents of the state where they wish to work at the time of appointment. Most state police agencies require at least a high school education, with some level of college education providing an edge in the employment process. Successful completion of the Civil Service Examination and a subsequent oral panel interview is usually required by many state police agencies throughout the nation. The interviewee is rated on such factors as verbal communication skills, tact, physical appearance, and the ability to exercise sound judgment. An in-depth medical exam is always required, and a psychological evaluation is usually required. All state police agencies have standards of height, weight, and vision, and applicants will be tested in strength, agility, and stamina. As with other law enforcement agencies, the state police applicant must pass a thorough background investigation to determine general character, honesty, employment history, and suitability for this position.

Police Officer (Municipal)

- High stress potential
- Uniformed officers
- Protection of lives and property of the public
- In addition to patrol work, many other areas of specialization
- Generally requires rotating shifts and some weekend work
- Potentially dangerous
- Requires use of firearms
- Requires excellent health
- High school diploma and examination or interview required for appointment
- Some college education may be required for appointment or advancement

The uniformed police officer is perhaps the most highly visible position of any career within our criminal justice system, with more than 600,000 sworn officers in our cities and towns.

Basically, the primary function of the police officer is to protect the lives and property of the public. Of their many responsibilities, the patrol function is the most common. Police officers on patrol perform a variety of diverse tasks. They may be assigned to patrol a designated area in a car, on a motorcycle or on foot in order to become familiar with area conditions and residents. Patrol officers observe and investigate suspicious or illegal behavior, question suspects regarding violations of laws and, if the situation arises, arrest persons believed to be breaking the law. When an arrest is made, police officers transport the suspect to the police station for booking and detention. The police officer is then expected to testify in court to provide evidence for the prosecuting attorney during the trial. While on patrol, police officers are also responsible for traffic control and direction to ensure safe and rapid movement. They observe parked and moving vehicles for evidence of traffic violations and will issue summonses when necessary. Police officers are trained to administer first aid to accident victims and arrange for dispatch of medical units. The patrol officer responds to radio calls ordering them to the scenes of incidents such as burglaries, bank robberies, homicides, rapes, suicides, assaults, and crimes in progress. The patrol officer is virtually a generalist whose day-to-day activities provide the essential services upon which the public depends. In some jurisdictions there is the opportunity for assignments to specialized units, such as the Bomb Squad, Community Relations, Canine Patrol, Crime Prevention, Emergency Services, Hostage Negotiations, Juvenile Bureau, Mounted Police, Harbor, Aviation, Sex Crime Analysis, Police Academy, and Vice Squad.

To demonstrate a further degree of specialization within some departments, consider that the cities of Washington, DC, San Francisco, and New York each have their own transit department. Still another example of police specialization is the Port Authority of New York and New Jersey Police Department and its law enforcement responsibilities for the bus terminals, waterways, and airports of the New York-New Jersey metropolitan area.

Students should not consider a career in police work without being aware of the practicalities of this job. Police work is considered physically demanding and has, without a doubt, the potential to be extremely dangerous. It can be both exciting and tedious. There is a very real possibility that an officer can spend an entire career working around the clock and on weekends and holidays.

While requirements vary across the nation, there are some general minimum standards. A high school diploma is necessary, with some departments requiring 15 to 60 college credits. The age of application requirement is typically between 20 and 29 years, and candidates usually must pass the Civil Service Examination. Most departments have strict medical, physical, and psychological requirements, with poor vision being a frequent cause for a candidate's disqualification. Finally, potential police recruits must pass a thorough background investigation which, among other things, testifies to the applicant's character in such areas as honesty and integrity.

Chapter 3

Careers in the Courts

All virtue is summed up in dealing justly.
—Aristotle

In the previous chapter, law enforcement careers were described as the first step in the administration of the criminal justice system. Law enforcement was defined as the prevention and investigation of crime, with the arrest and bringing to trial of those who break the law. Careers in the courts play a significant role in this process.

The main responsibility of those who work in the courts can be defined as the administration of justice in a swift, fair, and efficient manner. While most are familiar with such high-profile positions as judge and attorney, and have a basic knowledge of the organization of the American judiciary, they may not be aware of some of the relatively low-profile, yet critical, professional opportunities that exist in the court system. Included in this section are some well-known and lesser-known career positions that work to facilitate the efficient operation of the judicial system.

Opportunities within the court system are ever-changing and growing, as there is a continual call for court-related reform and reorganization. As this general change in our judicial system takes place, the personnel staffing needs of the federal, state, and local court administrations will require educated and able people with diverse skills and abilities to contribute and be a part of this task.

Attorney/Lawyer

- Interpret laws, serve as advocates/advisers
- Conduct research and write legal briefs
- Represent clients in civil or criminal court
- Can serve to prosecute, regulate, and enforce laws

- Must have Juris Doctor degree
- Entrance into law school extremely competitive

The system of laws in a democratic form of government is extremely important, yet complicated. Laws affect every aspect of our lives. They regulate relationships among individuals, citizens, groups, businesses, and governments. They define our rights and restrictions, protect and defend our freedoms, and ensure our safety as individual citizens and as a society.

Lawyers are the professional experts who connect our system of laws to society by developing, interpreting, and regulating them. Lawyers generally work as advocates or as advisers. As advocates, lawyers represent parties in criminal and civil court trials to resolve disputes. As advisers they inform their clients as to their legal rights. In either case, a lawyer must be extremely familiar with the laws and their application to each specific situation or case.

As a lawyer you can expect to be involved in active and in-depth research and report writing to clearly substantiate a particular position. Much of your work will be in an office or law library. You should not expect that court appearances will be a frequent responsibility unless you are a trial attorney.

Although many lawyers serve as generalists, a substantial number of lawyers specialize in a particular branch of the law, i.e., international law, family law, business law, probate law, civil law, environmental law, entertainment law, to name a few. Most lawyers, approximately 75 percent, are in private practice working either in law firms or in solo practices. Others are employed by private business and others work for non-profit organizations, i.e., legal aide societies, and public interest law.

A substantial number of lawyers are employed in various levels of government. Lawyers who work in government service represent an integral part of the criminal justice system. At the federal level each department or agency employs lawyers whose function is to prosecute, regulate, and enforce laws. For example, at the federal level, you may investigate cases for the Department of Justice, the Federal Bureau of Investigation (FBI), or the Treasury Department. Each state may have administrative or regulatory agencies staffed with lawyers that work for the State Attorney General's office, a prosecutor, or a public defender. At the county or municipal level, a lawyer might work as a district attorney representing the prosecution in criminal cases or handling post-conviction matters (i.e., motions for a new trial) at the trial court level. If you are a lawyer in government service, you are likely to work less hours than those in private practice, although the pay is generally lower.

Your preparation for a career in law should begin as early as the first year of college. Although there is no recommended pre-law major, certain courses and activities are considered more helpful than others. For example, courses that help you develop writing skills, communicate verbally, and help you to analyze and think logically are most important. Pre-law advisers often suggest enrolling in courses such as English, history, government, law, and philosophy. To be eligible to attend law school, you must demonstrate an aptitude to study law, usually evidenced by the grades you obtained in college. Law schools will also look at your Law School Admissions Test (LSAT) score, as well as recommendations from professors, and a personal statement is also given consideration. Law schools vary in the weight they attach to each of the above. Graduates of law school receive a Juris Doctor (J.D.) degree. All lawyers must pass the bar exam in the state in which they plan to practice. To qualify for this exam, a candidate must graduate from a law school approved by the American Bar Association or the state authorities.

Large national and regional law firms will continue to be selective in hiring new lawyers for associate positions that offer the potential for partnership status. Graduates of prestigious law schools and those who rank high in their classes should have the best opportunities for such positions. Graduates of less prominent schools and those with lower scholastic ratings may experience difficulty in securing associate positions with partnership potential, but should experience an easing of competition for positions with smaller law firms. Due to competition for jobs, a law graduate's geographic mobility and work experience assume greater importance. The willingness to relocate may be an advantage in getting a job, but to be licensed in a new state, a lawyer may have to take an additional state bar examination. Establishing a new practice probably will continue to be easiest in small towns and expanding suburban areas. Nevertheless, starting a new practice will remain an expensive and risky undertaking that should be weighed carefully. Most salaried positions will remain in urban areas where government agencies, law firms, and large corporations are concentrated.

Bailiff (Court Officer)

- Uniformed law enforcement; provide courtroom security
- Assist judge
- Escort prisoners, jury members
- Requires high school diploma and passing grade on Civil Service Examination

Similar to the Deputy U.S. Marshal, who provides courtroom security and protection during federal court cases, the bailiff or court officer retains similar responsibilities in the courts on the state and local levels.

Essentially, the bailiff is the uniformed law enforcement person present at trials and hearings in the court. The bailiff assumes the responsibility of the protection of judges and courtroom participants. Working under the direction of the judge, bailiffs perform daily courtroom searches and reports. They remain on guard to take corrective action on any security violations or to respond to potentially dangerous situations that may arise. Bailiffs often escort and take charge of prisoners and jury members in and out of the courtroom.

In typical courtroom procedures, bailiffs call defendants and witnesses to the stand and generally act as a liaison between the jurors and the court. Bailiffs are responsible for a variety of routine assignments. Each day they inspect and prepare the courtroom to assure that all necessary equipment is in operable condition. They may perform a variety of clerical and/or administrative tasks including report writing, screening visitors, answering the telephone, making appointments, and generally being available to service the needs of the judge.

Becoming a bailiff requires graduation from high school, with college preferred and required in some areas. In most cases applicants will be required to pass a written test, as well as an oral exam. Since the position entails constantly dealing with attorneys, witnesses, prisoners, jurors, and others, candidates will be examined for their ability to exercise tact, good judgment, and courtesy. Experience involving extensive contact with the public in a court system or in an agency providing administrative support services to the court system is helpful and may be substituted in lieu of education requirements.

Court Administrator

- Perform administrative and management functions within the court
- Assist judge with court calendar, case flow, personnel management, research, and evaluation
- Maintain court facilities
- BA/BS in public administration
- Administrative court experience
- Knowledge of law important

The primary function of the court administrator is to assist the chief judge with the overall operation of the court to which they are assigned. The person in this position can oversee a wide variety of areas as they relate to the administrative support areas of the day-to-day workings of the judicial system.

At minimum, the education for a court administrator requires graduation from an accredited college with a specialization in judicial studies, business, public administration, or management. Applicants should have at least five years of progressively responsible experience in a staff or administrative capacity with a criminal justice agency. Ideally, the court administrator holds a graduate or professional degree in the above-mentioned fields and should have extensive knowledge of calendar management techniques, case law and procedures, and human relations management skills and abilities.

The court administrator establishes policies and procedures for the centralized control and coordination of all court calendars and programs; directs the evaluation, development, and direction of activities pertaining to the automation of calendar operations; coordinates the court's data processing activity with other criminal justice agencies; directs the preparation of reports, statistical studies, and other documents pertaining to calendar matters; evaluates and modifies existing calendar procedures; initiates and oversees the preparation of procedural manuals; has responsibility for reports showing the arraignment, detention, adjudication calendars, including original department designations and transfers of cases; meets with the chief judge, judges, attorneys, and other related personnel to assure the proper assignment, transfer, and disposition of cases; holds chief responsibility for the coordination and planning of court security facilities and activities; and could attend meetings as a representative of the chief judge or serve as a member on various internal and external committees concerned with the judicial system.

Court Clerk

- Clerical assistant with a variety of administrative responsibilities
- Maintain case records
- Prepare statistical reports
- Prepare and receive court documents
- Explain court procedures to parties involved in court cases
- High school diploma required
- BS/BA degree or business school training a plus

The court administrator oversees a number of professionals who help to ensure the efficient daily operations of the court calendar. Court clerks are excellent examples of this type of support personnel.

Generally, court clerks are considered clerical assistants who host a variety of administrative responsibilities. Two titles from the U.S. District Court and the U.S. District Court of Appeals provide an example of the responsibilities of this position.

A case processing clerk is responsible for the maintenance of the official case records in both civil and criminal cases for the court. This person also provides pertinent information, either in person, by telephone, or by correspondence to the public. Other case-processing tasks are performed by this person as assigned.

A docket clerk reports to the director of courtroom services and is responsible for maintaining the official case records in both civil and criminal cases. This person prepares statistical reports on cases commenced and closed, furnishing information, either in person, by telephone or by correspondence, as to the status of cases.

To attain a job as a court clerk, individuals should have at least a high school diploma, combined with some form of clerical work experience. Training at a business school is often viewed favorably, particularly if the job applicant has typing skills. A college degree is also favorable. All court clerks are required to have knowledge of the law, court procedures and policies, and a general understanding of court operations. As in the case of most court careers, the ability to communicate effectively is considered a prerequisite. There is room for advancement if the clerk is a concerned and competent employee.

Court Liaison Counselor

- Assist and counsel defendants charged with crimes
- Evaluate and initiate treatment plans
- Make referrals to support agencies
- BA/BS in social work/counseling
- A desire to be helpful to others required

There are a number of specialized pretrial intervention projects or alternatives to detention programs throughout our nation's courts. Many of these projects employ the court liaison counselor.

The basic responsibility of this counselor is short-term counseling of the program participants. The participants are defendants charged with criminal and penal offenses who have been released by the court into the project's supervision before entering their plea. In addition to counseling, the court liaison counselor is responsible for referring the participants to appropriate community agencies, maintaining case files, evaluating client's motivation for help, determining problems that clients have, and formulating and implementing the treatment/counseling plan to prevent conditions that could lead to recidivism or re-arrest.

One of the most important qualifications for this job is that the court liaison counselor possess strong human relations skills. He or she must show the ability to express thoughts on paper in a concise and organized manner and also must be able to assess the client's situation and formulate a counseling plan from this assessment. Interpersonal skills are also important because the court liaison officer will be interacting with professionals such as social workers, probation officers, and other staff members. Finally, the counselor should be able to accept supervision, make use of community resources and be able to work with program participants whose lifestyles may differ significantly from their own.

Counseling/correctional-type experience for two to three years in the above areas, when combined with a BA/BS in criminal justice, social work, counseling, or psychology provides the required background for application to this position.

Court Reporter (Short-Hand Reporter)

- Record all trial proceedings with the use of a stenographic machine
- Must pass certifying exam as court reporter
- Knowledge of legal vocabulary essential

The court reporter is a "specialized" stenographer who records all statements made at trials and hearings, then presents their recording as the official transcript of the court. The position requires the utmost in skill, accuracy, and speed. Only the most experienced and highly trained reporters are recruited for court recording work.

In the recruitment of court reporters there is a preference for reporters who possess the ability to use a stenographic machine, which prints symbols as certain keys are pressed. They must also be knowledgeable in the vocabulary of the legal profession.

As mentioned previously, only the most highly skilled stenographers are employed with the courts. In many states, a court reporter must be certified through the passing of the certified shorthand reporter (CSR) test, which is administered by a board of examiners. The mark of excellence in this profession is to earn the designation of registered professional reporter. This is accomplished through further education and testing.

While employment in the stenographic field is expected to decline, the demand for skilled court reporters is expected to remain strong as federal and state court systems expand to handle the rising number of cases being brought to the court.

Students interested in this field should consult colleges and business schools that specialize in this area.

Court Representative

- Ascertain eligibility for alternative to detention sentences
- Heavy interaction with defendant population
- Requires some related experience and education for appointment

Another position in the area of alternative-to-detention programs is the court representative, who is responsible for reviewing court papers in order to identify and compile a daily list of defendants whose arraignment charge, criminal history, residence, and disposition make them "paper-eligible" for a community service sentence. These defendants have already been convicted of a property crime but instead of serving a jail term, they serve a community sentence based on a court representative's finding.

Once these "paper-eligible" defendants are identified, the court representative then conducts interviews with them and keeps a record of the defendant's sentence. Finally, the court representative conducts participant-orientation interviews with the defendant as well.

The court representative must have the ability to interact effectively not only with court personnel, but also with the defendant population. Generally speaking, this position requires at least one year of work experience in the criminal justice system or a college degree, or a combination of education and related experience.

Domestic Violence Counselor

- Assist/counsel victims of domestic violence
- Possess strong human relations skills
- Administrative/organizational skills vital
- Varied work hours

Many family courts throughout the country operate domestic violence units in which victims of domestic disputes are assisted. These counselors provide court advocacy, crisis intervention, short-term counseling, and assist victims in the petition room for filing for Orders of Protection, and concrete services and referrals as needed. There are a number of duties associated with this position. In the actual courtroom setting they may provide the victims with an orientation to the family court and escort the clients to court when necessary. They can assist their clients with other direct services such as placement into shelters, relocation, transportation, public assistance, or other assistance when necessary. Finally as in most every position within the criminal justice system, they are responsible for and must maintain accurate case records and statistics.

Domestic violence counselors must have strong interviewing and interpersonal skills, good organizational ability, the ability to work day/night shifts, and an understanding of the issues of domestic violence. A degree in criminal justice and prior experience or internship background in the social services would usually qualify candidates for an entry-level position in this field. In some areas of the nation, bilingual ability would be considered an advantage.

Judge

- Oversee legal process in courts of law
- Safeguard rights, determine legal positions, instruct jury
- Many judges appointed/elected thus part of political process
- Determine sentences, set bail, award damages
- Most judges hold the Juris Doctor degree

The job responsibilities of a judge may vary according to his/her jurisdictions and powers. In general, a judge oversees the legal process in courts of law. They ensure that trials and hearings are conducted fairly and that the legal rights of all parties are safeguarded. They ensure that rules and procedures are strictly adhered to with respect to such items as the admissibility of evidence and methods of conducting testimony. In the initial phase of a trial called a "pretrial," a judge will listen to allegations to determine whether a particular case has enough merit to warrant a trial. In criminal cases, a judge may decide whether a person should be remanded to jail prior to trial or decide whether, and in what amount, bail will be set in order to release the accused. In civil cases, a judge may determine specific conditions to be upheld by opposing parties until the trial.

A judge may decide the outcome of a case when laws do not require a jury trial. In cases requiring a jury trial, a judge will instruct the jury on applicable laws and direct them to deduce the facts from the evidence presented to determine a verdict. In a criminal case, a judge may determine the sentence, and in a civil case, award compensation for the litigants.

There are different types of judges whose responsibilities vary according to jurisdiction. Trial court judges of the federal and state court system generally try civil cases that transcend the jurisdiction of lower courts and all cases involving felony offenses. Federal and state appellate court judges have the greatest power and prestige. They review cases handled by lower courts to support or nullify the verdict of the lower court. The majority of state court judges preside in courts whose jurisdiction is limited by law to certain types of cases. For example, traffic violations, small claims, misdemeanors, and pretrial hearings constitute the bulk of the work. Administrative judges or hearing officers are employed by government agencies to rule on appeals of agency administrative decisions regarding such issues as: workers' compensation, and enforcement of health and safety regulations.

Judges do most of their work in offices, courtrooms, and law libraries, and generally work a 40-hour week. Much of a judge's time is spent preparing for trial, researching the law, and preparing rulings and judgments for trial. Judges held approximately 40,000 jobs in 1988 with about one-half working at the state level.

In most cases, to become a judge you must first be a lawyer. All federal judges are appointed by the President with the consent of the Senate. About one-half of state judges are appointed while the remainder are elected in partisan or nonpartisan elections. The prestige associated with serving as a judge should ensure continued intense competition for openings on the bench.

Paralegal/Legal Assistant

- Perform clerical and administrative duties for lawyers
- Research and prepare cases
- Obtain and draft legal documents
- Interview defendants and witnesses
- BA in legal or paralegal studies, certificate desired

In effect, paralegals function in very much the same way that lawyers do, except that they do not give legal advice or represent clients in court. They assist in all phases of case preparation. Duties include collecting evidence, drafting legal documentation, and researching and summarizing information about laws pertinent to cases, as well as those tasks that are relatively routine in nature (i.e., clerical responsibilities). Paralegals commonly attend and schedule hearings, interview defendants, witnesses or citizens, and obtain legal documents such as sworn affidavits.

At the present time, no standardization exists for employment or certification of paralegals. Those employed in this field have qualifications that range from high school graduation with work experience to those who hold college degrees emphasizing courses in criminal justice and law.

There has been a growing trend towards meeting specific educational and/or training requirements. Today there are a number of educational institutions such as business schools, colleges, and paralegal training institutions that provide specific legal education training and experience vital to obtaining a position in this field. Students should evaluate the variety of these programs for their educational content and job placement success before enrolling but, by all means should seek additional educational expertise, as the trend to hire students with some formal training is expected to rise.

In addition to acquiring knowledge about legal forms, procedures, and terminology, students must be able to write clear and concise reports. Good English and legal vocabularies are essential. It is also important for paralegals to be able to work effectively with people, because they meet and communicate regularly with a variety of other professionals in the course of their job.

Pretrial Services Officer, U.S. District Courts

- Investigation and supervision specialist
- Advises court on pretrial release and detention, release condition supervision, monitoring, pretrial diversion, and public safety
- Duties may be similar to probation officer
- Requires a college degree, and specialized experience for appointment at Judicial Salary Plan level 7/9

The pretrial services officer has duties and responsibilities similar to those of a probation officer on the federal level. He or she will conduct background investigations of those alleged to have violated federal statutes and refer these investigations to the courts, will recommend release or detention after the investigation, and will supervise those defendants who are released.

The officer is also responsible for notifying the courts of violations of pretrial release, assisting persons under supervision with social service referrals, monitoring pretrial release reports for the U.S. Attorney, and maintaining effective interagency liaisons when required.

The pretrial services officer is expected to participate in ongoing personal training and education, cooperate with community agencies and, if deemed necessary by the court, carry firearms.

To qualify for a position as a pretrial services officer, a person must be a college graduate from an accredited college or university with a degree in a social science or in a field appropriate to the subject matter of the position and must have a minimum of one year of specialized experience. Specialized experience for this title can be defined as progressively responsible experience in the investigation, counseling, and guidance of offenders in community correction or pretrial programs, or in closely allied fields such as education guidance counselor, social worker, caseworker, psychologist, substance abuse treatment specialist, or correctional researcher. A person interested in such a position may apply to the Federal Court District Office of Pretrial Services in which he or she desires to work.

Release-on-Own-Recognizance (ROR) Interviewer

- Interviews and collects background information on defendants
- Makes release recommendations to judge
- Frequent court appearances
- BA/BS degree required

A position found in some areas of the country, and one that is relatively new, is that of the release-on-own-recognizance (ROR) interviewer. The ROR interviewer emerged as an offshoot of judicial reform that attempted to enhance the efficiency and fairness of the pretrial process in two ways. The first was an effort to decrease the number of days spent in detention by defendants who could safely be released to the community while awaiting trial. The second was to reduce the rate of nonappearance in court by defendants released from detention and awaiting trial.

The ROR interviewer's main task is the interviewing of defendants to verify information regarding their background and community ties to determine whether they could qualify for release on their own recognizance. In this position, the ROR interviewer interviews the defendant shortly after his/her arrest, usually at central booking. Information on the defendant's residential, employment, and family status is collected, and attempts are then made to verify this information by telephone. Additional information from police department arrest reports, prior convictions, and outstanding warrants are added to all that has been collected. Upon completion of this process, the ROR interviewer makes a release recommendation based on the strength of the community ties, and the likelihood of voluntary return to court. This information and recommendation is forwarded to the judge, who in turn examines this data, and in conjunction with other factors in the case, arrives at a bail or release-on-own-recognizance decision.

Other typical tasks may involve appearing in court and responding to questions relating to defendant's eligibility for ROR or interpreting information for the judge, district attorney, and defense attorney. The ROR interviewer might also assist defendants in following directions to ensure that they appear in court, maintain contact with defendants and provide them with any information necessary to successfully complete court appearances, and contact defendants for whom warrants have been issued to make arrangements for a voluntary return.

The basic qualifications for this position include at least two full years of college and two years of full-time work experience in some form of court contact (interviewing, counseling, job placement referrals) in a social service or criminal justice agency. In some cases, a bachelor's degree from an accredited university is a substitute for the experience.

Research Analyst/Statistician

- Prepare and evaluate statistical research reports designed to improve effectiveness and operation of agency or department
- BA/BS minimum requirement, master's degree preferred
- Strong math and computer skills essential

Research analysts perform a vital function within the overall administrative and management systems of the courts. Usually working under the direction of the chief judge's designee or the court administrator's deputy, research analysts prepare and evaluate statistical research and management reports designed to improve the structure and flow of court services, programs, and procedures. Analysts concern themselves with the improvement of existing programs and help to create and implement new ones.

Common areas for research include case flow through the courts, cost control, probation and parole services, grant writing, court procedures, space and equipment management, and other vital services.

A BA/BS degree is the minimum educational requirement for an entry-level position. In most cases, a research position in the courts requires, at minimum, a master's degree in criminal justice, public administration, business administration, or statistics. A strong background in math, statistical theory, research techniques, and computers is essential. Depending on the jurisdiction, applications for this position are made directly to the clerk of the court or by taking an appropriate Civil Service Examination.

Support Services Coordinator

- Assist nonviolent misdemeanant in alternative sentencing programs with social service needs
- Requires knowledge of social service programs
- Ability to work with hard-to-employ population
- Experience in counseling
- Excellent entry-level position for correctional counseling

The support services coordinator is responsible for assisting nonviolent misdemeanants in alternative sentencing programs in finding employment, education, housing, health, or other necessary services that these clients might require. In order to perform this duty, a support services coordinator must first evaluate a client's needs by conducting assessment interviews and administrating basic educational exams such as math and English. The support services coordinator also must develop a network of social and health agencies that could provide the required resources for the client. The coordinator also provides employment counseling and accompanies the client to interviews. Finally, the support services coordinator is responsible for collecting data and writing reports on the services provided for each client, as well as enforcing the client's sentence.

Since the participants are considered difficult to employ, experience working with and a desire to assist this group is paramount. Further qualifications for this type of position include extensive contacts with and knowledge of referral agencies, effective communication skills, ability to work well in a small group setting, and possession of a valid driver's license. Educational requirements can vary with each jurisdiction.

Site Supervisor

- Supervise defendants in community service sentencing projects
- Possess handyman skills and motivational abilities
- Good entry-level position for social service, corrections, alternative-to-detention field

In some court jurisdictions, an alternative to detention sentence might involve assigning the defendants to rehabilitation of public property. Site supervisors are responsible for the supervision of the defendants involved in this community service. This supervision involves teaching proper work techniques in cleaning out buildings, painting and plastering interiors, and other forms of restorative construction.

The site supervisors are also responsible for continuous on-site inspections in order to observe not only the level of work being done, but to ensure that a high level of safety and productivity is being maintained. Site supervisors also write reports on each worker and on the progress of the work being done, and distribute stipends to the workers. Finally, the site supervisors are expected to maintain effective communication and constructive ties with the community and community groups.

This position requires experience in manual labor, good interpersonal and motivational skills, supervisory experience, ability to handle pressure, and familiarity with the problems of ex-offenders.

Victim Services Personnel

- Provide assistance to crime victims
- Exposure to disturbing crisis situations
- Must work well under pressure
- Provide counseling service and casework
- College degree usually required
- Background in social work/counseling
- Mature, calm, and caring personality needed

Victim services personnel provide supportive assistance to victims of crime and their families. In certain regions, these professionals find employment in municipally sponsored victim services agencies; however, more than likely, opportunities will be found in private not-for-profit agencies affiliated with local police departments, district attorney offices, hospitals, and through the courts.

Victim Services Specialist

The duties of the victim services specialist generally fall into two particular areas of the judicial process: complaint and arraignment. In the complaint room, the victim services specialist interviews victims to determine service needs; provides orientation to central booking, complaint room and arraignment proceedings; collects notification information for possible future court appearances; screens cases for restitution; advocates for victim needs in the District Attorney's complaint room; and assists with property releases and affidavits. Ability to accurately record information and a high level of organizational ability are required. A college degree is required, and prior work or internship experience is helpful.

Child and Youth Counselor

There is a compelling need for child and youth counselors. To meet the problems confronted when children are victims of crimes, the victim services agencies have developed a number of programs in which child and youth counselors can help children and parents overcome the trauma of the crime as well as the possible criminal proceedings that follow.

In many areas, victim services agencies operate children's centers, which provide structured day care for child victims and children whose parents are involved in court proceedings. For child victims who must testify in court, child and youth counselors explain the process and accompany the child to meetings with lawyers and into the courtroom. These counselors help court officials understand the child's cognitive abilities and emotional state before the case proceeds. Child and youth counselors also help children express and dispel fears resulting from the crime. They prepare them for dealing with such threatening situations as what to do when they see the defendant in the neighborhood or courtroom, or how to tell friends about their experiences.

Child preventive services programs are programs that are designed to protect children from abuse. In these programs, child and youth counselors assist families with a history of violence, where children are at risk of abuse or neglect.

A third program in which the child and youth counselor is involved in aiding child victims is in the child victim unit. This project helps child victims and their families deal with the family court system and cope with the crime. The child and youth counselor accompanies the child to court and acts as a liaison between the attorney and the victim's family. The child and youth counselor also helps the child deal with the emotional consequences of the crime.

The child and youth counselor also assists in school victim assistance programs, which provide individual and family counseling for students who have witnessed violence themselves or been victims of crime at school, at home, or in the street.

Finally, a child and youth counselor may assist in group counseling for children who have experienced or witnessed violence at home, and in support groups for the brothers and sisters of murder victims, where these youths can discuss their feelings and help one another cope with the trauma of their losses.

The basic qualifications to work as a child/youth counselor include an advanced degree in social work and/or counseling, or in some cases a bachelor's degree in a relevant field combined with some social service work experience. Preferably, such work should be with children and families. Sensitivity and concern for others is necessary, and working knowledge of the courts and criminal justice system is helpful.

Crisis Counselor

The responsibilities of crisis counselors basically consist of providing services to victims of domestic violence, incest, rape, or runaway youths, and youths contemplating running away. A crisis counselor provides services such as crisis intervention, short-term counseling, concrete services, and information and referral for victims and their families. They also assess victims' needs and formulate treatment plans for victims.

In addition, crisis counselors coordinate and conduct educational programs and develop support groups for victims and their families. They also assist in establishing and maintaining service linkages with other social services and community agencies, and assist in staff training. Finally, a crisis counselor maintains case records and statistics on services provided, and performs other related tasks as assigned.

The qualifications needed to become a crisis counselor are an advanced degree in social work or a related field, or a BA and two years of relevant experience, or an equivalent combination of relevant course work and experience. Other important qualifications include telephone counseling experience, knowledge of the police and the criminal justice system, and the ability to work with others as a team.

Runaway Counselor

The job of the runaway counselor is to assist runaway children by discussing with them the dangers of the streets and the options for improving the situation at home through counseling, family mediation, and peer support groups. Runaway counselors also assist parents of runaways by giving support and advice on how to search for their children or how to respond should their child call or return home. In addition, runaway counselors counsel parents whose children are at risk of running away about the warning signs and how to cope with them.

Runaway counselors usually work via a hotline number that is given out by the police, churches, hospitals, and city agencies. Runaway counselors may also reach out to young people who are involved or who are at risk of becoming involved in juvenile prostitution by taking to the streets. The counselors may go to a specific area in the afternoons and evenings and try to identify and establish contact with teenagers on the streets.

Once the runaway counselor has gained the confidence of the young people, he or she can provide them with support, guidance, and information. The counselor also offers food and clothing and arranges for emergency medical care, shelter, and transportation.

Qualifications for runaway counselors include a combination of education and experience, preferably in the area of counseling, peer counseling, or human services.

Homicide Victim Counselor

These counselors assist families of homicides victims, providing comprehensive services including advocacy with representatives of the criminal justice system.

Responsibilities are similar to other victim services personnel in providing individual, family, and support group counseling; helping in obtaining available entitlement; liaison and advocacy with representatives of the criminal justice system; maintenance of accurate records and timely statistics.

Basic qualifications are a BA/BS in Criminal Justice, Human Services or a related major; experience in conducting individual (including children and teenagers) counseling; and the ability to work as a team member demonstrating extreme flexibility with excellent interpersonal and organizational skills.

Chapter 4

Careers in Corrections

Humane treatment may raise up one in whom the divine image has long been obscured. It is with the unfortunate, above all, that humane conduct is necessary.

—Dostoyevsky

Individuals in the field of corrections deal with incarcerated persons or those who obtain alternatives to incarceration. These professionals have a goal of rehabilitation and prevention of recidivism. Jobs are found in the general areas of detention, rehabilitation, and administration. Required for any aspect of this field is the ability of the candidate to be concerned about people in difficulty, and to have the desire to compassionately assist individuals who have experienced conflict with fellow human beings.

Correctional Treatment Specialist (Federal Prison)

- Provide guidance/support to inmate population
- Requires BA/BS plus graduate credit or experience
- Appointment at GS-9 level
- Work solely within prison confines

On the federal level, correctional treatment specialists perform correctional casework in an institutional setting. They develop, evaluate, and analyze program needs and other data about the inmates; evaluate progress of individual offenders in the institution; coordinate and integrate inmate training programs; develop social histories; and evaluate positive and negative aspects in each case. Correctional treatment specialists also provide case reports to the U.S. Parole Commission; work with prisoners, their families, and interested persons in developing parole and release plans; and work with U.S. probation officers and other social agencies in developing and implementing release plans or programs for selected individuals. The work may include individual and group interviews or discussions and extensive correspondence; and may involve contact and coordination with prisoners, relatives, interested persons, former and prospective employers, courts, social agencies, boards of parole, U.S. probation officers, and law enforcement agencies. Applicants for the correctional treatment specialist position must be U.S. citizens, less than 35 years old at time of appointment, and will be required to successfully complete an employment interview, physical examination, and full-field security investigation.

Additionally all candidates must have a bachelor's degree with at least 24 semester hours of social science. The applicant must also have two years of graduate study in social science or two years of graduate education and casework experience. Qualified applicants are appointed at the GS-9 level with promotion potential to GS-11 after one year. For further information applicants should contact the Federal Bureau of Prisons, Examining Section, Room 400, 320 First Street, N.W., Washington, DC 20534.

Corrections Counselor

- Guide and counsel inmates during their incarceration
- Assess and develop appropriate rehabilitative programs for each inmate
- Conduct individual and group counseling sessions
- BA/BS and/or master's degree in counseling, social work, or psychology
- Strong interest in helping others

Corrections counselors (educational, guidance, vocational) are individuals with educational background and expertise in casework techniques. Along with other professionals in a correctional facility, they are involved in the selection of individual educational and vocational programs and treatment for inmates, in planning and coordinating inmate rehabilitation programs, and in intensive inmate counseling. Corrections counselors interview new inmates, study their case histories, review reports from various sources, summarize this material and make program recommendations. Areas in which inmates receive counseling are family, institutional, educational, vocational, financial, parole, and disciplinary matters. Counselors may also participate in parole and disciplinary hearings.

These positions, depending on the jurisdiction, generally require a written examination to be considered for appointment. These exams are designed to test for knowledge, skills, and abilities in the areas of correctional counseling and preparing written material, with emphasis on clarity and organization.

Other important minimal experiential and educational requirements must also be met. A bachelor's degree is necessary, usually in a relevant discipline, in addition to three years of experience as a caseworker or group-worker in a recognized social service, correctional, criminal justice, community or human welfare agency, or in a position providing program services to incarcerated inmates. An alternative to this requirement would be a bachelor's degree in social work, sociology, criminal justice, psychology, probation and parole, or a closely related social services field. Some agencies permit holders of a master's degree in criminal justice, social work, or a related field to substitute this advanced education for up to two years of work experience. The experience should involve casework or program services that includes the establishment of an ongoing one-on-one relationships between counselor and clients. The groupwork experience must include responsibility for conducting group sessions designed to provide the participants with therapeutic services for significant social problems, such as alcohol and drug abuse, mental and emotional problems, family disturbance, and delinquency.

Corrections Officer

- Guard, observe, and supervise inmates in correctional facility
- Ability to enforce rules and regulations
- College degree helpful, but not required
- Sensitivity to people
- Rotating shifts
- Element of danger to be considered

A career as a corrections officer is a very demanding, yet potentially rewarding position for someone with a strong sense of authority, responsibility, and sensitivity toward others.

Corrections officers are primarily responsible for the safekeeping of prisoners either awaiting trial or previously sentenced to a federal, state, or municipal correctional facility. A correctional facility may be large, such as a penitentiary, or small, such as a jail or detention center. The level of security at these sites can range from minimum to maximum with each classification reflecting the relative level of supervision inmates receive. The major responsibility of corrections officers involves the continued observation and supervision of inmates. Corrections officers must be alert for signs of disorder, tension, and rule infractions by inmates, and be prepared to enforce these rules and regulations, should such a situation arise. This involves settling disputes, administering discipline, and searching of inmates on a regular basis. The element of danger is considered part of the job, particularly when corrections officers respond to emergency situations involving riotous inmate behavior or escape. The use of firearms, chemical agents, or other emergency equipment may be required.

Corrections officers may be required to report orally and in writing regarding such matters as inmate conduct, their work habits, and progress. Therefore, good writing skills are helpful. Another common task is the inspection of prison cells and other facilities to ensure that proper health, safety, and security are maintained.

By virtue of their close and continued contact with the prison population, corrections officers are an integral part of the rehabilitation process of inmates. It is not uncommon for corrections officers to participate in a variety of programs with other professionals such as counselors, social workers, and psychologists, who work to help inmates adjust to prison life in the institution and in the process of preparing for life outside.

Because the custody and security of inmates is a 24-hour-a-day job, corrections officers may be required to work night shifts, holidays, weekends, and overtime during emergencies, working both indoors and outdoors and spending long periods of time on their feet.

In the coming years, employment prospects in this field are expected to rise. As inmate populations increase, more corrections officers will be needed.

Promotional opportunity in this field is generally good. Corrections officers may advance to corrections sergeant, lieutenant, captain, or assistant warden. With additional education, corrections officers may qualify for related jobs such as parole and probation officers, corrections counselors, and a variety of administrative positions within the institutions.

Most corrections departments have civil service regulations that require corrections officers to be at least 21 years of age, possess a high school diploma or its equivalent, and be in sound physical health. Strength, good judgment and the ability to think and act quickly are assets. Some states may require candidates to pass a written examination. Others require candidates to have some experience in corrections or police work. In the federal prison system, college education can be substituted for general experience.

The Federal Bureau of Prisons provides two weeks of formalized training for all new employees. In some states, newly hired corrections officers are required to complete similar formal training programs. Most states and local governments use experienced officers to train new employees informally, on-the-job.

Juvenile Justice Counselor

- Counsel juveniles assigned to state youth division
- Work with juveniles ranging from Persons in Need of Supervision (PINS) to more hard-core troubled adolescents
- Work frequently performed in an institutional setting
- Generally requires BA/BS degree (jurisdiction can require high school diploma plus experience)
- Requires compassion and sensitivity

Most states have a division for youth or similar agency which is designed to promote the physical, emotional, and social well-being of the state's youth. Its mandate is to provide a unified system of youth development and juvenile justice services that assist the youth to become productive, fully integrated members of society.

A major responsibility of a youth service division is the rehabilitation of youths found guilty of crimes against persons or property. These youths are placed with the division by the county and designated as juvenile delinquents or juvenile offenders, depending on the severity of their actions.

Juvenile justice counselors also work with persons in need of supervision (PINS), also referred to as "status offenders," who are placed with the division for youth by the family courts. Such youths include runaways, truants, and those who must be removed from their homes because of family difficulties. Often victims rather than offenders, PINS are now protected by federal statutes which prohibit their confinement in detention facilities or with youths who have been indicted for more serious offenses.

Juvenile justice counselors basically work under the jurisdiction of a program coordinator. Counselors can be expected to perform any or all of the following tasks: providing support and counseling to residents; participating in the development and execution of treatment plans; interacting with staff members regarding the needs of residents; participating in recreational and cultural activities; providing a safe and clean environment for residents; maintaining discipline and order among residents; providing safe transportation for residents; participating in ongoing meetings, conferences and training; maintaining records and case files; and preparing and presenting oral and written reports.

Minimum requirements for this position include a bachelor's degree with a major in psychology, criminal justice, social service or a related field, and preferably some related experience in the counseling or social service field. Information on application procedures generally can be found with the personnel office of the state division for youth or its equivalent.

Parole Officer

- Employed in correctional facility or private agency
- Guide inmates in their preparation for and adjustment to community life
- Investigate and take action for parole violations
- BA/BS degree required; master's degree helpful
- Training in firearms
- Social work and counseling background necessary

Parole is defined as a system of discretionary release of inmates from correctional facilities and jails prior to the maximum expiration of their sentences. Parole is also the community supervision of offenders who have been released to parole. Parole is usually implemented through an administrative body or board composed of members who are appointed by the governor of a state to serve a term, the length of which varies from state to state. The parole board is broken down into panels of perhaps three to four members who visit the correctional facilities to make parole decisions.

An inmate is eligible for parole consideration when he/she has served the minimum period of imprisonment as imposed by the court. The parole board conducts an in-depth personal interview in which it considers all of the available information concerning the inmate. Factors taken into account might include such factors as the crime, criminal history, adjustment while confined, and release plans.

In an institutional assignment, the parole officer guides and directs inmates during their incarceration to help them develop positive attitudes and behavior, to motivate their participation in appropriate programs of self-improvement, and to prepare inmates for hearings before the parole board and for their eventual release to the community.

If assigned to the field, the parole officer guides and directs parolees during their period of adjustment from incarceration to community life. They help them comply with the terms and conditions of parole, investigate, and take appropriate action concerning parole violations. As peace officers, parole officers are trained in the use of firearms and are required to apprehend and arrest parole violators.

While this career has been categorized under counseling or social service, parole work involves both social work and law enforcement responsibilities, requiring firearms training and knowledge of arrest procedures. In most parole agencies, all appointees will be required to participate in and satisfactorily complete a training program including classroom instruction in such areas as basic law, social work practice and case management, firearms training, and arrest procedures.

The applicant must pass a thorough character investigation, with a previous felony conviction barring appointment. Physical and medical standards include vision requirements in some parole departments, along with the ability to function effectively in possibly arduous and physically demanding field assignments. As travel to their field assignments is frequent, most parole agencies require possession of a valid driver's license at the time of appointment.

The parole officer title will minimally require a bachelor's degree with a major in the social sciences and one to three years of experience as a social caseworker or group worker in a recognized social services, correctional, criminal justice, or human welfare agency. Qualifying casework experience involves the establishment of an ongoing, one-on-one relationship between the caseworker and client, with the development of treatment plans and implementation of appropriate treatment services. Groupworker experience shows abilities in conducting group sessions designed to provide the participants with therapeutic services for significant social problems such as substance abuse, mental and emotional problems, family disturbance, and juvenile delinquency.

As a substitution for education and experience, many parole agencies will favorably consider a law degree or a master's degree in social work, probation and parole, sociology, criminal justice, or psychology.

For those who meet these requirements, many states require passing a written test designed to elicit knowledge, skills, and abilities in such areas as preparing written material, interviewing techniques, principles, and practices of casework, counseling in a correctional setting, and a knowledge and understanding of social issues relating to minorities, the poor and ethnic groups and cultures.

Contact the State Civil Service Commission, the State Correctional Services Department or the Division of Parole to receive applications for this position. On the federal level, the role of parole officer is incorporated with that of federal probation officer.

Finally, cities, counties, and other jurisdictions have their own parole programs, and the local criminal justice agencies for these areas should be contacted for employment information.

Pre-Release Program Correctional Counselor

- Counsel clients
- Help in transition from custody to society
- Work is within confines of the facility
- Must be able to interact well with inmates
- May require BA/BS degree, plus experience in social service field

Pre-release program correctional counselors work with residents of state prison pre-release centers. They assist in orienting residents to the facility and its procedures in order to provide emotional support. Pre-release program correctional counselors also provide individual and group counseling under the supervision of the center's administration. Furthermore, the counselors accompany residents to job interviews, hospitals and assist the employment counselors in helping the resident find meaningful employment. Finally, the pre-release counselors also assist in the general operation of the facility at the request of the administrators.

To qualify for employment as a pre-release center correctional counselor, one must have, at minimum, a bachelor's degree in addition to two years of social service related counseling experience. Résumé and employment inquiries should be addressed to the personnel office of the state prison system.

Pre-Release Program Employment Counselor

- Provide vocational guidance for those soon to be released from incarceration
- Requires BA/BS and experience in career/vocational counseling
- Work entails placement of hard-to-employ clients
- Job site usually located within a detention center or halfway house
- Requires strong communication skills

Pre-release program employment counselors work with residents of state prisons by attempting to provide a range of vocational counseling. The duties of the employment counselor can vary, but usually involve interviewing and assessing prisoners; developing and maintaining job placement and training contacts; administering, scoring, and interpreting vocational aptitude and standardized tests; maintaining written records; developing and coordinating a program of workshops on vocational issues and verifying the place of prisoners' employment through site visits and telephone contact with the employers.

Requirements for the employment counselor include a bachelor's degree plus two years of experience in the labor market or vocational counseling field. However, these qualifications can be substituted in some prison systems by a satisfactory combination of education and experience coupled with evidence of the knowledge skills and ability to perform these tasks well. Inquiry can be made at the state, county, or local correctional facilities administrative headquarters.

Pre-Release Program Halfway House Manager

- Similar to a corrections officer/prison administrator
- Residents will be easier to work with than those in prison
- Requires strong administrative skills
- Must be willing to work all shifts and weekends
- College degree or equivalent combination of education and experience preferred

Pre-release program halfway house managers can be employed in state-run pre-release programs. Additionally, they can also be employed as contract employees in federally financed probation programs designed to aid prisoners in their return to society.

Halfway house managers maintain custodial responsibility for the facility and are accountable for the whereabouts of the residents. They conduct personal searches and dispense supplies and medication. In addition, they can supervise daily clean-up duties and oversee all visitors entering and leaving the building on a daily basis. Finally, halfway house managers write reports on the prisoners along with census and population statistics.

This position usually requires a high school diploma. However, college credits or a bachelor's degree may be required, depending on the size of the halfway house program. Candidates must be willing to work mornings, evenings, nights, and weekends, as 24-hour/seven-day coverage is required. The ability to work well with people and effectively deal with an inmate population is essential.

Probation Officer

- Conduct presentence reports and evaluations concerning release conditions
- Work to rehabilitate and supervise offender once released
- Counseling and referral to community agencies
- Some law enforcement background helpful
- BA/BS in social sciences; master's degree and/or work experience helpful
- Human relations skills a must

A probation officer provides supervision of offenders in the community instead of prison. Their task is to help protect the community by supervising adult and juvenile offenders and aiding them in leading a law-abiding life. Probation officers also service individuals and families with problems that may come to the attention of the family court.

Similarities do exist between probation and parole officers. Ideally, they have a dual role, that is, protection of the public while also helping the offender interact successfully in the community.

Probation officers can be employees of the federal, state, county, or city government. They are responsible for the delivery of professional probation services to clients and courts, and they perform a wide variety of duties related to court proceedings and to the delivery of correctional services to juveniles and adults.

These duties include intake evaluations, completion of reports and investigations, and the supervision of persons sentenced to probation. Peace officer status can be connected with the probation officer position, which may include some law enforcement responsibilities such as execution of warrants, searches and seizures, and making arrests. This work is usually performed under the supervision of a higher-level professional employee.

Probation officers should possess a genuine respect and concern for people. They should be able to communicate with all types of individuals. Since the job is stressful, the probation officer should be emotionally strong and able to cope with difficult situations. This requires strong leadership skills and the ability to be at times both gentle and assertive.

The minimum qualification is a bachelor's degree, preferably in one of the social sciences. Many positions found on the city, state, or county level will probably require a written and oral examination designed to test the applicant's ability to provide client services. As the probation officer gains work experience and additional formal education, he or she can move to higher-level positions, usually in supervision of administration.

Juvenile Probation Officer

- Provide intake, investigation, and supervising services to family court for juveniles
- Requires desire to work with youths and their families
- Generally requires BS degree in related field in addition to two years of casework or counseling-type experience
- Ability to manage heavy caseload and work effectively with an offender-type population

A juvenile probation officer, an employee of the probation department, provides intake, investigation and supervision services to the family court for juveniles generally up to the age of 16 who appear as the result of delinquent acts or as Persons In Need of Supervision (PINS).

In the intake process, the juvenile probation officer assesses the total situation of the petitioner when first making contact with the family court. The officer weighs the attitudes and strengths, and evaluates the risks of the petitioner. Based on these decisions, the juvenile probation officer may present an alternative plan that is consistent with protecting both the community and the needs of the petitioner. If the petitioner is a PINS project participant, the juvenile probation officer helps determine the eligibility and suitability of the PINS respondent as well as the needs of his family. The juvenile probation officer also has the possible alternative of referring the respondent to community service and ensuring that initial appointments are kept with the service provider.

The investigative process is intended to provide the court with a comprehensive picture of the offender and the offense. The investigative report reviews and analyzes social factors, as well as the details of the current offense and the respondent's legal history. The juvenile probation officer then submits a recommendation to assist the court in reaching an appropriate disposition. Because of the special skills and knowledge of the resources needed to best meet the needs of juveniles, the juvenile probation officer also has responsibility for all presentence investigations on youthful offenders before higher courts.

In supervision services to the family court, the juvenile probation officer conducts interviews with the juvenile after he or she is placed on probation. The main purpose of this contact is to explain the conditions of probation as specified by the court and to establish a preliminary supervision plan. After placement on probation, the officer, probationer and parents become involved in further developing the supervision treatment plan and defining goals for the probation. The juvenile probationer will also identify community services that are available, and plans are made to utilize them if necessary.

Finally, the juvenile probation officer may make visits to the probationer's home if necessary, and if the probationer fails to comply with the conditions of probation, the juvenile probation officer may file a violation and explore other dispositional alternatives. In most jurisdictions, a juvenile probation officer is required to have a bachelor's degree in a related field such as psychology, human services, social work, or criminal justice. Some probation departments also may require a master's degree in social work or counseling. Experience in paid casework-type counseling is also extremely important, with some jurisdictions asking that the applicant have at least two years of experience in this work. Other requirements include strong analytical abilities, excellent written and oral communication skills, ability to manage a sometimes heavy and stressful caseload, possession of a valid driver's license and, perhaps most importantly, a willingness and ability to interact effectively with an offender/ex-offender population.

Warden

- Overall supervision and administration of correctional facility
- Plan, direct, coordinate programs
- Responsible for all rehabilitative, security, disciplinary, and educational programs
- Oversee and supervise staff
- BA/BS degree, master's degree preferred
- Excellent managerial skills
- Knowledge of all phases of corrections operation

Wardens function to oversee all operations and programs that are a part of life within the correctional facility. However, they do not work alone, nor do they always have direct involvement in all phases of corrections operations. Because their job responsibilities are so all-encompassing, they must successfully delegate responsibilities to a host of administrative professionals who serve under their direct supervision. Through these subordinates, wardens direct, plan, and coordinate operations and correctional facility programs in such areas as security, discipline, education, rehabilitation, budget and fiscal management, staffing, and inmate care.

They meet regularly with the staff members to develop and establish policies and regulations, review inmate records and behavior, prepare written reports, gather statistics, and evaluate all components of a facility's operations.

Wardens must possess a complete knowledge and understanding of correctional programs and the operation of a correctional facility, including knowledge of the methods and techniques of inmate care, rehabilitation, and custody. In addition, wardens need to be good supervisors, administrators, and managers.

The position of warden, a senior-level position, is designed for someone who has gained experience through a working knowledge of the correctional system. A limited number of qualified individuals rise to this rank. Students striving toward this occupation should have, at minimum, a bachelor's degree, with a master's degree preferred. Coursework in sociology, psychology, criminology, and penology is recommended.

Other Related Corrections Occupations

When considering that a correctional institution is in many ways like a small community, it is understandable that a wide variety of career specialists are employed to care for and rehabilitate the inmate population, as well as maintain the services of the correctional facility. Within the institution, a number of specialists are employed to help in the rehabilitative process.

Clinical psychologists work closely with inmates. Often as members of an interdisciplinary health care team, they participate in administering a wide variety of psychological assessment techniques (intellectual, personality, aptitude, vocational, and educational), interpret results and prepare comprehensive reports. They are also involved in the development and organization of individual and group therapy and other rehabilitative programs for the treatment of prisoners with many kinds of problems. Specific emphasis may be geared toward vocational planning, so as to prepare the inmates for successful return to community life. Students interested in a career as a correctional psychologist should receive training in the area of criminal psychology. A doctoral degree is required, as well as the appropriate state licensing or certification.

Vocational counselors provide educational programs in vocational specialties. For example, they might teach a course in carpentry, automotive repair, electronics, or provide other career training through work programs that sell their products or services to federal agencies. Vocational instructors determine learning needs, abilities, and other facts about inmates. They may participate in discussion with other members of the treatment team and staff professionals to assess and aid in the overall rehabilitation of individuals.

Recreation counselors conduct and supervise the social activities of inmates, such as team sports and games, hobbies and dramatics, designed to promote the emotional, physical, and social well-being of inmates. Recreation leaders work with individuals of all ages and races. The ability to organize and motivate participation and interest through their own excitement and concern is a highly desirable personal quality.

Academic teachers are employed on all levels within a correctional facility. They might instruct in basic remedial courses designed to increase rudimentary English, reading or math abilities, or be employed to teach on a college level. In either case, a teacher within a correctional facility is a special kind of professional who must be able to communicate with inmates, convey knowledge, monitor and encourage progress, and adjust to the varied interests, abilities, and personalities of this kind of population. Time is spent grading papers, preparing lesson plans, and attending meetings with other support staff.

Caseworkers/HIV specialists are increasingly in demand to provide support services to the growing number of residents of traditional and non-traditional correctional facilities who are testing positive for the HIV virus.

Caseworkers help HIV-infected inmates cope with their emotional and health-related concerns while incarcerated. They also work closely with inmates soon to be released to help make their transition to society more manageable. This usually involves helping to coordinate many community support services as well as regular home visits. Caseworkers/HIV specialists are often responsible for facilitating educational programs. It is essential that caseworkers be able to deal with HIV issues pertinent to men and women, mothers and fathers, minority communities, substance abusers, homosexual, heterosexual, and bisexual clients. Equally essential is that candidates possess a genuine concern/caring for others. A bachelor's degree and experience in social services are required.

Education counselors are responsible for providing counseling services to aid inmates in making an effective adjustment to the facility educational programs. Working with inmates and staff, they help to ensure that the inmate's choice of program is in relation to his or her long-term goals. They periodically evaluate the progress of inmates to provide suggestions and make recommendations for continued educational training and supportive services.

Substance abuse specialists can be found in correctional institutions, pre-release and other alternative detention programs. These professionals primarily function as substance and alcohol abuse education and prevention workers. Working with criminal offenders, parolees, and other high-risk groups and their family members, these professionals provide individual and group counseling that focuses on the issues and problems surrounding alcohol and/or drug abuse. These positions usually require a college degree, in addition to a familiarity with the addictive personality and withdrawal process. Some agencies and institutions require a C.A.C. (Certified Alcoholism Counselor) certificate or specific training in substance abuse.

On an administrative level, a variety of other career specialists are available to help plan, direct, research, and evaluate the many programs and activities found within a correctional facility.

Classification and treatment directors and other management coordinators apply the principles of management to the overall planning, coordination, and evaluation of correctional programs. They assign inmates to particular programs, review inmate case reports and consult with other staff members to recommend parole, educational or vocational training, medical treatment, and other services for the inmate. The ability to organize and direct the work of others is an essential requirement of this position. Additionally, they should be well informed about all phases of inmate care, custody, rehabilitation, and operations.

Inmate records coordinators supervise personnel with records and other correspondence. They maintain responsibility for receiving and transferring of inmates, prepare inmate reports and written work regarding such matters as court proceedings, legal affidavits, furloughs, leaves of absence, and escapes, to name a few.

Correctional facilities specialists engage in on-site visitation to local and state correctional facilities to determine that proper standards and regulations have been followed. They investigate and report on complaints involving state and local correctional facilities referred by officials, organizations, residents, or other interested parties. They may also participate in the plans for the building or remodeling of a facility or to develop programs or policies that are seen as promoting the rehabilitation process.

Prisoner-classification interviewers interview new inmates and compile social and criminal histories. They collect such data as work histories; school, criminal, and medical records; evaluations from correctional staff; information from relatives; and data surrounding each offender's crime and criminal background. With this thorough background investigation, and after a personal interview with each offender, prisoner-classification interviewers construct profiles of each new inmate with a recommendation to work assignment and the degree of custody recommended.

In the field of corrections a variety of specialists are employed to help research and evaluate correctional programs, policies, the inmate population, and crime in general.

Penologists conduct research and study the control and prevention of crime, punishment for crime, management of correctional facilities, and rehabilitation of inmates, with an emphasis on treatment programs and parole procedures. These professionals work closely with other specialists such as economists, anthropologists, statisticians, physicians, social workers, and historians. Students who are interested in this kind of career should pursue master's-level training and education in the specialization of penology or sociology with an emphasis on research and design skills. Often a doctoral degree is required for directorships of major research projects or higher-level positions in this area.

Occupations within the field of corrections can be considered similar to nearly every kind of job found outside the system. There are positions that range from those requiring a high degree of formal education and experience to those that require more modest ability and education. Advancement within the system is possible with continued training and education.

Chapter 5

Careers in Forensic
Science/Criminalistics

The hopes of the world must rest on the habit of form-
ing opinions on evidence rather than on passion.
                                    —Bertrand Russell

Criminalistics

For purposes of this book, the term "criminalistics" is used to describe the area of forensic science specific to criminal justice work, and the terms "forensic scientist" and "criminalist" are used interchangeably.

By employing standardized scientific analysis, forensic scientists use their expertise to examine evidence vital to an investigation. Essentially, their findings can be used by investigators, prosecutors, and defense lawyers to support someone's guilt or innocence.

As compared to other fields in the criminal justice system, forensic science is perhaps the most technical. The process of analyzing physical evidence involves the abilities of a highly skilled professional trained to apply the principles of chemistry, physiology, biology, and other sciences in the analyzation, identification, and classification of evidence.

Perhaps the most well-known career in the field of forensic science is that of the medical examiner. Medical examiners work closely with law enforcement personnel; they provide valuable evidence as to the "cause of death" of individuals and, thus, are instrumental to the investigative process. The academic preparation for this career is extremely rigorous, requiring completion of medical school in addition to advanced specialized training in pathology and forensic pathology. Should you not want to consider such a demanding career preparatory track, other opportunities to work as a criminalist exist. Requirements for these careers vary. Generally, advanced graduate education in the sciences and/or specialized training and experience gained in the field of law enforcement is required. Because of the variation and complexity of the evidence to be analyzed, a criminalist may specialize in one area.

Ballistics Specialist

A ballistics specialist is primarily interested in the weapons used in the commission of crimes. This specialist conducts examinations that range from the basic identification of the gun from which a particular bullet was fired to the operational and functional tests of firearms. The work also would include everything from the determination by gunpowder and shot pattern tests of the distance from which a shot was fired, to finding the type of weapon used in firing a questioned bullet or cartridge case.

Toolmark Specialist

This specialist employs the same principles used in firearms identification and can identify the tools or objects used by criminals at the scene of a crime. The toolmark specialist also is involved in the investigation of motor vehicle theft. If, for example, a thief alters the original serial number of a stolen car and re-stamps a fictitious one, the toolmark specialist might identify the stamp.

Serology Specialist

The serology specialist conducts laboratory analyses of body fluids (such as blood, urine, semen) collected as evidence during a criminal investigation. This technician performs extensive chemical tests to determine such things as blood or semen type, or the presence and content level of drugs or alcohol.

Fingerprint Specialist

Employed by either the FBI, the State Civil Identification Bureau or the local police department, the fingerprint technician is responsible for collecting, classifying, analyzing, and identifying fingerprint impressions.

The purpose of this work can range from uncovering a prior criminal record, indicating whether an individual is sought by another enforcement agency or identifying missing persons or amnesia victims.

The fingerprint technician should be detail-oriented and able to exercise patience. This is methodical work that is usually obtained on the state and local level by taking a civil service examination. The FBI, the largest single employer of fingerprint technicians, requires applicants to be high school graduates and pass its written examination for initial employment.

Arson Specialist

The arson specialist is employed by various police or fire departments, or works independently for insurance companies. He or she basically arrives at the scene of a fire to determine its origin and cause, through the collection and evaluation of evidence, which may lead to a full-scale investigation.

Document Specialist

Document investigation involves a minute comparison of questioned handwriting with known handwriting. The document specialist can determine if handwriting and signatures are forged. Analyzation would include the paper, ink, instrument, etc. to determine when and by what means a document (or part of a document) was created.

Polygraph Specialist

This specialist uses an instrument known as a polygraph to conduct examinations of individuals to learn if their verbal responses are truthful. The polygraph is frequently called a lie detector, although the instrument does not actually determine if a person is telling the truth or lying. It merely measures physical responses such as blood pressure, respiratory rate, etc.

A polygraph specialist observes the patterns of such responses to questions to determine if the reactions indicate the presence of stress due to lying. A good polygraph specialist should understand the dynamics of psychology, response, and human behavior; special skills and training received in an approved lie detection school are mandatory.

The Crime Laboratories

Four federal law enforcement agencies are highlighted below whose modern laboratory facilities provide the workplace for many of these forensic specialists. It is hoped that descriptions of these agencies will further clarify understanding of how the role and functions of these professionals serve as an integral part of the criminal justice system.

Federal Bureau of Investigation

The FBI crime laboratory is divided into several sections and units. Because work in the FBI laboratory is highly specialized, each of their scientific experts must limit their activities to a relatively narrow field. In looking at the organization of the FBI crime lab, one will realize just how specialized and complex it can be.

Scientists working in the document section would involve dealing with scientific examinations of physical evidence including ink, paper, alterations, obliterations, infrared, ultraviolet, handwriting, handprinting, typewriting, shoe prints and tire treads, conducting scientific research with respect to these areas, and keeping abreast of new developments and maintaining reference files for use and assistance in conducting examinations. This section also assumes major responsibility for the translation and interpretation of a wide variety of written and oral foreign language material into English, examines evidence in gambling and extortionate credit transaction cases and conducts crypto-analytic examinations of secret/enciphered communications.

The scientific analysis section is composed of several units that handle a variety of highly specialized types of examinations. These units include chemistry, toxicology, firearms, toolmarks, hairs and fibers, blood, metallurgy, petrography, number restoration, glass fractures, and spectography.

The special projects section of the laboratory assists in the investigation and prosecution of cases by conducting forensic photographic examinations of physical evidence and by means of visual aids used as demonstrative evidence. This section also plans, designs, and constructs special purpose equipment used as investigative aids for special agents in the field.

Finally, there is the engineering section. Formerly part of the FBI laboratory, it is now part of the FBI's technical services division. Even though it is not part of the laboratory division, it is involved in the examination of physical evidence. This section consists of units that design and develop new radio communications for use in the field, set up and maintain a network of radio stations for use in the event of an emergency, and serve in a consulting capacity in a large number of other matters relating to radio communications. In addition, the section conducts forensic examinations pertaining to electronics, electrical and security devices, and performs audio analyses of magnetic boxes.

Bureau of Alcohol, Tobacco, and Firearms

In operation for close to a century, the Bureau of Alcohol, Tobacco, and Firearms (ATF) laboratory system provides scientific support services to the Bureau's combined responsibilities of law enforcement, industry regulation, tax collection, and state assistance. Some major concerns of the ATF scientists include product analysis, consumer protection, analysis of firearms and explosives evidence, and applied research to develop new analytical techniques in these areas. ATF scientists and technicians also provide expert testimony in court cases.

The ATF laboratory system is divided into three headquarters laboratories: chemical, forensic, and identification. These are located in Washington, DC. The headquarters office maintains a scientific library and a complete photographic laboratory. Four regional labs are located in Atlanta, Cincinnati, Philadelphia, and San Francisco.

In the ATF chemical laboratory, samples of all alcoholic beverages marketed in the United States are analyzed for both tax purposes and consumer protection. ATF regulates more than 100 different categories of products using industrial or denatured alcohol, from foods, drugs, and toiletries to embalming fluids and rocket fuels, and determines the eligibility of internal medicines, food products, and flavoring extracts for prepaid tax rebates.

Another task confronting the chemical lab is tobacco analysis, to distinguish between cigarette and cigar filler tobacco. Since the tax on cigarettes is more than five times greater than the tax on small cigars, the potential for revenue loss is great. The chemical laboratory is also responsible for calibration of alcohol-gauging instruments such as the hydrometer, a device used to measure the density of liquid.

The identification laboratory is responsible for examining a wide variety of physical evidence submitted in connection with criminal cases. These examinations encompass a broad spectrum of scientific disciplines and include questioned document verifications (handwriting, typewriting identifications), fingerprint identifications, firearms and toolmark identifications, speaker identifications by the voiceprint method, and ink and paper analyses.

The ATF's identification laboratory maintains the world's largest ink standards library. The library contains ink samples, results of chemical analyses and the first date of production of each standard ink sample. The ink library allows inks on questioned documents to be identified and dated, a valuable capability for the detection of fraudulent documents.

In discussing ATF's forensic laboratory, it is interesting to note that it performs about 80 percent of its work for state and local law enforcement agencies upon request. This laboratory performs mainly chemical and instrumental examinations of evidence.

In investigations of arson, incendiaries, bombs, and other destructive devices, the ATF forensic chemists attempt to determine the type of explosive used and the components of the destructive device, such as pipe, clock, or battery. These investigators are aided by such highly sensitive equipment as the Vapor Trace Analyzer, an explosives sniffer that detects vapors from commercial explosives both before and after detonation.

Many comparative analyses of evidence are performed by ATF forensic specialists, who match known samples of evidence with questioned samples. X-ray analysis and the emission spectrograph (enabling rapid comparison of metal fragments and paint samples), and neutron activation analysis (a process which detects elements at very low levels), provide fast and accurate results for these comparative analyses.

The largest single work area of the ATF forensic laboratory is the gunshot residue testing area. By examining residue from a suspect's hand for traces of barium and antimony, it may be established whether the suspect recently fired a gun.

Finally, the ATF forensic laboratories employ experts in serology, the examination of body fluids, to determine the blood types of various samples.

U.S. Customs Service

The customs laboratory system, like that of the Bureau of Alcohol, Tobacco, and Firearms, provides modern technological backup support for the law enforcement efforts of all customs offices, including enforcement of the tariff and trade laws.

The customs chemist plays a prominent role in protecting the health and safety of American citizens and the security of this country's commerce. During the course of their careers, customs chemists are called upon to analyze imported merchandise ranging from textile fibers to contraband narcotics. In many cases, the duty collected on imported products depends on the chemists' analytical report. Customs chemists also analyze samples of seized or suspect merchandise, and serve as expert witnesses in subsequent litigation.

Customs laboratories are located in Boston; New York; Savannah; New Orleans; Los Angeles; San Francisco; Chicago; Washington, DC; and San Juan, Puerto Rico. They are equipped with instruments that are used to analyze a wide variety of materials for tariff classification, such as determination of content in beverages, the metallographic characterization of an alloyed structural steel, the fiber content of textiles, and the lead oxide content of fine crystal.

Analyses involved in their law enforcement role include narcotics and dangerous drugs, products derived from endangered species, toxic chemicals or prohibited additives, mislabeled merchandise, and products in violation of United States patent laws.

The forensic capabilities of the field laboratories are being increased through training of field laboratory personnel in forensic science and purchasing specialized equipment needed for forensic analysis.

Drug Enforcement Administration

The Drug Enforcement Administration (DEA) employs forensic experts in its Office of Sciences and Technology. Over the past decade, scientific advances have enabled the DEA to improve its investigative techniques and equipment to the point that its investigators are using and relying more on these techniques and equipment, particularly in long-term, complex investigations.

The primary scientific areas that the DEA utilizes are in the fields of chemistry and communications and technical surveillances. This is not surprising since these areas are of extreme importance to narcotics, investigative, and forensic experts.

The DEA chemical units can provide a rapid indication of the presence or absence of a drug substance through their field-testing techniques. DEA research chemists have also devised techniques that can identify, within appropriate statistical confidence, where various drugs have been produced throughout the world. This enables their enforcement personnel to target their efforts towards the source countries. Communications technicians within the DEA are responsible for a satellite communications system that provides a digital communications capability for its investigative personnel who operate beyond the range of other DEA systems.

Qualifications for Employment

Though many of the criminalists and other forensic lab professionals originally began their careers through the experience derived from general police work and detective investigations (in such areas as fingerprint investigations, documents examination or crime scene photography and sketching), in addition to the taking of in-service coursework conducted by their respective agencies, there is a growing trend towards hiring civilian personnel who have formalized education in chemistry, biology, and physics. More recent additions are those who have bachelor's or master's degrees in the specific discipline of forensic science.

Students are advised that they should be able to successfully complete a strong college science background and in particular attend a college that will provide an internship component. Because requirements for each position vary according to the complexity and responsibility, and because federal, state, and local hiring practices for each agency or laboratory may differ, it is best to contact the civil service office or agency for the jurisdiction where employment is desired.

Chapter 6

Careers in Private Security

In examining the origins and development of security, it is both obvious and instructive to observe that security holds a mirror up, not to nature, but to society and its institutions.

—Gion Green

Private security represents one of the fastest growing fields of employment today. Security work (or as it is often called, loss prevention or risk management) is moving in a direction that will firmly establish itself as a separate career field within the criminal justice system.

Security may be thought of as proactive, in that it concentrates primarily on the prevention and management of our environment to deter crime and enhance safety. The field of private security implies that the protection, prevention and management responsibilities of this field are provided by entities other than our government. It might be helpful to think of private security as employment that is privately funded, usually beginning where governmental or public security leaves off. In many cities, the number of private security personnel exceed those employed as public police and related law enforcement personnel.

Most often, security work is associated with the uniformed guard who functions as a deterrent to crime in the local bank or shopping mall. This is perhaps because these workers provide a highly visible presence. Security guard positions are merely one component of the opportunities that exist within the security field.

Diverse Employment Opportunities

Because the need for security touches all areas of work and home life, security professionals are employed virtually everywhere. Hess and Wrobleski (1992) describe four major areas in which the services of the security professional will be called upon: (1) retail security, (2) commercial security, (3) industrial security, and (4) institutional security. Within these areas, a variety of challenging job responsibilities exist.

Retail Security

Burglary, shoplifting, vandalism, employee theft, credit card fraud, bad checks, etc., all have the potential to cripple the success of any retail establishment. Whether it is a small business or a large department store, safeguarding the establishment ensures its stability and security. Of particular concern is the rise of "mega-malls" throughout the country. As these retail stores centralize, they will pose unique safety challenges. Businesses will increasingly turn to professionally trained security managers and directors to coordinate mobile patrols, develop and install high-tech equipment, and improve communications and surveillance systems in efforts to deter crime, reduce financial losses, and protect the public from harm.

Commercial Security

The security of commercial buildings such as financial institutions, office buildings, hotels, recreational parks, transportation systems, airports, and airlines is becoming an increasing concern. These establishments will need to turn to professional security experts for their knowledge and leadership to ensure the safety of people and property. We need only to consider the tragic bombings at the World Trade Center and the Oklahoma City federal building to highlight the need for increased professional security.

Financial institutions are especially attractive targets to criminals. Robbery, unauthorized and fraudulent use of credit cards, and insider dishonesty result in millions of dollars in losses and increased harm to the public. Vandalism and theft in buildings, crowd control at public gatherings, terrorism at airports and other places threaten public safety. Commercial enterprises will need to increasingly rely on a professional security staff to meet this security challenge.

Institutional Security

Beyond the scope of commercial establishments exist a number of institutions that are open to the public, and pose their own unique security problems. These include hospitals, educational institutions, libraries, museums, religious facilities, etc. Hospitals, for example, are considered magnets for criminals – especially drug addicts – and present particular security risks and concerns. Internal theft of medication/drugs is big business and results in significant loss to a hospital. Hospitals present particular security risks and precautions. They are spread out over a large area with many open access points. Proper lighting, fencing, and access control will be needed to reduce crime. Also, the emergency room is considered a challenging security point. Here, assaults on patients, nurses/doctors, and visitors by unruly persons occur with some frequency. It is understandable that the security professional will be called upon to safeguard hospitals and other institutions with increasing regularity.

Industrial Security

Manufacturing plants have had an increasing need for the services of the security professional. Vandalism and theft of equipment, tool supplies, products, etc., result in huge financial losses. Theft of confidential information such as trade secrets is another area of security concern. The use of security professionals to carefully screen, monitor, and investigate personnel is essential. Additionally, utility and transportation companies, for example, need trained professionals who will design and set up complex security systems that function to reduce loss, monitor access, and control and deter crime. An understanding, as well as an ability to install closed circuit television and other high-tech surveillance equipment will be needed.

Beyond the position of security guard, there are many other job titles/ functions in this field.

Various Job Titles

Agent	Operative Watchperson
Alarm Investigator	Plant Protection
Armed Guard	Private Detective
Attendant	Private Investigator
Bodyguard	Private Police
Console Operator	Private Watchman
Courier	Railroad Detective/Patrol Officer
Credit Investigator	Runner
Detective (retail, undercover, private, hotel, hospital, etc.)	Security Director
	Security Guard/Officer
Electronic Protection	Security Manager
Guard	Security Representative
Inspector	Special Agent
Intelligence Officer	Special Investigator
Investigator (airline, hotel, insurance, etc.)	Special Police/Patrol Officer
	Store Detective
Loss Prevention Specialist	Truck Guard
Merchant Patrol Officer	Undercover Agent (or operative)

Job Responsibilities

Responsibilities of the job titles listed above can be divided into four broad categories:

1. Administrative/Managerial
2. Investigative
3. Technical
4. Protective

It is important to keep in mind that these job duties will frequently overlap.

Administrator/Manager

The security administrator/manager is a leadership position that combines the ability to make policy decisions with a fine sense of communication skills. A security administrator/manager consults and advises superiors in upper management on the design and implementation of an effective program. Subsequently, duties entail the follow-through of procedures that have been agreed upon.

The security administrator/manager is also responsible for personnel administration. He or she has overall authority for the hiring, training, and direction of subordinates. Other personnel duties could include wage and salary analyses and recommendations, labor relations, budgetary preparation, and overall record-keeping for the security program. Thus, interpersonal communication skills are essential.

Investigator

The concept of "investigations in private security" is broad-based, having similarities to public sector law enforcement in that certain skills and abilities are necessary to conduct a proper investigation. Talents such as being able to deal with people, collecting and assembling pertinent facts, preparing clear and concise reports, and an ability to function well under pressure (assume a role) are all critical to the success of an investigator.

In the retail business one might be asked to pose as an integrity shopper in an attempt to verify the honesty and efficiency of the store's cashiers and personnel. Another example of the investigation of the retail area would be an assignment as an undercover operative in the stockroom to determine possible employee pilferage. Banks and financial institutions employ personnel as investigators who might concern themselves with either internal auditing or accounting procedures, following up on the writers of bad checks, or the investigation of credit card forgeries. Attorneys frequently employ investigators to develop information that will be used either in defense of their clients or as evidence in a lawsuit.

Technician

The field of technical service as it applies to security work is rapidly advancing. Technical service can be thought of as the application and utilization of technological equipment such as computers, closed circuit television, alarm systems, locks, polygraph machines, photographic devices, and other electronic equipment used in crime prevention. In fact, it is difficult to imagine any sophisticated security system without the utilization of technological equipment.

With the tremendous advances in scientific equipment, the security field requires those skilled and knowledgeable security professionals who install, monitor, and repair this equipment. Career opportunities in this area of security work are diverse and dependent on one's skill and training. There is a vital need for skilled crime prevention experts trained in many areas. All personnel in the security field will be greatly aided by a working knowledge of how these systems impact and integrate into a comprehensive security system regardless of any direct involvement in their design, control, or repair.

Protective Specialist

The function of a protective specialist can vary greatly according to the level of importance and responsibility of the person or property to be protected. On a routine level, the functions of a guard in a factory or warehouse might be considered. Responsibilities might be to patrol a designated area. Duties may include checking gates, locks, windows, and doors to ensure against vandalism. Checking the identities of persons who enter and leave the area may be another duty. In another situation, a guard at a port of entry or railroad may be responsible for observing the ongoing loading and unloading of shipments. Guards might work to protect a company from pilferage and smuggling, or might have to notify authorities of potential fire hazards or emergencies. In a location, guards must be prepared to deal with all emergency situations and in some cases be ready to administer first aid procedures. In these types of security operations, guards may not need to carry weapons as the element of danger may not warrant it.

On a more complex level, as a part of an elite security force that functions to protect individuals or highly valuable or dangerous goods, the level of responsibility might change. The element of danger might require security personnel to be trained in firearms and self-defense. Guards might work to protect against extortion, terrorism, kidnapping, computer theft, bomb threats, or sabotage. These protection responsibilities require advanced skills and knowledge and a higher level of enforcement power.

Qualifications for Employment

Requirements for positions in the security field will vary depending on the nature of the job and responsibilities of the person in each position. At the entry level, a uniformed officer working, for example, in a contract guard agency would usually be required to have a high school degree, no prior criminal record, relatively good health, and effective communication skills. In a retail department store employing plainclothes store detectives, the candidate might also be required to have prior experience in retail undercover-type investigation. Moving up in responsibilities, there are shift supervisors who answer to an assistant director of security. They will generally be required to possess at least one year of guard-related experience plus either some coursework on the college level or be able to substitute prior related supervisory or military/law enforcement experience.

Advancement at this point, whether to an assistant director level or above, will usually rely on some formalized education combined with progressively more responsible experience and training. Because many institutions of higher education in the country recognize that the growth of the private security field will require more college-trained personnel, there has been an increase in the number of programs that offer coursework in this field.

Higher-level administrative positions in private security may require broader skills and abilities. Therefore, it is helpful for security administrators to be knowledgeable in such areas as cost control, accounting, law, electronics, computer usage, personnel administration and training, and employee relations, to name a few. An increasingly important requirement for high-level security, administrative-type positions is possession of the Certified Protection Professional Certificate granted by the American Society for Industrial Security (ASIS). To attain this certification, candidates must fulfill certain education, experience, and exam requirements. Membership in ASIS is not a prerequisite to meet certification requirements.

The future of the security professional appears bright. As college degree programs in security management continue to develop, you can expect an increasing trend toward specialization in this field. Governmental requirements regarding licensing and the adherence to standards for security personnel will be adopted. Qualified personnel will be sought after at all levels – especially at the management level. Increased opportunities and high salaries can be anticipated.

Chapter 7

Hearing from
Criminal Justice Professionals

The fool wonders, the wise man asks.
—Benjamin Disraeli

In the previous chapters, a variety of criminal justice careers were described, with focus on five major areas. The information contained in these career descriptions was culled from available civil service position announcements, brochures, and other information received from the agencies themselves.

In this chapter, you will hear from some of the people actually employed in these professions. From them, you will learn some of the realities of criminal justice employment as seen through the eyes of those who actually perform the work each day. Many professionals were asked to respond in writing to the following four basic and critical questions.

- Describe how a typical day is spent doing your work.

- What do you like most about your work?

- What do you like least about your work?

- What is the best advice you could give to a student who plans to work in your career field?

Responses to these key questions are reported exactly as the various professionals relayed them to us. They are presented in alphabetical order according to job title. Responses were anonymous and represent only a sampling of careers in the criminal justice system.

Assistant District Attorney

Describe a typical day. No day is typical – the cases are as varied as the people who commit, or are victims of, the crimes involved. You review your daily assignments (new and old cases), go to court, deal with judges and defendant's attorney. If on trial, last-minute preparation of witnesses and legal research, in addition to assisting your colleagues.

What do you like most about your work? Being able to control the situation and bring order out of disorder. Finding out the "truth" of a situation, and through logic and evidence, spelling it out for others to learn. Also, being able to help change laws that I think are unfair.

What do you like least about your work? The amount of paperwork involved.

What advice could you give to a student? Be prepared for the worst and all else is easy. Maintain a good sense of values, be patient with others and yourself. Maintain a good sense of humor, especially when the going gets tough and frustrations are high.

Civilian Aviation Security Specialist

Describe a typical day. I report to the airport and check and monitor security systems, participate in undercover activities designed to infiltrate restricted security areas, and gather intelligence regarding airport security.

What do you like most about your work? I enjoy the travel and overtime pay.

What do you like least about your work? Report writing. Since FAA is a regulatory agency, I am not allowed to carry a firearm.

What advice could you give to a student? Take several English classes and/or writing classes to develop writing skills. Keep grades high.

Confidential Investigator

Describe a typical day. Taking complaints, scheduling, and conducting interviews of complainants and/or witnesses, writing reports, retrieving data from agency records, municipal, county or federal records, and/or conducting surveillances.

What do you like most about your work? The ability to structure my work to suit my pace. Also the fact that many of my investigations result in positive changes being effected for the public good.

What do you like least about your work? The paperwork.

What advice could you give to a student? Do an internship with one of the city agencies, since it allows you to get a foot in the door.

Conservation Police Officer

Describe a typical day. Check out pet stores, check out fish markets, checking waste haulers for permits, speaking at schools. Endangered species investigation, wild bird law enforcement. May run across some penal law violations.

What do you like most about your work? Being outdoors and meeting people and protecting the environment.

What do you like least about your work? The pay.

What advice could you give to a student? If he/she loves the outdoors and wants to protect his or her own environment, this is the job for him/her.

Consumer Safety Officer

Describe a typical day. A typical day is spent evaluating systems and processes at establishments engaged in the production of foods, drugs, cosmetics, and medical devices used by the American public. The purpose of these evaluations is to assure that products used by the public are safe and effective.

What do you like most about your work? The non-routine nature of the work. Each establishment process, system, or product presents a unique challenge and opportunity to learn.

What do you like least about your work? The starting pay could be better.

What advice could you give to a student? Obtain a strong science background in school.

Correctional Officer

Describe a typical day. The day is fast paced and busy. Most of the time is spent supervising inmates, securing the safety of the institution, inmates, and staff during their day-to-day changing schedule.

What do you like most about your work? There is opportunity for upward mobility and training if you are motivated and interested. I enjoy learning the computer technology involved in aspects of this work.

What do you like least about your work? I don't think you ever get used to feeling like you are locked up all day as well. It is very stressful.

What advice could you give to a student? Be professional and have pride in what you do. Have a positive attitude, be willing to work hard to get ahead.

Criminal Investigator (senior level)

Describe a typical day. Setting up appointments; arranging travel schedule locally and overnight; studying and evaluating correspondence and files concerning allegation(s) involved; conducting interviews.

What do you like most about your work? Attempting to resolve cases and problems which usually includes obtaining indictments through the Assistant U.S. Attorney's office.

What do you like least about your work? Investigations without any allegations involved. Looking for criminal wrong-doing, strictly on our own, which we do a lot.

What advice could you give to a student? Attempt to obtain a basic knowledge (at least) of the operation of computers in dealing in white-collar crime matters. We are continually doing computer runs in white-collar investigative matters involving matters of fraud.

Customs Inspector

Describe a typical day. The job entails two primary areas of responsibility. You either examine cargo containers at various locations such as piers, airports, warehouses, container stations, or, examine passenger belongings at ports of entry.

What do you like most about your work? The contact and interaction with people during the course of the day.

What do you like least about your work? The job can be very tedious and boring, with long hours.

What advice can you give to a student? Keep grades high as there may be incentive programs for outstanding students, apply for co-op programs with Customs.

Deputy U.S. Marshal

Describe a typical day. Report to the office for my assignment for the day. Often, prisoners need to be transferred to and from federal and local jails for court appearances. Occasional seizures and arrests.

What do you like most about your work? The high degree of diversity from day to day.

What do you like least about your work? Often there are very long hours and mandatory overtime.

What advice could you give to a student? Keep your grades high, keep your record clean, join a co-op or internship program, and prepare for entry-level exam and job interviews.

Evidence Unit Technician

Describe a typical day. Morning staff meeting, process toxicology evidence and suicide notes, crime scene photos. Request medical and other hospital records, handle disturbances that might jeopardize building security. Receive all types of evidence from borough offices and police. Assist family members with any problems or questions.

What do you like most about your work? Working together with the federal, state, and city agencies.

What do you like least about your work? Trying to retrieve homicide clothing.

What advice could you give to a student? Get a BS degree in criminal justice. Volunteer to work with community organizations that deal with counseling or the police and community relations.

General Duty Road Trooper

Describe a typical day. Patrol of highways and interstate roadways. Criminal investigation and general police activities.

What do you like most about your work? The challenge.

What do you like least about your work? Shift-work.

What advice could you give to a student? Do some volunteer work or an internship at a police precinct to see if you like dealing with people in a crisis situation.

Internal Revenue Agent

Describe a typical day. Most of the day is spent examining corporate tax returns to determine tax liability.

What do you like most about your work? Dealing with people in all types of businesses and in all fields of employment.

What do you like least about your work? I become really angry when people who earn a lot of money try to cheat the government.

What advice could you give to a student? Have some knowledge about the job prior to application. Be prepared for the job interview. Demonstrate interest in the organization and in the work you will be expected to perform. Finally, be sure your own income tax records are accurate and reliable!

Loss Prevention Auditor/Investigator

Describe a typical day. My job mainly deals with enforcement of the company's procedures and policies. I audit each of the facilities for compliance. I train loss and prevention personnel. I investigate merchandise and cash losses.

What do you like most about your work? I enjoy conducting internal investigations. They are very challenging and each one is different.

What do you like least about your work? The amount of report writing.

What advice could you give to a student? Get an education that combines criminal justice and accounting. Some experience with computers is helpful. While in college, work part-time in some related entry-level job, or participate in an internship program.

Narcotics Agent (assigned to financial investigation of illegal narcotics trade)

Describe a typical day. Spend two hours on the computer, two hours making record requests from other agencies, three hours reviewing records received, one hour planning investigative moves based on the above.

What do you like the most about your work? The challenge of trying to outsmart the dealers. The excitement of the occasional raids and the satisfaction of seizing money/drugs from the dealers.

What do you like least about your work? The frustration of not getting to the major dealers. It becomes a game of trying to sweep the sand on the beach.

What advice could you give to a student? Get a strong background in accounting and business. Become literate in the use of the computer.

Personnel Administrator

Describe a typical day. Interviewing candidates for jobs, writing position descriptions, developing tasks and standards for job titles.

What do you like most about your work? I enjoy the human relations aspect of the work. In other words, the people contact.

What do you like least about your work? Working within a bureaucracy.

What advice could you give to a student? Gain a related undergraduate experience. Develop your communication skills and writing skills. Complete an internship where you get exposure to personnel practices and procedures.

Police Officer

Describe a typical day. As a police officer, you assume many different roles during the course of a day. You could help a lost child, settle a family dispute, investigate a crime, issue a traffic ticket, assist the victims of an auto accident, or simply patrol in a police vehicle without receiving a single call.

What do you like most about your work? The most appealing aspect of a police officer's job is that there is no typical day, each day is a new experience.

What do you like least about your work? Working different tours of duty is very difficult to get accustomed to and it is the cause of many family breakups.

What advice could you give to a student? The best advice anyone could give a student is to stay in school and continue your education. The best police officers are well-educated officers.

Police Officer/Recruiter

Describe a typical day. Talking to police candidates, via telephone, letter, formal group presentations or individually in regard to signing up for the Civil Service Exams. Also, informing lateral transfer candidates (police officers) of possibly transferring to our department. All the administrative record-keeping and paperwork associated with producing the aforementioned.

What do you like most about your work? Being able to meet and talk with different types of people.

What do you like least about your work? The paperwork.

What advice could you give to a student? Stay out of any kind of personal and legal trouble. Get good grades in college and keep trying until you get what you want.

Principal Court Analyst

Describe a typical day. Reviewing matters of alleged discrimination. Handling issues impacting on disability, i.e., reasonable accommodations. Reviewing proposals pertaining to human resource management. Responding to inquiries from the public.

What do you like most about your work? I really enjoy providing assistance and helping in the cases of individuals who have been discriminated against, especially in the workplace.

What do you like least about your work? The paperwork.

What advice could you give to a student? Study hard for entry-level exams. Know about the function of the agency and the judicial branch of government. Know how the structure impacts on operations. Know the types of court positions for which one can qualify.

Probation Officer

Describe a typical day. Monitoring cases, performing investigation procedures, court reporting, providing rehabilitative services/referrals, working with the courts, legal aid, district attorneys, police, families, substance abuse programs, mental health programs.

What do you like most about your work? Help people gain/regain control of their lives to grow and develop into healthy, productive members of society. Protect the community.

What do you like least about your work? High caseloads; limited resources.

What advice could you give to a student? Do an internship with the Department of Probation.

[U.S.] Probation/Parole Officer

Describe a typical day. Primarily paperwork: writing presentence reports for U.S. District Court. Casework entries, field work, release plans from the Bureau of Prisons, paper, paper, and more paper.

What do you like most about your work? Counseling clients in the field . . . social work with families.

What do you like least about your work? Too much paperwork (federal forms, etc.).

What advice could you give to a student? You must be able to wear two hats, one is a police hat, the other is a social workers'. Not always easy. I would recommend getting some sort of volunteer or observational experience before embarking on this career since it is a highly emotional and demanding job.

Special Agent

Describe a typical day. Conducting numerous interviews, a great deal of report writing, a great deal of time is also spent in your government vehicle traveling throughout the city and surrounding suburbs (much of this time can be stuck in traffic). After culmination of an investigation, hours can be spent interrogating and processing a prisoner. This can go into long hours into the night. However, after a successful arrest, I feel job satisfaction.

What do you like most about your work? Diverse types of investigations versus the same thing every day. Meeting people from all walks of life, travel worldwide versus always going to the same office everyday. The opportunity to work with other local, state, and federal agencies. This lets me make professional contacts and personal friends. This is very important, for instance, you could just call on the telephone and obtain information versus going through 'red tape.' Liaison is a very important function in law enforcement and can be most enjoyable.

What do you like least about your work? One feature that is very frustrating is too much paperwork. If your expertise is needed in another geographical area, you may have to relocate at an undesirable time. For instance, children in school or a personal problem, so you may have to move unaccompanied for a few months.

What advice could you give to a student? Take an opportunity to learn languages or obtain specialized training. Try to enter a co-op program with a law enforcement agency while in college; to meet individuals in the field and get 'a foot in the door.'

Special Agent/Defense Investigative Service

Describe a typical day. I interview individuals for access to classified information, and also to determine leaks of classified information. Interviews are followed up by writing extensive reports.

What do you like most about your work? Interviewing people from all walks of life and being exposed to all kinds of situations I'd not normally be exposed to.

What do you like least about your work? Government 'red tape.'

What advice could you give to a student? Don't neglect your English classes: good verbal skills and excellent writing skills are mandatory for any investigative position. No matter how good an investigator you are . . . or think you are . . . if you can't put the information in writing, you're useless!!

Special Agent, Secret Service

Describe a typical day. A given day for many may consist of advance work for a presidential visit, police liaison, surveys of area hospitals, logistical planning or dealing with a protectee's staff. A special agent involved in criminal investigation as opposed to protection, may find himself in consultation with prosecution and defense attorneys, testifying in court, preparing written reports, conducting investigations and making arrests.

Agents frequently spend entire days sitting in courtrooms, conducting surveillances, and engaging in lengthy meetings with attorneys, White House staff, press representatives, probation officers, embassy officials, or local police.

What do you like most about your work? The service provides a significant opportunity for a new special agent to mix with the public, fostering greater self-confidence and responsibility. An agent is frequently away from his (or her) desk, up and about of the office and responsible for his (or her) own time and productivity.

What do you like least about your work? During the course of a 20-25 year career, an agent is subject to frequent travel assignments and perhaps two, three, or four permanent relocations.

What advice could you give to a student? Complete your college studies. Upon graduation request an application from the local U.S. Secret Service Office. As soon as possible, obtain full-time employment. Learn as much about the U.S. as possible, be persistent, and continue to improve your qualifications by obtaining post-graduate education if possible.

Chapter 8

Testing the Waters:
The Value of Internship Experience

An ounce of work is worth many pounds of words.
—St. Francis DeSales

In the previous chapter, you read what professionals working in criminal justice careers had to say about their jobs. Finding out about the working world in this way is a good start. The best way to gain relevant work experience is to arrange for internship experience (sometimes they may be called externships or co-op programs).

The Importance of Internships

An internship is an educational opportunity where students beginning their career development in college have an opportunity to receive some direct experience. An internship is designed to give you the opportunity, while earning credit, to spend time working in the field related to your major course of study and career interests. This provides you with first-hand knowledge that cannot be experienced in classroom lectures or gained from faculty members and textbooks. It is the student's personal encounter in a particular career field.

An internship experience provides the opportunity to derive a realistic and practical view of the system. Even if the internship does not involve much responsibility, it provides the opportunity to view the career from within, in order to determine whether a particular job offers what you expect. All criminal justice majors should be aware of the immense value of this type of exposure and experimentation.

A sample of possible career-related internships will bear this out. Many cities (e.g., New York, Chicago, Miami, Washington, DC, Baltimore, St. Louis, Detroit, and New Orleans) have established work-study programs in the law enforcement field. These programs allow college students to split time between college studies and paid work within a police department. These "Cadet Programs," as they are referred to, provide excellent on-the-job training and experience. Many communities have similar programs in this and other fields. Internships might very well be set up in other such diverse criminal justice career areas as correctional institutions, probation departments, investigative agencies, courts, law offices, forensic science labs, and security management firms. As a result of observations and participation in the work world, a student can begin to evaluate his or her impressions and be better able to affirm career goals or change them if need be. To do this, you will need to consider important questions, such as: Is this field what you expected? Did you like or dislike what you observed others doing? Was there any one job that interested you? Did you feel excited about what you were assigned to do? Did you feel the internship was a good experience, or were you wasting your time? Did you feel bored observing others in their work? Did what the professionals have to say disappoint you? Is there too much report writing for you?

An internship experience is an excellent way of obtaining a realistic exposure that can help you decide if a particular field is really for you. It is also a way of building up experiences that can help make you marketable for employment. Students who are most successful in the job search usually possess a combination of education and job-related experience. Oftentimes, internships or other work-related experiences may lead to job offers. Even if you are not offered a job, you are developing a network of experiences and contacts that may make the job hunt easier and future employment more attainable.

Where to Arrange for an Internship

Probably the best place to start finding out about internship possibilities is to contact the office within the college designated to handle such matters (probably the career placement office) or your academic counselor for assistance. Also, it is possible that your library or career planning office has directories that describe programs available beyond the scope of the contacts your school provides.

Find out as much as possible prior to accepting a position so that you will not be disappointed. Most likely, you will need a résumé, and you need to prepare yourself for the interview, which probably will be a part of the screening process. The next chapter will focus on résumé preparation and interviewing skills.

How to Make the Most Out of an Internship

The value of an internship experience depends largely on your attitude and work habits, in addition to the adequacy of supervision. Understanding and accepting this premise will help make your experience more satisfying, even if the tasks you are requested to perform are not as thrilling as you had hoped. What can you do to make the internship experience more valuable and rewarding? Peggy Schmidt, in her book, *Making It On Your First Job*, provides several suggestions:

- Find out what your responsibilities will be before you start. Knowing what will be required of you prior to starting is a tremendous help. It will assist you in deciding if this is an internship you really want to do. Get clarification from your prospective supervisor as to what will be expected of you. If possible, talk with previous interns who worked at this job to gather more information and find if this is really an area you want to learn more about.

- Use your initiative. If at times during the course of your internship you find yourself feeling bored, or with little or nothing to do, try to be resourceful. Offer to help someone or perform some task that might be useful to the sponsoring organization. Keep your ideas simple and manageable. This is a wonderful way of gaining recognition and appreciation.

- Find out what various departments do. If your internship experience doesn't provide you with exposure to various departments within the agency or organization, you may want to formally request a tour of these other areas. You may find that another area's work appears more interesting. It will also increase the network of your contacts as well as provide you with a better overall perspective of how the agency or organization runs, thus making your experience more valuable.

- Get to meet the brass. Meeting those individuals at higher levels of decisionmaking can be rewarding.

- Ask people about their jobs. Find time to talk with co-workers about their job duties. You may want to ask them questions similar to those outlined in Chapter 7. You may find this is an excellent way to learn about a career, thus helping you to decide if it is really what you would want to do in the future.

- Go to professional activities. If your organization is sponsoring or participating in any professional forums, workshops, conferences, etc., see if you can attend. You will meet interesting people, gather up-to-date information pertaining to your career, and perhaps make contacts for future employment. As difficult as it may be, introduce yourself, ask questions, and share your opinions when it is appropriate. Attending these functions indicates your level of commitment to the organization, your school, and to the goal you have set for yourself.

An internship experience can validate your career choice, and open your eyes and ears to new possibilities of which you may be unaware. It might also force you to rethink your choices, and you may need to make new decisions. Whatever the outcome, the experience is a way for you to assess your strengths and weaknesses prior to graduating.

Chapter 9

Getting a Foot in the Door –
Cooperative Education Programs
in Criminal Justice

*To travel hopefully is a better thing than to arrive,
and the true success is to labor.*
—Robert Louis Stevenson

Similar to internship experiences, cooperative education programs can be a very important tool in a student's quest to prepare for a career in the criminal justice system. If you are fortunate enough to secure a position in a cooperative education program, you will be happy to know that there is a great chance you will end up being offered a job upon college graduation. The National Commission for Cooperative Education reports that 80 percent of co-op students receive offers of permanent employment.

The idea of cooperative education was introduced in 1906 at the University of Cincinnati and is in place now in more than 1,000 colleges and universities throughout the nation. Cooperative education programs exist in almost every academic major and discipline including Criminal Justice, and can best be defined by Ralph C. Porter, former President of the National Commission for Cooperative Education, who said, "Cooperative Education is a process of education which formally integrates a student's academic and/or career interests with productive work experiences in cooperating employer organizations. Through this interaction, students enhance their academic knowledge, persist in the continuation of their education, and improve their personal and professional development. The teaching faculty, cooperative education coordinators, and the employing supervisors all share in the intellectual and personal development of the student. The resulting effect is remarkably synergistic, with all of the parties benefitting from the collaborative effort."

The National Commission for Cooperative Education reports an estimated 50,000 employers in both the public and private sectors hire co-op students, with the Federal Government being the largest employer, having 16,000 students working in 36 agencies at more than 2,000 work sites.

The benefits of cooperative education for the student are similar to the benefits of internships: career exploration is facilitated; textbook knowledge is compared with the real world of work; students must employ job search skills in a successful manner to secure the co-op; co-ops provide pay to assist with undergraduate expenses and finally and most importantly, after graduation job prospects are markedly upgraded after the cooperative education experience.

The Agency also gains in this arrangement by availing itself of an excellent source of paraprofessional manpower; by observing actual on the job performance by the co-op student prior to consideration of a permanent job offer; by increasing ability to diversify the agency and lower the cost effectiveness of recruiting and training.

Finally, the college itself enjoys advantages resulting from the cooperative education program through an enhanced relationship with its Criminal Justice majors and the agency; by agency interaction allowing the college's Criminal Justice curricula to remain up to date; and by increasing enrollments of students attracted to cooperative education programs which foster better job placement opportunities.

From the above, then, it should be obvious that cooperative education can be critical to a Criminal Justice major realizing his or her career satisfaction. We should point out that the competition for cooperative education program vacancies can be brutal. It should also be noted that on the Federal level, as in any actual law enforcement/agent/criminal investigator positions, relocation might be required. Also, as will be seen in the following Federal Cooperative Education profiles, the anticipated date of a student's graduation will probably be delayed from six months to one year because of the way each agency's co-op is structured. In either case, whether of geographic considerations or graduation time frames our counsel to students has invariably been to accept the Co-op if offered and work through the inconvenience it might pose. The jump start to a student's career offered by a cooperative education appointment far outweighs any temporary discomforts.

Students interested in developing further information on cooperative education should contact their cooperative education coordinator and in the absence of a coordinator, might look to their Career Services office, Internship Program, the Dean/Chairperson of the Criminal Justice program, or a member of the Criminal Justice faculty. While we will discuss cooperative education on the Federal Government level, students should know that Criminal Justice Co-op Agreements could very well exist between their college and State, city, county, township, or private sector security offices. Once again the student is asked to inquire with your designated campus co-op representative.

Finally, these contacts would also be the most likely people to speak with if your institution lacks a cooperative education program with a Criminal Justice agency in that they have the contacts and authority with which to approach an agency in the hope of initiating a Cooperative Education Agreement.

Federal Agency Cooperative Education Programs

Following are descriptions of cooperative education programs on the Federal level for the Federal Bureau of Investigation, the United States Secret Service, the United States Customs Service, the United States Marshal's Service, the Drug Enforcement Administration, the Federal Bureau of Prisons and the Department of Justice Inspector General. We have taken the liberty of considering the FBI and the DEA as cooperative education programs when in fact the FBI actually has a paid summer honor internship and DEA calls its programs the "Q Appointment Student Aide Program." Both of these programs, however, are very similar to cooperative education and we feel both offer many, if not all, of the advantages found in traditional cooperative education.

The Federal Bureau of Investigation Summer Honors Internship Program

Each summer, a special group of outstanding undergraduate and graduate students are selected to participate in the FBI Honors Internship program in Washington, DC. The program offers students an insider's view to FBI operations and provides an opportunity to explore the many career opportunities within the Bureau. At the same time, the program is designed to enhance the FBI's visibility and recruitment efforts at colleges and universities throughout the United States.

Qualifications

Due to the very selective and highly competitive nature of the Honors Internship Program (more than 2,000 applicants a year), a limited number of internships are awarded each summer. Only individuals possessing strong academic credentials, outstanding character, a high degree of motivation, and the ability to represent the FBI upon returning to campus will be selected. In order to be considered, individuals must meet the following qualifications:

- Undergraduate students should be enrolled in their junior year at the time they apply to the program

- Graduate-level students must be enrolled in a college or a university and attending full time

- Students must return to their campus following the program

- Students must have a cumulative grade point average of 3.0 or above

- All candidates must be citizens of the United States

Application Requirements

If you are interested in the FBI Honors Internship Program, contact the FBI field office nearest to your campus for applications and additional information. Each applicant must complete and provide the following information:

- FD-646a application form

- Current academic transcript

- Personal résumé

- Recent photograph

- Written recommendation from appropriate dean or department head

- A 500-word essay expressing your interest in the program

Application Time Frame

July – August
Obtain an application package from the FBI field office nearest to your campus. Request the letter of recommendation from the dean or department head. Obtain a copy of your current academic transcript.

August – September
Complete your application, prepare your résumé, write a 500-word essay, and obtain your letter of recommendation from the dean or department head.

September – October
Review your Honors Internship brochure to ensure that all important documents have been obtained and completed.

Submit your completed application package to the FBI field office nearest your campus by November 1.

Selection Process

Once applications have been received at each respective field office, FBI representatives from that field office will arrange interviews with competitive candidates. Each field office will then nominate a designated number of candidates to the Personnel Division at FBI Headquarters in Washington, DC by December 1. A Headquarters selection committee will then make final determination of successful candidates. These finalists must undergo an extensive background investigation and drug-screening test. Final approval will be given by the Director of the FBI, and appointments will be rendered in the Spring of each year. Selections are based upon academic achievement, area of study, life/work experiences, and interest in law enforcement. Due to the FBI's specific long range needs, individuals with skills and education in the areas of engineering, computer science, foreign languages, political science, criminal justice, law, accounting, and the physical sciences will receive special consideration. The FBI also actively seeks women and minorities for participation in the program.

Things You Should Know

Once selected, FBI interns can look forward to three extremely rewarding and interesting months. Upon arriving in Washington, DC, Honors Interns will attend an orientation at FBI Headquarters. Interns will then be assigned to an FBI Headquarters division based on their academic discipline, potential contribution to the division, and the needs of the FBI. All interns will be under the supervision of the Assistant Director of their assigned Division. By the end of your internship, you will have a thorough understanding of the inner workings of the FBI.

The Honors Internship Program will begin on approximately the first Monday in June and will terminate on approximately the third Friday in August. All expenses for Interns traveling to and from Washington, DC to participate in this program will be reimbursed by the FBI. Each intern is paid at the GS-7 grade level on the Federal government pay scale. (Contact your Career Services Office for the most recent copy of the Federal Government pay scale). Information and assistance on housing is provided by FBI Headquarters. However, Interns are responsible for finalizing their own arrangements. Interns who own vehicles are encouraged to bring them to Washington, DC to facilitate travel related to particular assignments (some assignments are outside of Headquarters, though all are in the Greater Washington, DC area).

U.S. Secret Service Cooperative Education Employment Opportunity

In this program, selectees will participate in a two-year work-study program consistent with their field of study. The Cooperative Education Program provides an excellent avenue for the Secret Service to identify and train highly motivated individuals. The student gains job training, monetary responsibility, federal employee benefits, the potential for full-time employment after graduation, and an understanding and appreciation for the work environment at the federal level. The goal of the program is to bring together classroom training with a participatory work environment to produce capable employees. Positions are limited.

Students may choose from numerous professional occupations related to their field of study such as: Accountant, Budget Analyst, Computer Specialist, Computer Research Specialist, Criminal Justice, Electronic Engineer, Intelligence Research Specialist, Management Analyst, Personnel Management Specialist, Telecommunications Specialist, and Visual Information Specialist.

Baccalaureate Degree students must complete 1,040 hours of study related work requirements.

Criminal Investigator (Special Agent Co-Op Positions)

The selectee will pursue a two-year practical training program which will provide him or her with the necessary rudiments for the Special Agent position. The selectee will be introduced to the many investigative and protective techniques and resources utilized by Special Agents in carrying out their important responsibilities. They will work closely with Special Agents to gain practical experience in the origination, administration, and adjudication of criminal investigations. Positions are limited to the Washington, DC area for the Special Agent Co-op.

General Qualification Requirements

- Student must be enrolled full time in an accredited educational program

- Student must be enrolled in the school's cooperative education program

- Student must maintain a 3.0 GPA in undergraduate or graduate studies

- Student must be a U.S. citizen

- Student must be enrolled in a field of study related to the position for which they are applying

- All applicants tentatively selected for a position must submit to urinalysis screening for illegal drug use prior to appointment. Actual appointment to the position will be contingent upon the receipt of a negative drug test result.

- All Secret Service positions require top secret security clearances. Students may be appointed based on the results of a preliminary background investigation; however, continued employment is contingent upon completion of the full field background investigation. Some positions require a polygraph examination.

- The final goal is to bring the students into full-time positions upon graduation.

- Male applicants must certify that they have registered with the Selective Service System, or are exempt from having to do so under Selective Service law.

A signed working agreement between the educational institution and the Secret Service is required before the student is eligible for employment. The agreement documents the student's work schedule, program criteria, and requirements for future non-competitive conversion to full-time federal employment.

Work Schedule

Students work part time (no less than 16 hours per week and no more than 32 hours per week). However, during the holidays and school breaks, the student is eligible to work full time.

How to Apply

All applicants must submit either a Form OF-612, Optional Application for Federal Employment; or a résumé that includes the information cited in the Office of Personnel Management (OPM) Brochure OF-510, Applying for a Federal Job. This brochure is available from OPM or the Secret Service Personnel Division. Applicants can also apply through their cooperative education coordinator. This material should be sent to:

U.S. Secret Service, Personnel Division
Recruitment and Staffing Branch Room 912, 1800 G Street, N.W.
Washington, DC 20223
Attention: CO-OP Coordinator

U.S. Customs Inspector Cooperative Education Program

This is an innovative and highly competitive program that enables college students to obtain valuable law enforcement experience while completing their undergraduate degrees. Participation in the Cooperative Education Program enables students to experience all aspects for the Customs Inspector position and at the same time allows them to determine if they are interested in pursuing a career as a Customs Inspector after graduation.

Application Procedure and Requirements

In order to apply, students must have a cumulative GPA of 3.0 or above and be nearing the end of their second year of college. Interested students should complete Federal Employment Form OF-612 and attach a cover letter which includes the following information:

- Cumulative GPA

- Date of birth

- Foreign language capabilities

- Prior law enforcement experience (Internships are given serious consideration

- Computer skills

- Anticipated graduation date

- A narrative explaining why the applicant would like to be considered for the Customs Inspector Cooperative Education Program

Completed applications should then be submitted to the college Cooperative Education Coordinator for forwarding to the appropriate liaison with the U.S. Customs Service.

U.S. Marshals Service Centralized Student Career Experience Program

This cooperative educational program prepares potential Deputy Marshals to enter the Service. It is a work/study program for college students pursuing degrees in criminal justice or political science.

Co-Op Requirements for Deputy U.S. Marshal

- Be in attendance at an accredited school and be enrolled on a full-time program leading to a Bachelor's degree in criminal justice.

- Be enrolled in the college's cooperative educational program

- Have completed at least 90 credits towards the college degree

- Be nominated by the cooperative education coordinator

- Attain at least a 3.0 cumulative GPA and pass an oral interview by the Service

- Pass an extensive background investigation

- Be physically able to perform the duties of the Deputy U.S. Marshal and be able to pass the pre-employment physical examination

- Be a citizen of the United States

U.S. Marshals Service
Co-Op Student's Participation

Orientation

You will have the opportunity to meet Marshals Service personnel and become familiar with the duties and responsibilities of the Service.

Warrant Section

You are introduced to the intricacies of case preparation, legal precedence, applicable law, and actual arrest procedures. You will participate with sworn personnel in the field, as an observer, during actual arrests. Discretion of the Chief and/or the Marshal will be used.

Court Support Section

You will be involved with prisoner movements, booking procedures, and restraining prisoners in custody. This gives you exposure to persons confined within the prison system. There will be a chance for you to gain valuable law experience in the courtroom from observing case presentation by the Government. You will study courtroom security and protective services for Federal Judges. There will be exposure to trials that are highly publicized or of a sensitive nature. Finally it allows you the opportunity to observe testifying techniques by Federal Agents.

Criminal Section

Now that you have been involved with the actual arrests and trial procedures, the criminal section will expose you to the legal documentation issued by the court to complete the process. You will be engaged with court process (i.e. Court Orders, Judgment & Commitments, etc.), and learn how to interpret and execute these documents. You will have familiarization with national prisoner movements. There will also be the opportunity to see the gathering and preparation of statistical data used to prepare headquarters for future budget and manpower needs.

Civil Section

You have now completed the criminal procedure and will be ready to learn the functions of the civil sections. You will recognize that, at times, civil matters coincide with criminal matters in relation to various types of forfeitures. You are exposed to all facets of the civil field to include service of process, forfeitures, and seizures. You will participate in the highly complex methods of seizing expensive property in response to government of private litigants. You will participate in admiralty cases where vessels are seized, learn how to document accountable items on the vessel and how to appoint a substitute custodian for the property. This section also provides an overall view of the Comprehensive Crime Control Act of 1984 and its application as to forfeiture of seized assets.

Drug Enforcement Administration "Q" Appointment Program (Formerly Special Agent Cooperative Education Program)

The "Q" Appointment Program replaced the Special Agent Cooperative Education program in 1992. Because of the budgetary considerations within the Drug Enforcement Administration at that time, DEA was not able to offer appointments to Special Agent status after a Co-op Student completed her Co-op hours. The current "Q" Appointment allows students to work full time with the DEA for six months to a year in such units as communication, recruitment, diversion, and administration. While the prospective offer of full-time employment no longer exists, our experience has been that students who desired to become Special Agents have eventually been hired and that this experience as a "Q" appointment has been able to qualify in application for other Federal law enforcement agencies.

Requirements

- Student should have between 60 and 90 credits
- Minimum GPA of 3.0
- United States Citizenship
- Meet the physical and medical requirements for that of Special Agent

- Submission of OPM Form OF-612

- Pass an oral interview

- Pass an extensive background investigation

Federal Bureau of Prisons
Cooperative Education Case Manager

These Co-op positions can exist in Federal Prison Camps and the incumbent would act as aid to professional Case managers who are assigned to provide the inmates with such guidance as counseling the inmates to understand and accept work within the boundaries of a correctional setting; conducting group workshops; preparation of special progress reports for such consideration as parole, transfer, and restoration of forfeited good time; act as court liaison for inmates; and the development of inmate release plans.

Requirements

- Be enrolled in a college cooperative education program

- Maintain good academic standing; GPA 2.0/4.0

- Possess strong interest in working in the corrections field

- Major in criminal justice, psychology, or social sciences

- United States Citizenship

Method of Application

Submit cover letter stating your interest in this position along with your résumé or Form OF-612 to your college Cooperative Education Coordinator.

U.S. Department of Justice
Office of Inspector General, Cooperative
Education Investigative Clerk

Students assigned to this position provide clerical and administrative assistance to Special Agents working criminal investigations; assist in gathering and analyzing various types of intelligence data from federal, state, local, and public agencies; assist in monitoring and evaluating various types of bank, telephone, utility, and other records including grand jury material; receive and review correspondence from other federal agencies; monitor base radio stations; and complete other assignments as directed by the Special Agent in charge.

Requirements

- Must maintain minimum 3.0 GPA
- Must successfully complete minimum of 60 college credits

Method of Application

Submit Form OF-612 and two-page essay describing your career goals. Selected students will be brought in for an interview and ultimately will undergo a full background check.

Chapter 10

Test Taking: An Important Aspect
of Criminal Justice Employment

Beware the man who knows the answer before he
understands the question.

—C.M. Mancuso

Seeking Out Job Openings and Test Dates

Many employment opportunities within the law enforcement and criminal justice fields require that you pass an exam to be considered for the position. Your first and most important responsibility will be to find out what tests are being given, whether you are eligible to sit for these exams, and where and when these exams will take place. It is a good idea to begin the process by directly contacting the agency by whom you wish to be hired to see if they maintain the authority to test and hire you. Many federal law enforcement agencies have the authority to hire directly. You can contact these agencies directly to learn about upcoming exam dates and other conditions of employment.

Other employment opportunities in the criminal justice field (i.e., police and correction officers, border parol agents, drug enforcement agents, U.S. Marshals, to name a few), work through the Office of Personnel management (OPM) to announce, recruit, and administer the appropriate tests for a variety of criminal justice positions. OPM administers the exam and they subsequently submit all qualified applicant names to the appropriate agency for consideration. The OPM has sites termed "Federal Job Information Centers (FJIC)" in each state that provide this service (see resource section for listing). These offices announce position openings, when and where tests are given and what information and qualifications are required to apply. The application process for OPM is discussed in detail in Chapter 11.

Other job openings in criminal justice are announced in employment offices operated by city or state agencies or are announced in local newspapers or magazines. In some larger cities, there is a civil service newspaper that announces all upcoming exams (e.g., *The Chief* in New York City). And finally, use the Internet to find out about current vacancy openings. With the right equipment you can download all the info needed and in some cases apply for the position directly through the Internet.

It is a good idea to learn about upcoming exams well in advance so that you have time to prepare yourself correctly. Your first step is to ensure that your application is filled out neatly and correctly and that you follow all the steps carefully. Always mail applications in by certified mail. Make sure that you keep copies of everything and file all papers in a convenient and safe place. Pay particular attention when reviewing job vacancy announcements to what subject areas in which test questions will be given. In some cases, all you will need to do is pass the test to become eligible – in others, your score will determine your employment eligibility. At this point let's begin to see how you can improve on your test scores so that you enhance your chances for employment.

Beginning the Test Preparation Process

As stated previously, taking a test is never an easy or even enjoyable task. It creates anxiety, apprehension, and even physical discomfort. This occurs most frequently in students who have never developed a comprehensive strategy for taking tests. Unfortunately, many high school students are never taught how to prepare for tests, and this lack of training can become a major problem in test performance.

Taking a test is like any performance activity. You need preparation, forethought, and a plan of action to do well. In fact being truly prepared for a test is the best defense against feelings of test anxiety. Lets first look at some generally suggested test taking strategies before we look more carefully at the test as they apply to criminal justice careers.

As mentioned earlier, it is a good idea to give yourself plenty of time before taking the test in order to best prepare. Now here are some tips regarding how to ensure you will do your best:

Tips to Prepare for the Test

- Write down and verify testing date/site – find out as much as possible about the format of the test. How long is it? Do people usually finish on time? What topics are covered on the test? How is it graded? What is considered the best way to prepare?

- Find out if there are any classes that will help you prepare – many colleges/police departments offer preparation classes.

- Develop a study plan and make a commitment to study each day – Your plan is contingent on how much time you have before the exam. If the exam is soon you may have to put everything else on hold while you prepare. If you have several months you can create a more leisurely study plan.

- Create the best study environment you can – find a quiet place free from distractions.

- Purchase study/test guides – *this is essential* – we will talk more specifically about this later.

- Form a study group if you have friends also taking the exam.

- Begin to find out your areas of weakness and pay more attention to these areas.

- Talk to others who have taken the exam if possible.

- Good night sleep – give yourself plenty of time to arrive on time.

- Practice relaxation techniques – visualize success.

- Pack up all your materials the night before; pencils, directions.

Tips to Help You During the Test

Once you arrive at the test site, there are a few things you should keep in mind.

- **Budget time – pace yourself** – It is helpful to take a few seconds to preview the test – Don't automatically start to rush. Always make sure that you have enough time to complete the test. This may sound easy, but it takes practice and a few helpful hints to master. First, make sure that you always bring a wristwatch. Second, when you first receive the test, check to see how many questions are on it so that you can quickly calculate how to pace yourself. If the test consists of 50 multiple-choice questions and you have 50 minutes to complete the test, plan to answer approximately one question per minute. If the test consists of two essay questions and you have 50 minutes, you should complete the first essay at approximately the 25-minute mark of the test period.

- **Follow directions** – Many students do poorly on their exams because they fail to follow directions. Read the directions carefully. If you do not understand the instructions, ask the instructor to explain them to you. DO NOT begin the test until you know what is expected!

- **Do the simple questions first** – This strategy will allow you to get started with a positive attitude, maximize your test score, and allow you more time for difficult questions. Make sure you mark clearly those questions that you skipped.

- **Focus on the test** – If you find it difficult to concentrate during the test and your mind begins to wander, shift your thoughts to question- or subject-related information. Ask yourself, What do I know about this? If you are not sure, go on to the next question.

- **Answer all questions** – If you don't mark an answer, you have NO chance of getting it correct. NEVER LEAVE AN ANSWER BLANK!

- **Changing answers** – The research seems to indicate that, if you think or feel that an answer should be changed, your instinct is usually right. However, if you are going to change an answer make sure that you have a reason for doing so. Don't get into the habit of changing answers all of the time. It wastes time and can affect your concentration.

- **Use process of elimination** – If you don't know the answer, eliminate those that you know are definitely wrong. Then choose the most logical response from the remaining choices.

- **Underline key words/phrases** – Many people lose points because they misread a question or the right answer because they fail to underline while test taking.

Specific Test Preparation for Law Enforcement Careers

Most entry-level positions within the civil service system require that you have some fundamental knowledge in the area of basic areas of reading, writing, and mathematics. However, depending on the nature of the position you are applying for you can expect to be tested on qualities and skills deemed essential for the work you will perform. We have outlined several general areas you can expect to be tested in if you are seeking employment in the criminal justice/law enforcement field. Each area is considered vital to job performance.

Test questions may be multiple choice and are often based on reading comprehension. Brushing up on your reading and writing abilities is strongly recommended.

Preparation/Practice Books Help

There are specific books designed to help you prepare. Many people are familiar with the ARCO series, which can be purchased at most bookstores. We would also like to alert you to the preparation texts available through the:

Learning Express
900 Broadway
Suite 604
New York, New York

Books by the Learning Express provide customized law enforcement and other civil service test preparation exam guides. What makes them special is that they specifically design some exams to target certain states such as Illinois, New York, Texas, etc. They also have many study skills and test preparation guides that are comprehensive, yet easy to use. Check your local bookstore. They also have a Web site: www.learn.com

Six Important Skills on Which You Will Be Tested

There are six important skills vital to the work of a law enforcement professional: memory/observation, judgment, verbal comprehension, map reading/spatial orientation, interpretation/reasoning, and general math. Below we will describe these areas, inform you of the general kinds of questions you are likely to be asked in each area, and offer some suggestions regarding how to respond to them. You should, of course, purchase samples of the actual tests you plan to take if available and then practice, practice, practice. Consult the books previously recommended.

Memory/Observation Skills

The ability to observe and memorize information/detail is vital to the work of the criminal justice professional. As a police officer, you will need to observe potential suspects, remember geographical locations and roads, memorize portraits of potential suspects and details of a crime scene, etc. To test you on your long- and short-term memory, you can expect the following possibilities:

In this skill area you may be given a picture to study for several minutes before it is taken away. You may be provided a picture of a busy street scene – then asked to recall certain details about the facial expressions of individuals or what you have observed in the scene. You may be asked to read a short passage and then asked to respond from memory. You may be sent something to read and study in advance of the test, and then you may be queried based on your memory of factual information covered. You may be asked to look at WANTED posters and later may be asked to recall specific identifying features of a criminal.

Tips for Answering These Questions

Inspect all pictures carefully as you may not have the opportunity to see them again. Remember the obvious details, but also pay attention to details that may appear more subtle. Keep your eye on specific indicators such as signs, windows, doors, and clocks. It is suggested that you draw mental lines in the picture to divide it into four quadrants and then proceed to study one at a time. This organizes your memory and provides needed structure. Visualize events, situations, and people in your mind with pictures or words. See if you find a pattern of events to describe the scene. Organize these events in your mind. Be positive – tell yourself to focus and that you are going to remember as much as possible as you begin the task. Read the questions that you will be asked before looking at the picture.

Sample Memory/Observation Question:

The sketch appearing to the left of the line represents the face of an alleged criminal, based on witnesses' descriptions at the crime scene. One of the four sketches to the right of the line represents the way the suspect looked after changing his/her appearance. Assume that NO surgery has been performed on the suspect. Select the sketch that most likely represents the face of the suspect.

Explanation of Example Question:
The correct answer is "D." All critical features match the features of the suspect. In addition, all other alternatives have at least one critical difference.

> "A" is incorrect, because the lips are too small.
> "B" is incorrect, because the lips are too small AND the nose
>   is too short (or high on face).
> "C" is incorrect, because the chin is rounded.

Judgment Skills

Obviously the ability of a criminal justice professional to exercise sound judgment is paramount to his/her professional responsibility. Good judgment is the process of combining knowledge and understanding with common sense and it is considered fundamental to the nature of working this field. Not only is this skill area a part of one's routine work in the criminal justice field, but becomes extremely vital in emergency situations which you are likely to encounter.

To test how well you are able to make good decisions, you may encounter a number of possible questions: You may be given certain laws and ask to apply them to specific situations. For example, armed with legal information about the appropriate use of "restraint/handcuffs," you might be asked to determine whether handcuff restraint is warranted in a particular situation.

If you are applying for a position as a correction officer, you may be asked how to handle a particular situation with an inmate while on duty (i.e., you found something in an inmates cell or on his person). Judgment questions often deal with emergency situations and public safety. As a highway patrol officer you may be asked how you might handle a situation at a accident/disaster scene. In these cases you are primarily asked for your judgment as you portray the role of the position for which you are applying.

Tips for Answering These Questions

Paramount in your mind should be the issue of safety. In short, trying to prevent harm or injury to someone or the public is often the best answer for these questions. It is often the right choice to avoid the use of force if possible. Don't project your thoughts and feelings into the answer or read more into it than needed . . . use only the information provided and trust your common sense.

Sample Judgment Questions:

Use the following information to answer the questions below:

Officers frequently handle domestic disturbance calls. Because these calls are dangerous for both the families involved and the officers, officers called to the scene of a domestic disturbance should carry out the following steps in the order listed:

1. Inform the dispatcher when they arrive.

2. Park the patrol car away from the residence.

3. Before knocking, listen carefully at the door to get an idea of what is happening inside.

4. Stand on either side of the door while knocking in order to be less vulnerable to gunshots or immediate attack.

5. Knock and identify themselves as police officers.

6. Once inside, restore order as calmly as possible by separating those who are arguing.

7. Administer first aid if immediately necessary.

8. Talk to the participants separately and find out what happened.

9. Let the dispatcher know if the situation is under control or if assistance is needed.

Judgment Questions:

1. Officers Charles and Washington have been dispatched to 2104 Maple Avenue. Neighbors called 911 and said that they can hear Jeff threatening his wife Sara and that they are afraid he is about to beat her. Officer Charles notifies the dispatcher that they have arrived. He parks the care in front of 2102 Maple, and he and Officer Washington begin walking up the sidewalk to 2104 Maple Avenue. What should the two officers do next?

    a. Knock on the front door and request entry.

    b. Listen at the door to see if they can tell what is going on inside.

    c. Talk to the neighbors who called before taking any action.

    d. Administer first aid to those who are injured.

2. Officer Wallace arrives at the scene of a domestic disturbance. After notifying the dispatcher of her arrival and parking her car a few houses away, Officer Wallace is at the front door of the house. She listens for a few minutes and hears a woman sobbing. The house is dark and quiet except for the sounds of the woman crying. The next step Officer Wallace should take is to:

    a. walk around to the rear of the house and listen at the back door.

    b. knock at the door and identify herself.

    c. call to the woman through the door to ask if she is injured.

    d. step to one side of the door before knocking.

3. Officers Stanley and DiMartino have just pulled up to the curb near 9000 Block Parkway on a domestic disturbance call. Neighbors are reporting sounds of breaking glass, yelling, and gunshots. What is the first thing the officers should do?

    a.   Listen at the door to see if they can tell what is happening.

    b.   Get the dispatcher to have a neighbor meet them outside to tell them what they heard.

    c.   Radio in to the dispatcher when they arrive at the scene.

    d.   Immediately run into the residence.

4.   Officer Roberts is dispatched to a domestic disturbance at 3412 Runnymeade. When he arrives, he radios in to the dispatcher and parks at 3410 Runnymeade. As he approaches the house, the door flies open and a woman runs out. She is bleeding heavily from a cut on her arm and collapses at his feet crying, "Help me, officer!" The next thing Officer Roberts should do is to

    a.   Apply first aid to the woman's wound.

    b.   Search the house for the suspect.

    c.   Separate the victim and the suspect.

    d.   Identify himself to the victim.

Judgment Answers:

1.   The correct answer is "b." The officers have accomplished steps 1 and 2. Step 3 is to listen at the door.

2.   The correct answer is "d." Standing to one side of the door before knowing is the next step in the procedure after listening at the door.

3.   The correct answer is "c." The first step is for the officers to tell the dispatcher that they have arrived at the scene.

4.   The correct answer is "a." The woman is bleeding and needs first aid. Choice "b" is not an option in the list of procedures. There aren't two people to separate, as is suggested in choice "c." The woman knows he is a police officer, so there is no need to identify himself, as is suggested in choice "d."

Verbal Comprehension/Expression Skills

You can expect to demonstrate your ability to read and understand the meaning of a series of sentences or paragraphs. Perhaps you will be given an offense report, manual, description of an event that took place, or asked to read a list of stated laws, then questioned on your understanding of general main themes/ideas expressed, as well as, your attention to smaller specific details, inferences, and conclusions you draw from the information provided to you. In terms of verbal expression, you might be tested on your ability to communicate information or ideas to people based on your understanding of words – their meaning and usage. For example, you may be asked how to explain a new policy or procedure to a new employee or victim of a crime.

Tips for Answering These Questions

To help you become aware of how to identify significant points while reading a fair amount of information, it is suggested that you first review the questions that will be asked – prior to reading the passage. Circle key words or phrases. Ask yourself questions as you read. Building your reading skills will obviously help, and there are many books that support skill building in this area. When asked to communicate your understanding regarding an event such as a crime you witnessed, it is important to communicate the main idea in a concise and accurate way. Do not add or omit details not yet established as fact. Also remember to present information in the appropriate/logical sequence.

Sample Verbal Comprehension Questions:

Record your answers to the two questions below on the Sample Test Answer Sheet.

Use the information in the following passage to answer the next two questions.

Two troop cars were dispatched to a rural home on the evening of June 12, at 9:47 p.m. The dispatcher stated that the owner of the home had reported a robbery which took place earlier that evening when he and his wife were out. The owner also stated that the suspects were still in the home when the victims arrived, but they fled the scene in a dark blue sedan.

Upon arrival at the home, Troopers Baker and Reigner began to question Mr. Corneal, the owner of the home. In the meantime, Troopers Lucas and Gentry conducted a preliminary investigation of the home to determine the activities of the suspects and the extent of damage. The questioning revealed that Mr. Corneal had several sets of antique jewelry. When questioned about who knew about the collections, Mr. Corneal stated that only friends of the family and members of the rifle club were aware of them. He was further questioned to determine whether any unusual events had occurred recently that might be related to this incident. Mr. Corneal stated that they had extensive remodeling done to the interior of the home during the past six weeks by several different companies. Trooper Reigner asked if they had reason to suspect any of the workers. Mr. Corneal stated that several members of the crew had shown an interest in seeing and discussing his collection of guns, but that it would be very difficult to determine which individuals, if any, may have been involved. Trooper Reigner requested the names of the companies and the services they performed.

After a few minutes, Troopers Lucas and Gentry returned from their search of the home. They had determined that the robbers concentrated their efforts on the two collections, since the only other areas that were disturbed were ones that typically contain money (e.g., dresser top, dresser drawers). They concluded that the robbers must have been aware of the collections before entering the home.

1. According to the preceding passage, when the Corneals arrived home on the evening of June 12, they discovered that their home had been:

   a. Ransacked, but nothing was stolen.

   b. entered, and the television, stereo, and computer were stolen

   c. entered, and the robbers were still in the home.

   d. robbed, and five antique guns and several pieces of exotic jewelry were the items that were taken.

2. According the preceding passage, considering the robbery and subsequent investigation described above, the ONLY statement that accurately reflects the information gathered is:

   a. Trooper Reigner requested the names of the companies doing the remodeling.

   b. Mrs. Corneal seemed to be the one to answer all of the troopers' questions.

   c. Trooper Baker helped with the search of the home.

   d. The robbers were reported to have fled the scene in a dark blue van.

Verbal Comprehension Answers:

1. The correct answer is "C." As stated in the passage, "The owner of the home had reported a robbery . . . "AND" . . . the suspects were in the home when the victims arrived." Although the information in the passage does not indicate the exact number and type of items taken from the Corneal home, Troopers Lucas and Gentry did determine that the robbers concentrated their efforts on the exotic gun collection, the antique jewelry collection, and the areas of the house that typically contain money.

   "a" is incorrect, because it states that nothing was stolen;

   "b" is incorrect, because the wrong items are listed;

"d" is incorrect, because it states specific numbers of items stolen which were not stated in the passage.

2. The correct answer is "a." Trooper Reigner was the trooper who "requested the names of the companies and the services they performed."

"b" is incorrect, Mr. Corneal seemed to answer all of the troopers' questions.

"c" is incorrect, because Troopers Lucas and Gentry searched the home. Trooper Baker assisted with the questioning of the owners.

"d" is also incorrect, the robbers were reported to have fled the scene in a dark blue sedan, not a dark blue van.

Map Reading/Spatial Orientation Skills

A good sense of direction is important to the work of the criminal justice professional. This skills helps prevent you from getting lost and losing valuable time that may, in certain situations, be the difference between life and death. Not only should law enforcement persons be able to know their location at all times, they should also be able to arrive at a different location using a map to determine the best route.

To assess your skill in this area, you may be provided with a map with certain symbols and keys to direct you. You will be asked to figure the most prudent/shortest legal way to get from one point to the next. You may be asked to follow directions which will give clues to your ability to understand and integrate knowledge of/perception of directions – North/South/East/West.

Tips for Answering These Questions

It is advised to study the map in a broad perspective. Trace answers lightly in pencil, and if wrong, erase so not to confuse you later. Move the map around in different positions to help you understand the directions. Take note of symbols such as street signs and other signs (e.g., one-way signs, compass for directions and arrows).

Mapping Questions:

The following mapping question appeared in the preparation guide for the Massachusetts state police, published by the Learning Express.

Answer the following questions based on the diagram and the information below.

A police officer is often required to assist civilians who seek travel directions or referral to city agencies and facilities. The diagram above is a map of a section of a city, where some public buildings are located. Each of the squares represent one city block. Street names are shown. If there is an arrow next to the street name, it means the street is one-way only in the direction of the arrow. If there is no arrow next to the street name, two-way traffic is allowed.

1. You arrive at the scene of a vehicular accident at the corner of Brown Street and 9th Avenue to find gasoline leaking from one of the cars. What is the most direct legal way for the fire engine to travel to the scene of the accident?

   a. east on Maple Street and north on 9th Ave. to the accident

   b. west on Maple Street, north on 12th Ave., and east on Brown St. to the accident

   c. east on Maple Street and north on 11th Ave. to the accident

   d. west on Maple Street, north on 11th Ave. And east on Brown St. to the accident

   The correct answer is "a." All other routes are illegal.

2. What streets run north and south of the park?

   a. Brown Street and Oak Street

   b. Maple Street and Park Street

   c. Brown Street and Park Street

   d. Green Street and Oak Street

   The correct answer is "c."

3. A civilian leaving the clinic needs to drive to the drugstore. If you were giving her directions from the clinic, what would be the most direct, legal route?

   a. east on Maple Street, north on 9th Ave., and west on Brown Street to the store entrance

   b. west on Maple Street, north on 10th Ave., and west on Brown Street to the store entrance

   c. west on Green Street, north on 12th Ave., and east on Brown Street to the store entrance

   d. east on Oak Street, north on 11th Ave., and east on Brown Street to the store entrance

   The correct answer is "a." All other routes are illegal.

Interpretation/Reasoning Skills

After being informed of certain laws, policies, and procedures you may be asked to apply them in particular hypothetical situations. For example, after being given guidelines for establishing roadblocks in order to identify prospective drunk drivers, you will be asked how to proceed in a situation utilizing the policy presented. You may be told under what condition pepper spray should be used to dispense a crowd and then asked what to do in a given situation. A law against a certain crime, such as shoplifting, may be outlined and subsequently you will be provided with situations to determine if the law was actually broken. You might be asked to distinguish between a burglary and a trespass what factors to take into account when drawing a weapon. You may be asked your position regarding whether to treat an injured person or to wait for medical support in a step-by-step manner, whether to call for back up, whether a person's explanation is believable or truthful. You may, for example, be provided with contradicting information from a victim and several witnesses. Based on the information, could you identify a potential problem in someone's account of the events?

Tips for Answering These Questions

Procedures are often presented in an order in which they must be performed. Pay close attention to the pattern, steps, or order of information you are given. Usually there is a sequence that must be followed in a rule or procedure for an answer to be correct. Sometimes it is a matter of arranging information in a logical order and at other times it is a matter of arranging information in order of importance.

Pay close attention to the rule or procedure in effect. It is possible that there are exceptions to the rule under certain conditions? Make sure that the correct answer applies to the given situation and time in question. Make sure your answer allows that all procedures are followed, and doesn't eliminate a vital step unless you are aware of exceptions.

Keep your eye on words like *unless*, *except*, *if*, and, *or*, and *only*. Underline all key words as they provide pieces of important information.

Sample Interpretation/Reasoning Questions:

1. **Example:** Trooper Dunn interviews four witnesses to a murder that took place in a crowded bar and grill. Each of the witnesses observed the perpetrator of the shooting as he was leaving the bar. They described him as follows:

   Witness 1 – "He was a white male, about 25 to 30 years of age, with brown shoulder-length hair. He was about 6' tall and weighed about 185 pounds. He wore blue jeans and a brown leather jacket. He had a small scar on his forehead."

   Witness 2 – "He was a male, white or Hispanic, late twenties, around 5'10," about 190 pounds, with long brown hair. He was stocky and wore dark pants and a brownish jacket.

Witness 3 – "He was a light-skinned male, possibly white or Hispanic, in his mid-twenties, about 6' tall and weighing about 180 pounds. He had a tattoo of a panther on his right forearm. He had moderately long hair and wore a brown shirt and dark pants."

Witness 4 – "He was a white male, around 25 years old, about 5'11" tall and weighing about 185 pounds. His hair was brown and over his ears, fairly long. He wore darkish clothes; I'm not sure of the color of his jacket or pants."

Based on the information above, Trooper Dunn should recognize that there is a problem with the description given by which of the four witnesses described above?

Explanation of Example Question:

"Witness 3" is the correct answer. There is agreement that the perpetrator was a white or Hispanic male in his mid-to-late twenties with long, brown hair who was approximately 6' tall and 185 pounds. In addition, his pants and jacket were dark in color. There were only two discrepancies across the descriptions. Witness 1 reported that the perpetrator has a small scar on his forehead. Witness 3 reported a tattoo of a panther on the perpetrator's right forearm. Of the two, it is much harder to explain how a tattoo of a panther could be overlooked by three of four witnesses AND how one witness could see it when the other three witnesses all stated that the perpetrator had a jacket on during the incident. Thus, "Witness 3" is the best answer.

2. **Disorderly Conduct** means with intent to cause public inconvenience, annoyance, or alarm; or recklessly creating a risk thereof; a person engages in fighting; or in violent, tumultuous, or threatening behavior.

For the crime of **Disorderly Conduct**:

Is it necessary to *intend* public inconvenience, annoyance, or alarm? No. The definition says "intent to cause . . . *OR* recklessly creating a risk thereof . . ."

Is it necessary to be *fighting*? No. The definition says "engages in fighting OR in violent, tumultuous, *OR* threatening behavior."

Practice using this strategy with the example below:

Example: Answer this question solely on the basis of the definition provided.

Criminal Mischief – the crime of criminal mischief is committed when:

1. A person intentionally damages property belonging to another and the amount of the damage is $250 or more; or

2. A person intentionally damages property, in any amount, by means of explosives.

According to the definition given above, the following represents the best example of criminal mischief.

a. Frank is playing baseball with his pals when he hits a ball that breaks the $2,000 window of Ford Motors.

b. Tony is chopping down a tree in his backyard. The tree falls the wrong way and hits the neighbor's house, causing $3,500 worth of damage.

c. Harold gets mad after an argument with his wife and throws his $600 TV through the $200 picture window of his house.

d. Lloyd decides to get even with a neighbor and throws an M-80 firecracker onto his neighbor's porch on Halloween night. The only damage is to his neighbor's milk box, about $15.

Explanation of Example Question:

The correct answer is "d." Intentional damage using explosives fits part 2 or the Criminal Mischief definition.

Answers "a" and "b" are incorrect because there was no intent in either case to damage property (the window or the house, respectively).

Answer "c" is incorrect because, although there was intent, no explosives were used AND the damage to property *belonging to another* did *not* exceed $250.

General Math Skills

In some exams, such as the Treasury Enforcement Exam, you will have to answer basic math questions. Many people worry about the math questions. To do well on the math problems, you will need to understand and perform some calculations but you will not be required to memorize complicated formulas. Some algebra is required, and you should expect to deal with fractions, ratios, basic problem solving such as figuring time/distance, add up dollar figures, calculating compound interest, Internet graphing info. You will have to analyze a paragraph in order to set up and solve a problem. The use of calculators is not permitted.

Tips for Answering These Questions

Your best advice is to purchase pertinent math study guides and to practice these questions in advance. Take your time when calculating the answer – never do calculations in your head, and check all your work.

Coming to Terms with Test Anxiety

Once you know the test date and have begun to practice, it is natural to feel some anxiety. If you are feeling some degree of tension about the prospects of taking and passing a test – relax – you are quite normal. After all, much is riding on whether you pass. You instinctively know how important this test is to being considered for your career. However, you must make some distinction between being a "little nervous" about the upcoming test or being truly "Test Anxious." It is common knowledge that some degree of tension can help you to keep alert and focused during a test. This kind of tension reflects anticipation of achievement and does not involve self-doubt. It is motivating! Athletes and other professionals get this feeling before performing – you are no different!

However, too much anxiety is not good. When your anxiety creates forgetfulness, confusion, mental blocks, and general apprehension, it is disruptive. It is important to understand two basic sets of behavior in response to tests; the first is that you attempt to perform as well as possible, and the second is that you react emotionally to being evaluated. It is often the emotional component that produces mental interference and makes the test situation threatening. Mental flexibility decreases, bodily tension increases, and your emotional responsiveness interferes with your performance.

What Are the Sources of Test Anxiety?

Research indicates that test anxiety is a learned response to evaluation. This response is conditioned or programmed very early in life. It is the result of conditions in your early environment over which you had no control. Fear of tests derives from some of the following kinds of learning experiences:

Steve (age six) sees that his mother becomes worried when he mentions that he has a test. His brother does very well in school.

Carla (age seven) notices that her teacher favors students who can answer quickly in English, her second language.

Andy (age eight) feels unable to do schoolwork after overhearing a conversation between two teachers talking about his problems.

Any of these sound familiar? These examples have elements of the origins of test anxiety: an environment of excessive worry, different and sometimes unreasonable expectations, fear of failure, and concerns about future security. Most people are unaware of the sources of their test anxiety. Until the sources are understood, the appropriate solutions cannot be applied. We think it will be helpful for you at this point to examine the primary sources of your anxiety . . . if any.

Complete the following inventory by placing a check (✓) on the line beside each response that describes how you feel about test taking.

Test Anxiety Inventory

_____ 1. I wish there were some way to succeed without taking tests.

_____ 2. Getting a good score on one test does seem to increase my confidence around others.

_____ 3. People (family, friends, etc.) are counting on me to do well.

_____ 4. I have always dreaded courses in which the teacher has a habit of giving "pop" quizzes.

_____ 5. People who do well on tests generally end up in better positions in life.

_____ 6. Before or during an important exam, I find myself thinking of how much brighter some of the other test takers are than I am.

_____ 7. Even though I don't always think about it, I am concerned about how others will view me if I do poorly.

_____ 8. Worrying about how well I will do interferes with my preparation and performance on tests.

_____ 9. Knowing that my future depends, in part, on doing well on tests upsets me.

_____ 10. I know I could outscore most people if I could just "get myself together."

_____ 11. People will question my ability if I do poorly.

_____ 12. I never seem to be fully prepared to take tests.

_____ 13. Tests make me wonder if I will ever reach my goals.

_____ 14. Tests do not really show how much a person knows.

_____ 15. If I score low, I am not going to tell anyone exactly what my score was.

_____ 16. I often feel the need to cram before a test.

_____ 17. I wish I could get into a vocation that does not require tests for entrance.

_____ 18. If I do not do well on this test, it will mean I am not as smart as I thought.

_____ 19. If my score is low, my parents will be very disappointed.

_____ 20. My anxiety about tests makes me want to avoid preparing fully and this just makes me more anxious.

_____ 21. Aside from what others may think of me, I am concerned about my own opinion of myself if I do not do well.

_____ 22. I do not feel confident and mentally relaxed before a test.

_____ 23. My friends will be disappointed in me if my score is low.

_____ 24. One of my problems is not knowing exactly when I am prepared for a test.

_____ 25. My test performance is directly connected to my future success and security.

The inventory items describe four main sources of test anxiety. They are not separate and do overlap. They are broad areas of focus rather than distinct categories. Use the following table to circle the items you checked.

ANALYSIS CHART
Sources of Test Anxiety & Item Numbers

1. Concerns about how others will view you if you do not do well
    3, 7, 11, 15, 19, 23

2. Concerns arising from threats to your own self-image
    2, 6, 10, 14, 18, 21, 22

3. Concerns about your future security
    1, 5, 9, 13, 17, 25

4. Concerns about not being prepared
    4, 8, 12, 16, 20, 24

Note: Test Adapted From *How to Beat Test Anxiety* by J.H. Divine and D.W. Kylen, 1979, Woodbury, NY: Barron's Educational Services, Inc. Copyright 1979 by Barron's Educational Services, Inc. Adapted by permission.

When you are finished, reflect upon which sources are strongest for you.

For example, a student who reflected upon his needs for others' approval became aware of his need not to disappoint his parents and girlfriend. A student who thought about her image of herself felt that she had to learn to accept that she was not perfect. Write down your thoughts with regard to these sources of test anxiety. You will want to reflect upon these sources as you begin to choose your coping mechanisms.

List your primary sources of test anxiety:

1. _____

2. _____

3. _____

How Do I Cope with Test Anxiety?

Acknowledging your source(s) of test anxiety and subsequently talking to someone about them (counselor/parent/friend) is a great way to begin to overcome your test anxiety. Talking about your feelings will reduce the stress and pressure you experience in a testing situation.

Following are some examples of students who learned to cope with their test anxiety and who became more comfortable with themselves. They learned to cope with their test anxiety while in college. Steve traced the source of his anxiety to his problems with self-image and confidence. He learned to relax and began working on bolstering his self-esteem by changing his thoughts and sharing his feelings with a good listening partner. Teresa traced the source of her anxiety to fears that passing mathematics would lead to a loss of her fiancé and of the security of marriage. She learned to face this fear and became more comfortable with the image of herself as a college graduate in a good relationship. As you become aware of your sources of test anxiety, you will be ready to learn strategies for dealing with your test anxiety. Listed below are some techniques that have been helpful to many people who previously experienced test anxiety.

Tips for Dealing with Test Anxiety

A. Get Rid of Negative Self-Talk

When taking exams, you are not helping yourself by constantly telling yourself negative thoughts. Negative self-talk is usually irrational but always sounds like the truth and can perpetuate or aggravate anxiety. You can learn to replace the negative with confidence-enhancing, supportive statements that will strengthen your ability to cope effectively.

You will need to identify the kind of negative self-talk in which you engage. Read the following statements:

1. I'll never score high enough to get appointed.

2. My mind always goes blank during exams.

3. I am a terrible test taker.

4. I'm the only one having trouble.

5 If I flunk, my career in criminal justice is ruined.

This is obviously pessimistic and erroneous thinking. The most effective way to deal with negative self-talk is to develop a series of positive countering statements and to practice saying these statements when the other thoughts emerge. In so doing, you are essentially programming yourself to think positively and eventually to feel more self-confident. Try these:

1. I know I can pass if I study.

2. If my mind goes blank, I will stay calm and focused.

3. In the past, I may not have done as well as I wanted, but with hard work and practice, I will improve.

4. Other people experience difficulty too.

5. If I fail, in many cases, I can retake the exam. If I work hard, I am not likely to fail.

B. Learn to Relax

Now that you have begun to work on your thoughts, it's time to work on your levels of physical or bodily tension. Many experts believe you can learn how to relax by doing a series of simple exercises that will clarify the relationship between tension and relaxation. Give the following exercise a shot . . . it really helps.

Begin by closing your eyes gently and focusing on your breathing. You will breathe deeply and evenly. Note the air flowing in and out and begin to think of your favorite activity. Note the sensations you enjoy, the smells, sights, sounds, feelings. You may notice that your breathing has become slower and more regular. Allow your shoulders to sink and your legs to lean against the floor. You are feeling the support and letting go of your tension. Your arms feel limp and heavy. You're going to begin relaxing your feet. You will point your toes up toward the ceiling and then toward the walls, moving around slowly, enjoying their increasing warmth. You begin to notice the tension leaving your calves, thighs, and hips and begin to feel more relaxed and comfortable. Your entire body begins to feel lighter.

You begin to focus on your back, arms, and shoulders. Sensing your regular breathing, you will notice how your back sinks into the floor and you will slowly feel your relaxation. You tense your shoulders by making a shrugging motion and then allow your shoulders to drop slowly, releasing the tension and allowing the relaxation to flow. You will hold your arms slightly above the floor and then allow them to rest gently on the floor. As you sense the warmth flowing into your arms and hands, you are aware of your regular and deep breathing and of the continuing relaxation of your entire body, especially of your abdominal muscles.

You will briefly tense the muscles of your stomach by holding them in. Then release those muscles and experience the sensations of relaxation. You will hold your breath and feel the tightness of your chest muscles. Releasing your breath will allow you to feel the comfort of regular and deep breathing once again. You will continue to breathe regularly and deeply, sensing the growing warmth of your stomach and chest and feeling the relaxation move upward toward your neck.

You will rotate your neck from side to side and feel the warmth moving upward toward your face. Your head feels weightless, sinking deeper and deeper into the floor. Your breathing remains even and slow and relaxed. The warm, relaxed feelings move upward toward your face, and your chin begins to drop as you feel the relaxation continue across your face, cheeks, forehead, and eyelids. Your eyelids begin to feel heavy and your slow, deep breaths wash away any remaining tension.

As you review the relaxation exercise, recall how you were feeling at the beginning of the exercise. Now consider how you are feeling. Practice relaxation daily for two weeks. After the two weeks, try visualizing a scene after performing the progressive relaxation. Try imagining the scene as you approach thoughts about test taking. Once you achieve deep relaxation, you are ready to apply your new relaxation skills to test situations using two other coping techniques, visualization and systematic desensitization.

C. Desensitize Yourself to Testing

Imagining certain anxiety-provoking thoughts while learning to place yourself in a state of relaxation will help you understand that you can control your physical response to stressful situation such as taking a test. To learn the systematic desensitizing process, you introduce anxiety-provoking statements about a testing situation from those that generally create low-anxiety to those that are likely to make you feel very anxious. Use the relaxation model above and once in a relaxed state begin to introduce these statements/thoughts into your thinking.

- First day you learned of job opening.

- A friend told you the exam is difficult.

- It is one week before the exam but you feel you need more time to be prepared.

- The night before the exam, you finished reviewing, but have difficulty going to sleep.

- Waiting for the examination door to open, seeing all the other prospective applicants.

- Looking at the exam, you read the first two questions and realize you are getting nervous.

- You hear that only 15 minutes remain, and you are far from being finished.

As you go through the list of anxiety-provoking thoughts/scenes, practice relaxation. As you become more comfortable with each given situation, move to the next while increasing your ability to relax and control the stress and tension you feel.

Visualize each scene, followed by periods of relaxation, until you feel in control of the situation and know that you can handle it comfortably. When you can imagine each scene without discomfort, move on. Once you can visualize the highest level scene, you may be able to see yourself as calm and alert and competently proceeding through the entire sequence of examination events with a sense of calm alertness and confidence. Good luck.

*cover letter — 3 paragraphs
*include a copy of the position applying for
perfectly fits   * background   / educational /work /Corps
                                    / mil experience
          * why interested   in the organization

Chapter 11

The Job Hunt

> *One secret of total success is that winners work at doing things the majority of the population are not willing to do.*
>
> —Denis Waitley

Successfully gaining employment is often the end result of working longer and harder than others have. Of course, you may need the support of the traditional placement services your college provides, but do not rely solely on them in your job search. Seeking employment involves selling yourself as a valuable asset. The key to success is the way in which you package and communicate who you are and what you have to offer.

Contacts: People Who Can Help

A contact is someone who can help you reach your objective of finding employment. Virtually anyone is potentially a key contact and should not be overlooked. Employers often prefer to hire people they know and like. If they are unable to do so, the next best thing is for them to turn to people they know, such as friends, co-workers, or family whom they trust and respect, for suggestions. Take the time to utilize and extend your network of contacts by sharing with people you know that you are in the process of looking for a job.

Start by contacting faculty, counselors, past employers, on-site internship supervisors, placement personnel, friends, and relatives. Sometimes the most unlikely person may turn into an important contact. It may be helpful to join professional and social organizations, clubs, and college alumni groups. However, be prepared to follow through effectively with the opportunities that your contacts provide. Contacts may guarantee an interview, but not necessarily a job.

157

The Résumé/Cover Letter Approach

In the criminal justice job hunt, as in any career quest, important and traditional tools are the résumé and cover letter. Keep in mind that the successful job applicant not only possesses a desirable combination of education, experience, and skills, but communicates this in an effective manner. What follows are some suggestions on developing your résumé and cover letter in ways that effectively communicate why you are qualified.

The Résumé

In French, résumé means brief history. It is generally agreed that a résumé should be limited to one side of one 8½" x 11" typewritten page. A common misconception is that the résumé alone will get you the job. This is not usually true. It is hoped that it will be helpful in obtaining the interview. The résumé is used by employers as a screening device to narrow the number of potential applicants. Thus, it is important that it be clear, concise, well-written, and free of typographical errors.

One of the most important traits employers are looking for is the applicant's ability to communicate clearly in oral and written form. The job applicant should write his or her own résumé because a personnel manager might question an applicant's ability in this area if a professional résumé writer has obviously been used. References to race, religion, politics, or controversial issues should also be avoided. An objective of the résumé is to portray yourself in a positive manner.

There are numerous formats/styles for constructing the résumé. Regardless of the exact style, certain information should always be included. (See pp. 160-161 for sample résumés.)

Basic Information

At the top of the résumé, list your full name, current address, and phone number where you can be reached or have a message taken.

Objective

If an employment objective is included, it should not be so specific as to exclude the entry-level applicant from other positions that might be available. A specific type of objective might exclude an applicant from other criminal justice career areas. Consider a general objective, such as "Seeking an entry-level position in the criminal justice field that will utilize my strong communication skills." This concept should be followed especially if the applicant is seeking his or her first position and might simply be interested in getting his or her foot in the door.

The narrowly defined objective is better used after the applicant has developed more extensive experience in an area.

Education

List on the résumé your highest or most recent degree or the degree currently being pursued. Then you may follow with the others. A brief overview of the course work on both the graduate and undergraduate levels might follow. However, remember that this is not a transcript but a short mention of courses that might be relevant to the job for which you are applying. Academic honors also may be listed here, such as "Graduated with high honors; Dean's List."

Experience

List jobs held, internships, work-study experience, with indications of start and stop dates. Such positions do not necessarily have to have been paid ones. Avoid using just the firm name and your title. You should include a well-written job description, citing positive experience and background.

Make use of dynamic and key words/phrases in describing your duties and responsibilities. Examples:

Created . . .	Managed . . .
Developed . . .	Hired . . .
Duties were . . .	Determined . . .
Responsibilities included	Supervised . . .
Designed . . .	Interviewed . . .
Implemented . . .	Researched . . .
Trained . . .	Recommended . . .
Organized . . .	Established . . .

Students frequently feel that they have no experience, but this is not usually the case. The goal or challenge of the résumé is to make the skills and experience you do have transferable, relative, adaptable, and applicable to the wide variety of occupational areas of the criminal justice system.

As mentioned earlier, internships and volunteering can be used as experience. They do not necessarily have to be paid positions. Holding an internship for the majority of criminal justice majors is an effective method of gaining practical, hands-on criminal justice-public administration experience, as discussed in a previous section.

Sample Résumé

Jane Johnson
1234 Main St.
Mobile, AL 36688
(205) 555-9876

EXPERIENCE: **Human Resources Administration,**
Bureau of Client Fraud Investigations (12-97 to present)
Fraud Investigator

Investigate allegations of fraud referred by public, federal, state, and city agencies.

Conduct interviews with clients, witnesses, and others to secure and document evidence.

Prepare written reports of the results with recommendations for referral or recoupment actions and testify at Administrative Disqualification Hearings.

Alabama Criminal Justice Agency,
Pre-Arraignment Services (5-97 to 9-97)
Release-On-Recognizance Intake Specialist

Interviewed and processed recently arrested defendants and verified their community affiliations.

Performed liaison work with attorneys and family members.

Reviewed and evaluated defendants' criminal profiles.

Input data entry.

Victim Services Agency,
Family Counseling Services (5-96 to 9-96)
Clinical Counselor

Provided individual, group, and family therapy to victims of domestic violence, serving children, adolescents, and adult populations.

Used techniques of play therapy with children for the purpose of determining the nature of the abuse where it was not clearly evident.

Provided crisis intervention, case consultations, and intakes.

Responsible for writing case reports, progress notes, and monthly statistics.

EDUCATION: Jacksonville State University, Jacksonville, AL
Bachelor of Science, June 1998
Major: Corrections   Minor: Psychology

ACTIVITIES: Sociology and Social Justice Club, President
Law Society, Co-Director of Programming and Information

REFERENCES: Furnished upon request.

Sample Résumé

Raymond Ramirez
1111 E. State St.
New York, NY 10465
Home (212) 555-1234
Business (212) 555-7788

EDUCATION
John Jay College of Criminal Justice
City University of New York

Master's Degree in Public Administration
Expected date of graduation: June 1999

Bachelor's Degree in Criminal Justice, June 1994

EXPERIENCE

4/97-Present
New York City Department of Investigation, New York, NY

Special Investigator
Investigate and prepare for prosecution cases of fraud, official misconduct, criminal misappropriation, and bribe solicitation. Obtain, analyze, and compile evidence through surveillance, computer analysis, record research, and field interviews. Conduct and plan studies of procedure, policy, and management within the office of the City Marshal. Prepare comprehensive reports of findings and recommendations.

7/94-4/97
Office of the Inspector General Department of Buildings, New York, NY

Confidential Investigator
Under the general direction of a Deputy Inspector General, with latitude for independent judgment, directed and coordinated sensitive investigations of corruption and misconduct in the New York City Department of Buildings. Reevaluated existing surveillance procedures for investigators. Implemented a corruption awareness program for employees. Prepared comprehensive reports of findings and recommendations. Appointed liaison to Bronx Borough Superintendent's Office.

9/93-2/94
New York State Office of the Attorney General, Harlem, NY

Student Intern
Under the general direction of an Assistant Attorney General, investigated cases currently under investigation by the New York State Department of Law. Duties included interviewing complainants and witnesses, evaluating existing state law, and participating in mediation among disputing parties. Received a letter of recommendation from the Assistant Attorney General.

REFERENCES
Available upon request.

Sample Cover Letter

Kevin A. Smith
333 Orange Ave., Apt. 3b
San Bernardino, CA 92407
(714) 555-0505

June 21, 1998

Mr. Frank Wilson, Personnel Coordinator
Child and Youth Services
1123 Second Street
Los Angeles, CA 90047

Dear Mr. Wilson:

I am a recent graduate of California State University with a bachelor's degree in criminal justice. I am interested in the position you currently have available for a Child and Youth Counselor, which I learned about through the state career placement center in Sacramento.

My experience prior to graduation includes one year with the Los Angeles Truancy Team, advising and counseling youths with behavioral problems, working in conjunction with parents and guidance personnel. This often involved communicating effectively with students and parents for whom English was a second language. I also provided counseling and supervisory guidance for one year to defendants through the District Attorney's Educational Outreach Program.

In addition to my practical experience, I possess strong interpersonal skills. I am a good listener and find that youths respond well to my patience and diplomacy.

If possible, I would like to arrange an interview at your earliest convenience to discuss this position. Please contact me at (714) 555-0505.

Thank you for your consideration in this matter.

Sincerely,

Kevin Smith

Kevin Smith

Extracurricular Activities

If there is room, these activities may be described. Particularly noteworthy would be activities that demonstrate traits such as leadership, organizational skills, and community involvement.

Personal

Definitely list technical skills, special licenses, language ability, or other traits that might place you above other applicants.

References

Simply state that references are "available upon request." As a matter of courtesy – and to ensure a positive recommendation – always ask permission of the person from whom you are requesting a recommendation before submitting his or her name as a reference.

The Cover Letter

A résumé should always be accompanied by a cover letter when it is sent to a prospective employer. Objectives of the cover letter are to introduce yourself to the employer, to indicate the position for which you are applying, and to explain briefly why you are qualified for that position. A good cover letter will highlight specific attributes you possess that distinguish you from other applicants. This is your opportunity to individualize your presentation to best emphasize the knowledge and skills you could bring to this position. Express your desire to schedule an interview at the employer's convenience, and provide a telephone number where you can be contacted.

A cover letter should not exceed one side of one 8½" x 11" typewritten page. Whenever possible, address the letter to a specific person by name and title. And always proofread your cover letter carefully to be sure it does not contain any grammatical or typographical errors. (See p. 162 for a sample cover letter.)

The Civil Service Approach

At a recent College/Public Agency Council Conference sponsored by the U.S. Office of Personnel Management, attended by career educators and public sector recruiting personnel, the general consensus was that neither college career counselors nor public agency recruiters will adequately provide available jobs to students. Students must learn the system and be able to seek out information themselves. While there will be positions that may only require a résumé to initiate the job application process, there will be other positions that will require filing an application to take an examination or to be rated for further consideration. Examples include applying to take a local police department exam or applying to federal positions such as the FBI or the DEA. It is important for those seeking jobs within criminal justice to realize that without a fundamental knowledge of how the civil service system operates in the area that you wish to be employed, you will be at a disadvantage in competing for positions.

In applying for any civil service position at any level of government, *timeliness* is a critical issue. Notices are given for the dates of upcoming exams, and there will usually be set filing periods for applying for such exams. If one is not aware of the exam or is late in filing the application, it means waiting until the next notice of filing is given, which might involve years.

Because it is important to know *when* certain criminal justice occupational categories might be open, *what* the requirements are, *who* may or may not apply, and *where* the exam will be held, individuals must be acquainted with public sector job information offices at all levels of government.

Federal career information can generally be found in federal job information centers, which are operated by the U.S. Office of Personnel Management. These offices are located throughout the United States and are responsible for announcing the dates, times, and requirements of examinations to be conducted.

The U.S. Office of Personnel Management

- Administers a merit system for Federal employment that includes recruiting, examining, and promoting people on the basis of their knowledge and skills, regardless of their race, religion, sex, political influence, or other nonmerit factors.

- Protects and promotes a merit-based federal civil service through an aggressive oversight program; identifying opportunities for improving federal personnel policies and programs; and helping agencies meet mission goals through effective recruitment, development and utilization of employees.

- Promotes maximum employment and job advancement opportunities within the federal government for disabled veterans and certain veterans of the Vietnam era and of the post-Vietnam era who are qualified for Veteran's Preference.

- Is responsible for regulations implementing the President's directive for assisting dislocated and surplus employees. These regulations require agencies to establish career transition plans and services, and to provide hiring preference to dislocated and surplus employees for those vacancies that do occur.

- In conjunction with the National Partnership Council, supports and promotes labor-management partnership throughout the Executive branch. Partnerships champion change in Federal Government agencies to transform them into organizations capable of delivering the highest quality of services to the American people.

- Supports Government program managers in their personnel management responsibilities through a range of programs designed to develop and encourage the effectiveness of the Government employee.

- Provides fast, friendly, accurate, and cost-effective retirement, health benefit, and life insurance services to federal employees, annuitants, and agencies. The competitiveness of these earned benefits allow the government to recruit and retain a high quality of workforce, capable to working better while costing less.

- Chairs the Interagency Advisory Group (IAG) of Federal Personnel Directors. This group provides leadership in identifying emerging government wide Human Resources Management policy and operation issues and proposing specific measures and approaches for dealing with them.

The New Road to Federal Employment

In 1993, the Vice President's National Performance Review recommended creating a flexible and responsive hiring system that was much more applicant friendly. By 1997, OPM announced the end of Form SF-171, the cumbersome and complex form that, in various guises, had plagued applicants since 1938. The job search for Federal career opportunities is now a 3-step process developed through the "Federal Employment Information System" to assist you along the way. We *obtained* the following information through contacting OPM through the Internet:

The system is composed of user-friendly components for conducting your personal job search. By using the system, you have access not only to Federal job listings, but to some state and local government, as well as private sector, listings. The system provides current information, is updated daily, and is available 24 hours a day, 7 days a week.

Step 1: Use Any of the Automated Systems on the Federal Employment Information Highway

Federal agencies list job opportunities on the Federal Employment Information System. The System is accessible from a number of user-friendly media:

- OPM's Career America Connection at (912) 757-3000, TDD Service at (912)744-2299, a telephone-based system that provides current worldwide Federal job opportunities, salary and employee benefits information, special recruitment messages, and more. You can also record your request to have application packages, forms, and other employment related literature mailed or faxed to you. Request Federal Employment Info Line fact sheet E.I.-42, "Federal Employment Information Sources," for a complete listing of local telephone numbers to this nationwide network.

- OPM's Federal Job Opportunities "Bulletin" Board (FJOB) at (912) 757-3100, a computer-based bulletin board system that provides current worldwide Federal Job opportunities, salaries and pay rates, general and specific employment information, and more. You must have a personal computer with a modem to access this system. Many of the jobs announced on the FJOB have complete text announcements attached which can be downloaded or viewed on-line, or you may leave your name and address to have application packages and forms mailed to you. You may also contact them on the Internet fjob.opm.gov for Telnet; or ftp.fjob.opm.gov for File Transfer Protocol. Information about obtaining Federal job announcement files via Internet mail should be directed to: info@fjob.opm.gov.

- OPM's Worldwide Web site at www.usajobs.opm.gov, like all of the components of the employment information delivery system, provides access to the Federal Job Data Base of worldwide opportunities; full text job announcements; answers to frequently asked Federal employment questions via delivery of Employment Info Line fact sheets; and access to electronic and hard copy application forms.

- Federal Job Information "Touch Screen" Computer, a computer-based system utilizing touch screen technology. These kiosks, located throughout the nation, in OPM offices, Federal Office Buildings and other locations, allow you to access current worldwide Federal job opportunities, on-line information, and more with the touch of a finger. You can also leave a request to have application packages, forms and other employment related literature mailed to you. Request Federal Employment Info Line fact sheet E.I.-42, "Federal Employment Information Sources," for a complete listing of the locations of their Touch Screen Computers.

- FEDFAX: By using a touch-tone telephone or fax machine, you may select from a variety of employment-related topics and forms you wish to have faxed to you. FedFax does not contain vacancy announcements or job listings. FedFax allows for the retrieval of hard-copy information at any fax machine in the world, 24 hours a day, 7 days a week. FedFax is available at the following numbers:

Atlanta (404) 331-5267; Denver (303) 969-7764; Detroit (313) 226-2593; San Francisco (415) 744-7002; and Washington, DC (202) 606-2600.

Since the system is updated on a daily basis, you are encouraged to check the system frequently for current listings and to allow time for processing when requesting application materials or information from the system. Full text vacancy announcements are available on the FJOB, USAFJOBS Web site, and Touch Screen Kiosks. In many cases it is possible to complete an application on-line and submit it electronically to the advertising personnel office.

Step 2: Obtain the Vacancy Announcement

Once you have found an opportunity that interests you, using STEP 1, you will need more information on the specific opportunity and appropriate application forms. You may obtain a copy of the vacancy announcement and a complete application package by leaving your name and address on the system or, when available, by downloading the actual announcement and any supplementary materials from the FJOB, USAFJOB, or Touch screens. The vacancy announcement is an important source of information. Most of the questions you may have will be answered as you read through the announcement. For example: closing/deadline dates for applications, specific duties of the position, whether a written test is required, educational requirements, duty location, salary, etc.

Step 3: Follow the Application Instructions

You may apply for most jobs with a résumé, or the *Optional Application for Federal Employment (OF-612)*, or any written format you choose. For jobs that are unique or filled through automated procedures, you may be given special forms and/or instructions in the job announcement. Although the Federal Government does not require a standard application form for most jobs, certain information is needed to evaluate your qualifications. If you decide to submit any other format, other than the OF-612, (i.e., a résumé), the following information must be included:

- **Job Information** – Announcement number, title, and grade.

- **Personal Information** – Full name, mailing address (with zip code), day and evening phone numbers (with area code), social security number, country of citizenship, veteran's preference, reinstatement eligibility, highest Federal civilian grade held.

- **Education** – High school name, city and state, colleges or universities, name, city and state, supervisor's name and phone number, starting and ending dates (month and year), hours per week, salary and indicate whether your current supervisor may be contacted. Prepare a separate entry for each job.

- **Other qualifications** – job-related training courses (title and year), job-related skills, job-related certificated and licenses, job-related honors, awards, and special accomplishments.

Excepted Service Agencies

Most Federal Government civilian positions are part of the competitive civil service. To obtain a Federal job, you must compete with other applicants in open competition. Some agencies are excluded from the competitive civil service procedures. This means that these agencies have their own hiring system which established the evaluation criteria they use in filing their internal vacancies. These agencies are called excepted service agencies.

If you are interested in employment with an excepted service agency, you should contact the agency directly. The U.S. Office of Personnel Management does not provide application forms or information on jobs in excepted service agencies or organizations. Below is a list of excepted service agencies, departments, and public international organizations. This list is not all-inclusive and is subject to change.

Federal Reserve System, Board of Governors
20th & C Street, N.W.
Washington, DC 20551
(202) 452-3038

Central Intelligence Agency
Office of Personnel
Washington, DC 20505
1-800-562-7242

Defense Intelligence Agency
Civilian Personnel Office
The Pentagon
Washington, DC 20340-3042
(703) 907-1724

U.S. Department of State
Foreign Service Positions, Recruitment Division
P.O. Box 9317, Rosslyn Station
Arlington, VA 22219

Federal Bureau of Investigation
JEH Building, Room 6647
10th Street & Pennsylvania Avenue, N.W.
Washington, DC 20571

Outstanding Scholar Program

What Is the Outstanding Scholar Program?

The Outstanding Scholar Program is a special hiring authority established for entry-level administrative positions at the GS-5 and GS-7 grade levels. The Outstanding Scholar Program is authorized under the terms of a consent decree (*Luevano v. Newman*) and can only be used for the specific series and job titles listed. It is not applicable for other entry-level professional jobs such as accountants, engineers, physical science careers, or jobs in the biological sciences or mathematics. The Outstanding Scholar Program is also not applicable at grades below GS-5 or above GS-7.

If you meet the requirements below, you may be offered a direct appointment by a Federal agency without having to go through the normal competitive hiring procedures. The direct appointment process cuts through all of the red tape and can save you weeks of time.

Requirements for the Outstanding Scholar Program

To qualify for consideration, you must be a college graduate and have maintained a grade point average (GPA) of 3.45 or better on a 4.0 scale for all undergraduate course work, or have graduated in the upper 10 percent of your class or major university subdivision.

A college degree in any major is qualifying for most of the career fields covered by the Outstanding Scholar Program. A few, however, require some course work in subjects related to the job. You may apply a few months before graduation, but you must have the GPA or class standing at such time as you are offered a job.

How to Apply as an Outstanding Scholar

You should contact Personnel Offices of Federal agencies directly to inquire about their hiring needs. Send a résumé or the Optional Application for Federal employment (OF612), attach a transcript and a cover letter identifying yourself as an Outstanding Scholar applicant. Frequently, Federal recruiters will visit college campuses, giving you an additional opportunity to make contact.

Following is a listing of common career fields for the Outstanding Scholar Program.

Law Enforcement and Investigative Jobs

- Park Ranger
- Security Administrations
- Intelligence
- Wage and Hour Compliance
- Internal Revenue Officer
- Civil Aviation Security
- General Investigations
- Criminal Investigations

- Game Law Enforcement
- Immigration Inspection
- Securities Compliance Examining
- Alcohol, Tobacco, and Firearms Inspection
- Public Health Quarantine Inspection
- Import Specialist
- Customs Inspector

Professional-Related Administrative Jobs

- Archives Specialist
- Archivist
- Archeology
- Community Planning
- Economics
- Educational Programming
- Foreign Affairs
- General Anthropology
- General Education and Training

- Geography
- History
- International Relations
- Manpower Research and Analysis
- Museum Management (Curator)
- Psychology
- Social Science
- Sociology

People with Disabilities

Job Opportunities for People with Disabilities

The Federal Government recognizes that people with disabilities have a right to full and fair consideration for any job for which they apply. It strives to offer an environment in which all can reach their highest potential and make a difference for our country.

Federal positions are filled by people with disabilities, as well as able-bodied persons. A Federal career can provide:

- Any individual the opportunity to excel;

- Challenges of a demanding job; and

- Advancement potential or individual growth.

Having a disability will not hinder your opportunities as an applicant for employment with the Federal Government or in pursuing career opportunities once you become an employee. Whether it is working on a cure for cancer, AIDS or heart disease, designing advanced avionics, or writing procurement contracts worth millions of dollars, the challenge is there for individuals with the right skills, motivation, and attitude.

Competitive Appointments

Most Federal employees obtain jobs competitively, through the following procedures:

You may apply for an establish eligibility on an U.S. Office of Personnel Management (OPM) (or agency-sponsored) list of eligibles, either by having your experience and education evaluated without a written test and/or by passing an appropriate written test. If passing a written test is required for consideration, special testing arrangements may be available, if requested. Then, when filling a vacancy, an agency requests a list of qualified people from the appropriate list of eligibles.

For some types of positions, you may apply directly to a Federal agency advertising the position. The agency may then interview and select you for the vacancy. Special interview "reasonable accommodation" arrangements may be made, if requested.

Selective Placement

The Federal Government's Selective Placement programs include special appointing authorities for people with disabilities.

Federal hiring officials are authorized to use special hiring authorities when considering certain people with disabilities (those who have a severe physical, cognitive, or emotional disability, or a history of having such disabilities, or are perceived as having such disabilities). The use of these authorities is not mandatory. These authorities evaluate the potential of an applicant to perform the essential duties of a position and whether reasonable accommodations are warranted.

How to Qualify for Selective Placement Opportunities

If you are interested in being considered under these special hiring authorities, you must contact either a state vocational or Department of Veterans Affairs rehabilitation counselor or Gallaudet University placement office and request their assistance. They will review and prepare the necessary documents. They should be asked to provide you with a "certification" statement that describes your ability to perform the essential duties for the position in which you are interested. Then, once you have obtained this certification statement, you should contact the Federal agency where you wish to work. Ask for the contact person who handles the Selective Placement Program. These agency representatives work closely with qualified people with disabilities and hiring officials with jobs. They help match applicant core skills and their employment accommodation needs to available jobs.

Disabled Veterans and Other Veteran Opportunities

Any disabled veteran can contact the Department of Veterans Affairs, Vocational Rehabilitation and Counseling Offices for information on veterans benefits and related employment services. Certain veterans may also be considered under special hiring programs for disabled veterans with disability ratings of 30 percent or more or Vietnam Era Veteran Readjustment Act opportunities.

Reasonable Workplace Accommodations

Sometimes it may be necessary or advisable for Federal hiring officials to make "a reasonable workplace accommodation," if requested, in either the duties of the job, or where and how job tasks are performed. Such forms of accommodation should make it easier to successfully perform the duties of the position. Examples of workplace reasonable accommodation include:

- Providing interpreters, readers, or other personal assistance.
- Modifying job duties.
- Restructuring work sites.
- Providing flexible work schedules or work sites.
- Obtaining accessible technology or other workplace adaptive equipment.

Federal Job Scams

Consumer Alert – Federal Job Fraud

Information on job vacancies with the Federal Government and the Postal Service is provided free of charge. However, many Americans are victimized by scam artists selling information about Federal job opportunities. These scam artists place classified advertisements in newspapers, magazines, and periodicals offering – for a fee – to help job seekers locate and apply for Federal jobs. Some companies go so far as to use names that imply affiliation with the Federal Government, such as the "U.S. Agency for Career Advancement," or "Postal Employment Service."

Many of these companies advertise the availability of large numbers of Federal jobs in local areas, while in reality few or none may actually exist. For example, the Postal Service has few vacancies for permanent, full-time jobs. Legitimate Postal Service hiring takes place through 85 district offices at the local level. Openings are announced for a very short time. Your local post office is the best source of information concerning current or anticipated openings. The U.S. Office of Personnel Management's Federal Employment Information System is the official source for employment information and contains Federal job listings as well as some state, local government, and private sector listings.

Remember, information about Federal job opportunities is available to the public free of charge, with the exception of local phone company charges for long distance calls. Federal agencies and the Postal Service never charge for applications, sell study guides for examinations, or guarantee that you will be hired. If an examination is required, the agency administering the examination typically offers free sample questions to applicants scheduled for the examination.

The Federal Trade Commission and the U.S. Office of Personnel Management urge consumers to protect themselves against job scams. Beware of advertisements or sales pitches containing:

- An implied affiliation with the Federal Government, a guarantee of high test scores or jobs, references to "hidden" or unadvertised job vacancies, or claims that "no experience is necessary."

- Referrals to a toll-free phone number. Often in these cases, an operator encourages you to buy a "valuable" booklet containing job listings, practice test questions, and tips for entrance examinations. These materials may be inaccurate, unnecessary, or available at no charge from the hiring agency.

- Toll-free numbers that direct you to pay-per-call numbers for more information. Under Federal law, any solicitations for pay-per-call numbers must contain full disclosures about cost. The solicitation must make clear if there is or is not an affiliation with the Federal Government. You must have a chance to hang up before you incur any charges.

If you have concerns about an employment advertisement or a company offering employment services, you may contact the following:

- Federal Trade Commission, (202) 326-3128.

- Postal Crime Hotline, U.S. Postal Inspection Service, 1-800-654-8896, available 24 hours a day.

- National Fraud Information Center (a project of the National Consumers League), 1-800-876-7060, available weekdays, 9:00 a.m. to 5:00 p.m. Eastern Standard Time, or on the Internet at www.fraud.org.

- Your State Attorney General or local Better Business Bureau.

Administrative Careers With America (ACWA)

In an effort to reduce confusion surrounding the process of seeking federal employment, the Office of Personnel Management (OPM) has recently initiated a program known as "Career America." As part of this program, OPM has published a 265-page *Federal Career Directory* designed to answer the most commonly asked questions about federal employment. The directory was developed primarily for new college graduates, career counseling professionals, current government employees, and college students who are in the process of choosing careers.

This directory has the usual information one would expect from such a source, including details on employee benefits, the federal pay and classification systems, and training and development opportunities.

The core of the directory, however, is a detailed profile of each federal department and agency, including its mission, functions, and the typical college majors and degrees required for entry-level jobs. Perhaps most importantly, it also gives the address and telephone numbers of each agency's employment office.

Another section of the new directory contains an index of college majors and areas of study referenced to the agencies that typically hire these graduates. By using this index, job applicants can get an idea which agencies are hiring which degree holders and thus can simplify the job search. By turning to the agencies, the reader learns what the agency does, where it is located, the telephone number of the personnel office and sometimes other relevant information—availability of student work/study programs, for instance.

While the directory provides information on the kinds of professional workers hired by the agency, it does not include the jobs that are currently available. To order the *Federal Career Directory* (stock number 006-000-01339-2) contact the Superintendent of Documents, U.S. Government Printing Office, Washington, DC 20402-9325.

To apply for an entry-level position with the federal government, you must first find out what category of jobs you qualify for and then determine how best to apply within the category selected.

Criminal justice related positions can sometimes be found in a large catchall group called "Administrative Careers With America" (ACWA), covering a majority of entry-level administrative and professional positions, sometimes not even requiring the degree recipient to have majored in criminal justice.

Administrative Careers With America covers a wide range of entry-level administrative and professional occupations and about 100 types of jobs are filled through this program using one of two application methods—a written examination or an application based on scholastic achievement, reflected by grade point average, 3.5 or above, or the top 10 percent of your class. You may apply for jobs under this program when you are within nine months of graduation, or upon completion of the qualifying academic courses or three years of experience. These positions usually start at the General Schedule (GS) grades 5 or 7 depending on qualification. Beginning salaries are eight percent higher in San Francisco, Los Angeles, and New York.

Under the program, written examinations are offered in each of six occupational groups and you can apply to take one or more test(s) from the following occupational groups:

Group I	Health, Safety, and Environment
Group II	Writing and Public Information
Group III	Business, Finance, and Management
Group IV	Personnel, Administration, and Computers
Group V	Benefits Review, Tax, and Legal
Group VI	Law Enforcement and Investigation

Each examination consists of two parts: A written test and a multiple-choice Individual Achievement Record (IAR) questionnaire. The written test is an assessment of job-relevant abilities, mostly reasoning. The IAR is a biographical questionnaire that is intended to assess job-relevant characteristics other than reasoning ability. When you apply to take an examination, you will get a descriptive booklet that includes sample questions. Examinations are conducted continuously for Groups III through VI and are announced for Groups I and II.

Although opportunities for employment under the ACWA program vary among occupations, Groups III through VI are likely to offer the greatest employment opportunities with the government.

For information on all entry-level opportunities available contact one of the OPM federal job information centers.

The Job Interview

There is much to learn about the job interview process if you are to compete effectively with other job applicants. An interview might simply be thought of as a conversation between yourself and a prospective employer. The goal of the interviewer is to see if a good match exists between your qualifications and the job responsibilities of the position. The interview is a time of mutual exploration. As the interviewee, your goal is to gather information about the position to decide if it is the job for you, while conveying the message, "Hire me," through information that you provide which is attractive and saleable to the interviewer. Expect the interviewer to ask about your skills, qualifications, and interests, the kind of person you are, etc.

A final point about the interview process is to know that you must be active and be prepared to participate fully, as a job interview is a cooperative endeavor. To help you prepare yourself for this experience, explore the interview process below, according to five phases.

Phase I: Preparation

The preparation stage is all the work you will have to do prior to coming to the interview. It would be an understatement to say that preparation is the key to having a good interview. Here are 10 tips on how you can prepare yourself:

1. Find out with whom, when, and where the interview will take place. Prepare to arrive at least 15 minutes early. If you are unfamiliar with the interview site, you may want to find the location the day before to avoid the difficulty and embarrassment of being late or getting lost.

2. Be prepared to fill out personnel forms.

3. Bring with you some form of identification, such as a Social Security card, samples of your work (if appropriate), and extra copies of your résumé.

4. Know things about the agency, position, organization, etc. that you wish to enter. Make it your business to collect and read the appropriate literature. It is possible that the interviewer will want to know what you know about the agency. This is the excellent opportunity to convey your preparedness and knowledge. This is critical.

5. Prepare several questions about the position, agency, or department that you would like to have answered. This demonstrates your curiosity and interest in the position/agency.

6. Know what the job requirements are and what the job demands, plus the training requirements, expected salary range, etc.

7. Know and be prepared to talk about your strengths, weaknesses, abilities, talents, values, accomplishments, prior work history, job expectations, and goals.

8. Be prepared to respond to questions posed to you. Below are some examples of more difficult-to-answer questions that may be posed; some may require a good deal of thought.

    - Tell me about yourself.

    - Why did you leave your last job?

    - Why did you choose this agency?

    - What do you know about our organization?

    - Why should we hire you?

    - How do you feel about working for a woman?

    - What are your strengths?

    - What are your weaknesses?

9. Be prepared to assume a relaxed yet attentive sitting position. Body language – a form of nonverbal behavior – plays a specific role in your evaluation. The evaluation of anxiety level is a significant factor in a criminal justice interview.

10. Dress appropriately. Dress on the conservative side, with a neat, clean, and professional appearance.

Phase II: Initial Meeting

This is the point at which you would first meet the interviewer(s). It is difficult to rehearse this situation, as you cannot predict what cues will be given to you. Your best advice is to rely on common sense and courtesy. Consider the following:

1. Greet the interviewer by name (title, last name) and be prepared for a firm handshake. Be sure to make eye contact with the interviewer. A pleasant smile always helps. Follow the interviewer's lead as to where to sit.

2. Sit comfortably, straight up, and avoid excessive movement. It is quite normal for you to be a bit nervous but you should avoid doing things that make your nervousness more obvious to those

interviewing you. You may want to keep your hands on your lap. Tapping of feet, gum chewing, and smoking should be avoided.

3. Be prepared for small talk. The interviewer might ask if you would care for a cup of coffee, how the trip to the interview went, or he or she might chat about something current in the news. Although the content of what is discussed seems unimportant, it is an excellent opportunity for your prospective employer to see you as friendly, calm, and confident. You should remain enthusiastic, talkative, and friendly. However, asking too much or too little could hinder your chances of employment.

Phase III: Information Sharing

Essentially, this is the question-and-answer period of the interview. Here you will be asked specific questions regarding your qualifications, interests, and experience. It is your opportunity to present the information about you. This is going to get the message across that you are the best candidate for the job. You can expect to be asked a variety of questions during this stage. Here, if you prepared your responses as suggested earlier, you will shine. This is also the time when you would want to ask the questions that you consider necessary to your decisions. Consider the following:

1. *Do not ask obvious or trivial questions* that could have been answered prior to the interview. Ask questions that are well thought through and that have been prepared earlier.

2. *Be a good listener.* Being concerned and attentive is important. An occasional nod of the head conveys your involvement. Your attentiveness is easily picked up as a positive quality.

3. *Speak clearly and to the point when asked questions.* Try to be factual, honest, and sincere, while making sure your good qualities are coming across. Do not be conceited, but do not be negative. For example, if asked about your weaknesses, turn them into a positive quality, e.g., "My weaknesses are that I care too much about my work and I sometimes work harder/longer than I need to." Do not reveal information that will damage your chances for attaining the job unless it is really necessary.

4. *Be positive in your responses.* Do not criticize former employers. Be diplomatic.

5. *Do not emphasize salary.* This can give the impression that you are overly concerned with this factor. Besides, many of the positions in the criminal justice system have standardized pay scales.

6. *Prepare for a "stress interview."* If you are considering a career within the criminal justice system, you can expect to encounter a number of experiences on the job that will require you to exercise sound judgment in the wake of some critical and tense situations. Your ability to respond appropriately and immediately is a vital part of doing your job well, a statement of the kind of character you possess and, in many cases, an indicator of whether you would respond well under pressure. Thus, a "stress interview" may be considered an integral part of the job acceptance process.

    Simply stated, a stress interview is a type of job interview that attempts to evaluate your reactions during the stressful situation the interviewer creates. The interview may involve a panel of interviewers whose task is to upset, confuse, annoy, or anger you to see how you will handle the stress. For example, you may be placed in a hypothetical situation that involves turning in your partner of many years, following appropriate legal procedures. Or they might place you in a variety of other "double bind" situations in which no right answer seems possible. You might even receive some verbal criticism. Generally, these questions are designed to measure your integrity, decision-making ability, and the extent to which you are able to control your emotions.

    Do not take the interview too personally or let your emotions control your thinking, regardless of what the interviewer tries to do. You must remain *calm* at all times and not feel personally offended or allowed to be influenced in your thinking. Never become loud, angry, or abusive. Look directly at the interviewer, maintaining good eye contact. Keep your body as still as possible. Honesty, calmness, and good common sense are the key ingredients to a successful interview. Many of the careers in criminal justice are stressful. Learning how to effectively handle this kind of situation will be good training. If you are a little nervous, it is natural, but if you think your emotions might overpower your ability to do well at an interview, get some help and practice.

Phase IV: The Closing

Usually when the interviewer asks you if you have any further questions, it is a signal that the interview is coming to a close. During this stage consider the following:

1. If you have any unresolved questions regarding the job, now is the time to ask. Perhaps you might want to know when you would expect to hear from them.

2. You may want to summarize your strong points.

3. If you really want this job, say so by again expressing your interest in an appropriate style. Do not ask what your chances are.

4. Before leaving, have a clear idea of what to expect. Find out if there are any remaining forms to be filed or completed.

5. Close the interview by expressing your appreciation.

Phase V: After the Interview

Although the interview has ended, your responsibilities have not. There are two more tasks to perform if you are to give your job search its best effort.

First, you should definitely send a thank you letter to your interviewer. It will serve as a reminder of who you are. As you may already know, many people are interviewed in the course of a job opening. Perhaps equally important, a letter reaffirms your interest in the job or agency. It demonstrates that you are serious and professional.

Second, use your interview to provide a learning experience. Go over each interview to evaluate its positive and negative aspects, so that with each interview you will improve. Use the experience to learn about yourself and the various responsibilities and agencies within the criminal justice field. Think about what you would do differently and practice, practice, practice. Start fresh with each new interview, but do not start until you are prepared.

Chapter 12

Using the Internet to Get a Job in the Criminal Justice Field

*As a general rule, the most successful people in life
are those who have the best information.*

—Disraeli

Finding a criminal justice job is more than an overnight venture. The entire process includes researching what jobs are available, applying for them, taking tests, interviewing, and deciding which one to accept. Each step is time-consuming, but there are some clever ways to accomplish more while cutting down on the amount of time you spend on the job search. One way is to work smarter, rather than harder, by using the Internet.

On the Internet, you can find out which agencies are hiring, the requirements for each job, as well as starting salaries and other interesting information. Some employers also answer questions and accept applications on-line. But before you can jump into this electronic wonderland, there are a few basics you'll need to know.

The Internet: What Is It Really?

You may have heard the terms **information superhighway, Infobahn, data highway, electronic highway, Net, or cyberspace.** They're all different ways of referring to the Internet, which is the world's largest communication network. It's made up of many local and regional computer networks that connect people and resources around the world.

A computer network is simply any two or more computers that are hooked up so that they can communicate with each other. Some consist of a central computer with remote stations that report to it. A police department's network, for example, might have a main computer plus screens and keyboards at the 911 call center, in the detective division and in each police car.

The Internet is actually a network of networks. College and university networks are part of the Internet, as are government agencies and corporations. It is estimated that about 40 million individuals use the Internet, and that number is growing every day.

Get Connected!

The number of companies and government agencies on the Internet is increasing quickly, too, making the Internet a more valuable job search tool every day. But to explore all the great information that's out there, you'll need to be able to access the Internet.

To get connected, you will need five things:

- a computer,

- a modem,

- an Internet service provider,

- an account user-name and password, and

- log-on and log-off instructions.

Because the Internet is a computer network, a computer is required in order to use it. But if you don't have your own computer, all is not lost. Computers with Internet access can be found at the computer center or library of almost every college and university. Alternatively, public libraries, community continuing education centers, cybercafés, and workplaces offer Internet services. Each place will have its own rules regarding computer access, so it pays to check them out before you settle in for a long spell in front of the screen.

Computers must be connected to a phone line with a modem in order to get on to the Net. External modems are separate boxes with power cords and cables that plug in to the computer and the phone line. Internal modems sit inside the computer and have just a cable to hook up to the phone line. Newer computers usually come with built-in modems.

The modem is used to call in to an Internet service provider, which in turn hooks your computer up to the Internet. There are a number of Internet providers to choose from, but if you're using a public computer, such as one at school, the server will already be in place.

To access the server, you will need an account user-name and password. You get these either directly from the service provider or from whoever owns the account, such as the computing center at school. The user-name allows the server to track usage. Your password is used to ensure that no one else can access your account, similar to the way your PIN number protects your bank ATM card.

Along with the user-name and password, you will receive log-on and log-off instructions. Each server's requirements are different, but most are simple and quick.

Full Internet Access

Being on the **Internet** means that you have full access to all these Internet services:

- electronic mail (E-mail);
- File Transfer Protocol (FTP);
- Telnet, or Remote Log-in; and
- World Wide Web (the Web).

E-mail is an electronic mail service that works with computers rather than with stamps and envelopes. With E-mail, you can send, receive, reply, save, file, and categorize messages. You can exchange messages with organizations more quickly than through conventional mail. You can send your résumé, for example, with one touch of a button (or one mouse-click). Or you can pose questions to an agency or request that a paper job application be sent to you.

File Transfer Protocol (FTP) allows files to be transferred from one computer to another. Protocols are a set of standards that allow computers to communicate. Using FTP, files or data can be uploaded, or sent to another site. Files and data can also be downloaded, or retrieved from a remote site.

Telnet, also called Remote Log-in, is one of the oldest Internet tools. It allows users to log onto another computer and use that computer's programs. By using Telnet, you can access a worldwide network of databases and services, such as libraries, bulletin boards, and interactive chats, which are not always available from an Internet provider. Telnet is not as interesting to look at as the Web, but it is essential to Net travel.

The World Wide Web is an Internet browsing and searching system that uses hypermedia, or multi-media, elements (text, images, video, and sound) to link documents and pictures. Moving around on, or surfing, the Web is as easy as a click of the mouse. Web browsers are programs that display the graphics of the Web. They use icons and pointers to make navigation fun and easy. The two best-known browsers are Netscape Navigator and Microsoft Internet Explorer.

Crawling Around the Web

You should know that the Internet and the Web are not the same thing. The Internet is the network used to transport information. The Web is the collection of standards and protocols that are used to access the information on the Internet. The Web uses three standards:

- URLs (Uniform Resource Locators);

- HTTP (Hypertext Transfer Protocol); and

- HTML (Hypertext Markup Language).

URLs, or Uniform Resource Locators, are the "addresses" where Net information can be found. The URL format is protocol//server-name/path. Most URLs look like this one: http://www.thelist.com, which is the address for a Web site that offers information about local service providers.

HTTP, or Hypertext Transfer Protocol, is the protocol the Web uses to move information. Web site URLs begin with the http protocol http:// and are followed by the server name.

HTML, or Hypertext Markup Language, is the programming language used to create a Web page. It is used for basic formatting and presentation of hypermedia documents and specifies links to other documents.

Cybersleuthing

The Internet is a useful tool in your job hunt because it allows you to find many different types of information. If you already know which agency holds the most interest for you, for example, often you can get employment requirements and application information from its home page. Or, if you're unsure about what kind of job you want within the criminal justice field, there are Web sites that list various job categories.

A **Web** site is a location on the World Wide Web. It is reached by typing in the URL. The Web site's home page is a "Welcome" page. Frequently, home pages list basic information about the company or agency to which it belongs, as well as a table of contents that lets you know what other information you can access on that Web site, such as the agency's field office locations or mission statement.

In order to find the Web sites that have information you might want or need, you will have to be able to find the URLs for these pages. If you do not already have the Web address for a site you want to explore, for example, the FBI's home page, which is http://www.fbi.gov, or if you are not sure where to start your search, the simplest way to go is by consulting a search directory or a search engine.

Search directories work in a similar fashion to computerized library catalogs. They offer descriptive subject indexes of Web sites, and they also have searching options. Some of the search directories available are Excite, Magellan, and Yahoo.

A search engine is something like an automated Yellow Pages. It searches World Wide Web sites as well as other Internet resources to find matches to your descriptor keywords. Keywords are words you type in that tell the search directory what information you are trying to find. If you were interested in finding a job with a state police agency, for example, you might type in the words "Arizona state police and employment." Many search engines rank the results according to a degree of relevancy, and most have options for advanced searching, which helps you to refine your search. Search engines include Alta Vista, HotBot, and Lycos.

A shortcut to avoid going to each search directory or engine individually is to visit a comprehensive directory, such as MetaCrawler (http://www.metacrawler.com) for one-stop searching. MetaCrawler conducts your search by tapping into Alta Vista, Excite, Infoseek, Lycos, Yahoo, and WebCrawler simultaneously.

Jump In – The Water's Fine!

Now you know the basic information you need to get on the Internet and what to look for once you're there, but if you're entering uncharted territory, it all might feel a bit overwhelming. To begin a smooth cyberspace journey into criminal justice job hunting, you may want to take advantage of some resources that we've already found for you.

As you travel from Web site to site, you will see fascinating new things and pick up ideas that may surprise you. If you take the time to follow your interests, you may discover things about yourself and your inclinations that you never knew before. That's all part of the career-shopping process, so enjoy the journey.

Sites with Links

The sites listed here are good places to start if your job search needs some inspiration. These Web pages provide links to other sites that you might find helpful.

CAREER OPPORTUNITIES IN SECURITY http://www.asisonline.org

CAREERS IN LAW ENFORCEMENT http://www.qni.com/~nixter

CENTER FOR INFORMATION LAW AND POLICY
http://www.law.vill.edu

CRIMINAL JUSTICE RELATED INTERNET SITES
http://broadway.vera.org/pub/ocjsites.html

FEDERAL GOVERNMENT AGENCIES
http://www.lib.lsu.edu/gov/fedgov.html

FEDERAL JOBS DIGEST http://www.jobsfed.com

FEDERAL TIMES http://www.federaltimes.com

DR. CECIL GREEK'S CRIMINAL JUSTICE LINKS
http://www.fsu.edu/~crimdo/feds.html

INFOSEEK: EXPLORE OCCUPATIONS
http://www.infoseek.com/Getting_It_Done/Find_a_job/Explore_
occupations?sv=N4

JUSTICE INFORMATION CENTER http://www.ncjrs.org

LAW ENFORCEMENT CAREERS http://www.gate.net/~fcfjobs

LAW ENFORCEMENT GUIDE TO THE WEB http://www.leolinks.com

LOCAL LAW ENFORCEMENT AGENCY SITES http://www.crisnet.com

OCCUPATIONAL OUTLOOK HANDBOOK
http://stats.bls.gov/ocohome.htm

THE POLICE OFFICER'S INTERNET DIRECTORY
http://www.officer.com

USING THE INTERNET IN YOUR JOB SEARCH
http://www.dbm.com/jobguide/jobsrch.html#why

WHAT COLOR IS YOUR PARACHUTE: THE NET GUIDE (R.N. BOLLES)
http://www.washingtonpost.com/wp-adv/classifieds/careerpost/
parachute/parafram2.htm

Other Law Enforcement Web Sites Worth Mentioning:

Center for Sex Offender Management
http://www.csg.org/appa/csom.html

Community Policing Consortium
http://www.communitypolicing.org

CopNet
http://www.copnet.org

Federal Bureau of Investigation's Ten Most Wanted Fugitives
http://www.fbi.gov/mostwant/tenlist.htm

Federal Bureau of Investigation's Fugitive Publicity
http://www.fbi.gov/fugitive/fpphome.htm

Federal Law Enforcement Training Center
http://www.ustreas.gov/fletc

Financial Crimes Enforcement Network (FinCEN)
http://www.ustreas.gov/fincen

Florida Department of Law Enforcement
http://www.fdle.state.fl.us

International Association of Chiefs of Police
http://www.theiacp.org

International Association of Law Enforcement Planners
http://www.dps.state.ak.us/ialep

Law Enforcement Agencies on the Web
by Florida State University Associate Professor of Criminology Cecil Greek
http://www.fsu.edu/~crimdo/cj.html

National Law Enforcement and Corrections Technology Center
http://www.nlectc.org

National Sheriffs' Association
http://www.sheriffs.org

Niagara Regional Police (Canada)
http://www.nrps.com/nrpsweb

Office of International Affairs Fugitive Homepage
http://www.usdoj.gov/criminal/oiafug/fugitives.htm

Partners OffDuty
http://www.murlin.com/~webfx/PartnersOffDuty

Police Executive Research Forum
http://www.PoliceForum.org

* see resource section at end of text for many other important Web sites.

See p. 188 for an example of information downloaded from one of these Web sites.

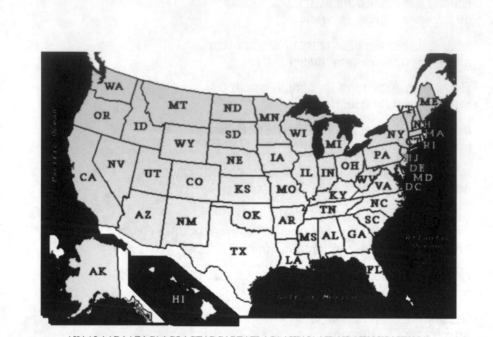

AK I AL I AR I AZ I CA I CO I CT I DC I DE I FL I GA I HI I IA I ID I IL I IN I KS I KY I LA
MA I MD I ME I MI I MN I MO I MS I MT I NE I NC I ND I NH I NJ I NM I NV I NY
OH I OK I OR I PA I RI I SC I SD I TN I TX I UT I VA I VT I WA I WI I WV I WY

Click on the label of any state on the map (or in the list above) to see the links for local law enforcement Web sites in that state. CRISNet maintains an extensive listing of local and state law enforcement agencies – now nearly **1,200** links! Every state is now represented!

We've updated our entire Web site! Please take a look around!

You'll probably want to bookmark YOUR home state
or use the form below to be informed of any changes to the page!

Enter your e-mail address and select your page(s) of interest.
[Hold the Ctrl and Enter keys to select more than one page.]
You will receive an e-mail message from **URL-Minder**
when the selected CRISNet Local Law pages are updated.

Your Internet e-mail address:

Page(s) of Interest:

This site is growing! We'll be glad to <u>add your site</u> (or others you know of) to our roster if you'll supply us the Internet address! And, please, visit us again soon! You're welcome to drop by ANY time!

Government Job Sites

FEDERAL BUREAU OF INVESTIGATION
http://www.fbi.gov/over.personel.htm

FEDERAL CAREER OPPORTUNITES
http://www.fedjobs.com

GOVERNMENT JOBS
http://www.govtjobs.com

LAW ENFORCEMENT AGENCY SITES
http://www.officer.com/agencies.htm

U.S. OFFICE OF PERSONNEL MANAGEMENT
http://www.usajobs.opm.gov/

Applying On-Line

Once you arrive at a job listing that appeals to you, take advantage of the information that is posted on the site. Read about the requirements as well as the job description. Check out the application process. While some sites will allow you to apply on-line, others require that you mail or E-mail them an application request. If you decide that you'd like to apply electronically, you'll need to have your basic information, such as your complete address and your Social Security Number, on hand when you apply. If you don't have it with you, note (or bookmark) the Web site address. Then, return when you have all the information together. If you submit an incomplete application, the hiring process will be slowed down.

An example of an on-line application is the Border Patrol Agent form (see pp. 190-191), which can be accessed at http://www.usajobs.opm.gov/bpa1.htm

Border Patrol Agent On-Line Application

Welcome. You have reached the U.S. Government's World Wide Web application process-ing system. We are now accepting applications for Border Patrol Agent positions with the United States Immigration and Naturalization Service.

The vacancies to be filled are General Schedule grades 5 and 7. You will be presented with a series of questions that must be answered. Some questions will require a simple Yes or No response, while others may require you to select from a list of options, or require you to type information using the keyboard.

Please enter your 4-digit extension number now. If your extension number has only 3 digits, add a leading zero. For example, if your extension number is 415, enter 0415. If you do not know the extension number, please enter 9999.

We are interested in knowing how you heard about this recruitment announcement for Border Patrol Agent positions. Indicate only one of the following numbers which was your primary source of information.

Ad in area newspaper.	O
INS employee.	O
INS Human Resources or Personnel Office.	O
Ad in military base newspaper.	O
Ad in college newspaper.	O
College Career Planning Office, College Job Fair, or Faculty Member.	O
USAJOBS, Federal Job Opportunities Board, Federal Job Information Touch Screen Computer Kiosk, or Career America Connection.	O
INS or U.S. Border Patrol's internet web sites.	O
OPM's USAJOBS internet web site.	O

Other internet web sites.   ○
State Employment Office.   ○
Job announcement on DOD Transition Bulletin Board.   ○
Exiting military personnel job fair.   ○
Other job fairs.   ○
Other sources.   ○

We request the following information in order to evaluate our efforts to recruit minorities and women. Providing this information is voluntary. This information will not be used to make selections nor will your chances for employment be affected if you do not answer these questions. Additionally, we treat the information that you provide to us as confidential, and we protect it from disclosure under the Privacy Act at 5 U.S.C. Section 552a(b). OMB Clearance Number 1115-0188, Expiration Date October 31, 1999.

A. Gender
                    ○ Male   ○ Female
B. National Origin
                    Are you of Hispanic/Latino Origin?   ○ Yes ○ No
C. Race
                    ○ White?
                    ○ African American?
                    ○ American Indian or Alaskan Native?
                    ○ Asian or Pacific Islander?
D. Veteran Status
                    Are you a Veteran of the U.S. armed forces who was
                    discharged under honorable conditions?   ○ Yes ○ No

We need your Social Security Number to maintain your records. Executive Order 9397 authorizes the Office of Personnel Management to use this number in keeping records. We may also use this number to make requests for information about you from employers, schools, banks and others. Giving us your Social Security Number is voluntary; however, we cannot process your application without it.

It is important that you enter your Social Security Number correctly. FAILURE TO DO SO WILL PROHIBIT OR DELAY THE PROCESSING OF YOUR APPLICATION AND WRITTEN TEST.

Now enter your Social Security Number: ☐☐☐ – ☐☐ – ☐☐☐☐

You must be available for employment within the next six months. If you will not be available during this time frame, you will not be considered. Are you available for employment within the next six months?   ○ Yes ○ No

When you have completed this portion of your application, click on the **SUBMIT APPLICATION** button. Your application will be reviewed for completeness. If it is complete, you will get the next part of the application. If there are errors, your application form will be returned with a list of the errors so you can correct and re-submit it. This may take from 10 to 30 seconds. Please be patient.

(SUBMIT APPLICATION)

Chapter 13

Pursuing Further Education
to Enhance Career Opportunity

Considering Graduate or Law School

After earning your bachelor's degree (BA/BS) you may want to consider attending graduate or law school in addition to or prior to attaining employment. Graduate and law school programs provide specialized concentrations of study leading to advanced degrees. A variety of graduate programs are associated with criminal justice education and its related disciplines. Some of the more common graduate or master's degrees include criminal justice, public administration, corrections, police administration, public policy, criminology, forensic psychology, juvenile justice, social work, human services, psychology, sociology, counseling, and security administration.

Usually the master's degree programs require 30-36 credits of academic course work in addition to the writing of a thesis or the passing of a comprehensive examination. Beyond the master's program, further advanced education leading to a doctorate (Ph.D., Ed.D.) is also available in many of these disciplines. Doctoral programs have rigorous admission standards and require several additional years (of post-master's study and research) culminating in the writing of a dissertation and/or other comprehensive oral and written exams.

The law degree, Juris Doctor (J.D.), is another example of a degree required for certain careers within the criminal justice field. With this particular degree, you would have an advantage when applying to criminal justice law-related positions within government service. The law degree (J.D.) typically requires three years of full-time study in addition to passing the bar exam, which licenses you to practice law in the state in which the exam was taken and passed.

Pursuing a graduate or law degree has many advantages with respect to successful career attainment and advancement within the criminal justice system. Quite simply, you may find that the entry-level requirement of the career you desire most when exploring your long-term or short-term plans requires it (e.g., FBI agent). Also, educational requirements for many criminal justice positions continue to increase, and this trend is worth noting. Enrolling in a graduate degree program makes you more competitive for many positions, as you will find many applicants with advanced degrees competing for jobs with applicants who hold bachelor's degrees. Having a graduate degree is also beneficial and often necessary in terms of eventual promotion, perhaps to a supervisory or managerial position.

Deciding on Graduate or Law School

You must actively engage in a decision-making process in order to decide if graduate school is for you, and if so, the type of educational program that is suited to your interests, abilities, and career goals.

It is not uncommon for students to drop out of graduate or law school. Common reasons shared by these students are that they find that graduate education: is too demanding, does not meet their expectations/interests, is too costly, is incongruent with their current lifestyle or that they were poorly prepared, and needed or should have taken a break from school prior to enrolling. Many of these problems could have been avoided if the student had taken the time to sort out some very difficult and important questions. Before deciding whether to attend graduate or law school, ask yourself the following questions:

- Where does the motivation to attend graduate or law school originate?

- What are my short- or long-term career goals?

- Is the decision to attend graduate school realistic in terms of my abilities? Current lifestyle?

- Is graduate or law school a necessary prerequisite to achieve my career goals?

- Can I handle the rigor of academic work?

- Would I benefit from some time off before starting?

- Why am I pursuing this path? Am I avoiding making a commitment to a career right now?

- What other options do I have?

- Am I willing and able to invest the time, energy, and money to pursue a graduate degree?

Faculty, career advisers, counselors, family, and friends are valuable sources of information and support. Also, there are many books, articles, and college bulletins that can help in making this decision.

Once you've decided to apply to a graduate or law school program, your next task would be to select the most appropriate school given your personal, academic, and career needs. This decision must be made with further careful research and discussion. Consider the following questions to begin the decision-making process:

- Does the graduate or law school have a good reputation?

- Can I realistically meet the academic standards for admissions?

- Is the law or graduate school fully accredited?

- What academic programs and curriculum are available?

- What are the requirements for graduation, i.e., number of courses, qualifying exams, usual length of time to graduate?

- Given my personal background, is this the type of school environment in which I will feel comfortable?

- Do I want to attend a large or small university? Is an urban or rural area preferred?

- Do I want to be near friends or family?

- What types of financial aid are available? Are there fellowships? Assistantships? Government loan programs?

- Is the institution consistently raising its tuition?

- What kind of career opportunities are available for graduates of the program? Salary? Do they help in the job placement of their graduates?

- Do they offer a flexible school schedule? Does it permit for part-time or full-time study?

Begin by addressing each of these questions and then proceed to collect any additional information necessary to make a prudent choice. Again, keep in mind that there are resources, books, and supportive individuals to help guide you through the decision-making process. For specific information about law schools, begin by reading the latest edition of *Barron's Guide to Law Schools* (Barron's Educational Series Inc.). This book provides a concise description of all the American Bar Association (ABA) approved law schools. *The Pre-Law Handbook* (Law School Admissions Council) includes for each school the programs of study, up-to-date admissions requirements, and a profile of the most recent class.

BIBLIOGRAPHY

Career Planning Sources

Adams, B. & Morin, L. *Complete Resume & Job Search Book for College Students.* Bob Adams Inc. Publishers, 1993.

Adams Electronic Job Search Almanac, Editors of Adams Publishing, 1998.

Adler, F.A. & Mueller, Gerhard O.W., & Laufer, William S. *Criminal Justice: The Core Criminal Justice Careers SourceBook.* The McGraw-Hill Companies, 1996.

Bolles, R.N. *What Color Is Your Parachute?* Ten Speed Press, Berkeley, CA, 1998.

Cohen, Paul & Cohen, Shari. *Careers in Law Enforcement & Security.* Rosen Publishing Group, 1994.

Coleman, Harvey J. *Empowering Yourself: The Organizational Game Revealed.* Kendall/Hunt Publishing Company, 1996.

Criscito, Pat. *Resumes in Cyberspace: Your Complete Guide to a Computerized Job Search.* Barron's Educational Series, Inc., 1997.

Henry, Stuart (Editor). *Inside Jobs: A Realistic Guide to Criminal Justice Careers for College Graduates.* Sheffield Publishing, 1994.

Hutton, Donald B. & Mydlarz, Anna. *Guide to Law Enforcement Careers.* Barron's Educational Series, Inc., 1997.

Kennedy, Joyce Lain. *Resumes for Dummies,* Second Edition. IDG Books Worldwide, 1998.

Law Enforcement Career Starter: Finding and Getting a Job. Learning Express Publishing, 1998.

Lee, Mary Price, Lee, Richard S., Beam, Carol, & Dilks, Carol. *100 Best Careers in Crime Fighting: Law Enforcement, Criminal Justice, Private Security, and Cyberspace Crime Detection.* MacMillan Publishing Company, Incorporated, 1998.

Lorenzen, Elizabeth A. (Editor). *Career Planning and Job Searching in the Information Age.* Haworth Press, 1996.

Messmer, Max. *Job Hunting for Dummies.* IDG Books Worldwide, 1995.

Moock, R.T., Jr. *Get That Interview!: The Indispensable Guide for College Grads.* Barron's Educational Series, Inc., 1996.

Morgan, Dana & Goldenkoff, Dana, & Goldenkoff, Robert. *Federal Jobs: The Ultimate Guide,* Second Edition. Arco Publishing, 1997.

Nelson, Jim. *Careers in Law Enforcement: Interviewing for Results.* Graduate Group Publishing, 1996.

Peterson's Internships, 1998: More than 40,000 Opportunities to Get an Edge in Today's Competitive Job Market, Eighteenth Edition. Petersons Publishing, 1997.

Occupational Outlook Handbook: 1998-1999 Edition. U.S. Department of Labor. JIST Works, Incorporated, 1998.

Steele, John E. & Morgan, Marilyn S. *Career Planning & Development for College Students & Recent Graduates.* VGM Career Horizons, 1990.

Stinchcomb, J.D. *Opportunities in Law Enforcement and Criminal Justice Careers.* VGM Career Horizons, 1996.

Warner, John W. *Federal Jobs in Law Enforcement: The Complete Job Bank for Law Enforcement Careers with More than 100 Federal Agencies, in-Depth Coverage of Each Agency, Job Descriptions, Activities, Famous Cases, Valuable Job-Getting Guidance, How to Qualify.* Macmillan Publishing Company, Incorporated, 1992.

Wood, Patricia B. *Applying for Federal Jobs: A Guide to Writing Successful Applications & Resumes for the Job You Want in Government.* Login Publishing Consortium, 1995.

Criminal Justice Sources

American Society for Criminology Membership Directory. American Society of Criminology, Columbus, OH.

Basic Sources in Criminal Justice. U.S. Dept. of Justice, National Institute of Law Enforcement and Criminal Justice, Washington, DC, 1978.

Bests' Safety Directory: Industrial Safety, Hygiene Security, Vols. 1-2, 1987. A.M. Best, Oldwick, MD.

Brown, S., Esbensen, F., & Geis, G. *Criminology: Explaining Crime and Its Context,* Third Edition. Anderson Publishing Co., Cincinnati, OH, 1998.

Compensation in the Security/Loss Prevention Field. Abbott Langer and Assoc., Crete, IL, 1990.

Criminal Justice Careers Guidebook. U.S. Dept. of Labor, Washington DC, 1987.

Criminal Justice Education: The End of the Beginning, Summary of Methods and Findings. John Jay College of Criminal Justice/SUNY, New York, NY, 1978.

Federal Law Related Careers. Federal Reports, Inc., Washington, DC, 1991.

Forensic Services Directory: National Register of Experts, Engineers, Scientific Advisors, Medical and Technical Consultants, and Sources of Specialized Knowledge. Forensic Sciences Directory, Inc., Princeton, NJ, 1993.

Gaines, L.K., Kappeler, V.E., & Vaughn, J.B. *Policing in America,* Second Edition. Anderson Publishing Co., Cincinnati, OH, 1997.

Gordon, G., & McBride, B. *Criminal Justice Internships: Theory Into Practice,* Third Edition. Anderson Publishing Co., Cincinnati, OH, 1996.

International Association of Chiefs of Police Membership Directory. International Association of Chiefs of Police, Inc., Arlington, VA, Annual.

Johnson, H. *History of Criminal Justice,* Second Edition. Anderson Publishing Co., Cincinnati, OH, 1996.

Juvenile and Adult Correctional Departments, Institutions, Agencies and Paroling Authorities Directory. American Correctional Association, College Park, MD, 1991.

Lombardo, L.X. *Guards Imprisoned: Correctional Officers at Work,* Second Edition. Anderson Publishing Co., Cincinnati, OH, 1989.

National Directory of Correctional Administration. American Correctional Association, Laurel, MD, 1990.

National Directory of Law Enforcement. National Police Chiefs and Sheriffs Information Bureau, Stevens Point, WI, Annual.

National Directory of Law Enforcement, Correctional Institutions and Related Agencies. SPAN Publishing, Inc., National Police Chiefs and Sheriffs Information Bureau, Stevens Point, WI, Annual.

National Jail and Adult Detention Directory. American Correctional Association, College Park, MD, 1991.

Nemeth, C.P. *The Paralegal Resource Manual,* Second Edition. Anderson Publishing Co., Cincinnati, OH, 1995.

Nemeth, C.P. *Private Security and the Investigative Process.* Anderson Publishing Co., Cincinnati, OH, 1992.

Niederhoffer, A. *The Police Family.* Lexington Books, D.C. Heath & Co., Boston, MA, 1978.

O'Block, R.L. *Criminal Justice Research Sources*, Third Edition. Anderson Publishing Co., Cincinnati, OH, 1992.

Osterburg, J.W., & Ward, R.H. *Criminal Investigation: A Method for Reconstructing the Past,* Second Edition. Anderson Publishing Co., Cincinnati, OH, 1997.

The Police Employment Guide. Sam Houston State University, Huntsville, TX, 1982.

Probation and Parole Directory, 18th Ed. National Council on Crime and Delinquency, Hackensack, NJ, 1989.

Ricks, T.A., Tillett, B.G., & Van Meter, C.W. *Principles of Security,* Third Edition. Anderson Publishing Co., Cincinnati, OH, 1994.

Security Letter Sourcebook. Security Letter, Robert McCrie (Editor), New York, NY, 1990-1991.

Stinchcomb, James D. *Opportunities in Law Enforcement and Criminal Justice.* Lincolnwood R., VGM Career Horizons, 1990.

Stojkovic, S., & Lovell, R. *Corrections: An Introduction,* Second Edition. Anderson Publishing Co., Cincinnati, OH, 1997.

Sullivan, John L. *Introduction to Police Science,* Third Edition. McGraw Hill Book Co., New York, NY, 1977.

Travis, L. *Introduction to Criminal Justice,* Third Edition. Anderson Publishing Co., Cincinnati, OH, 1998.

Trojanowicz, R. & Bucqueroux, B. *Community Policing: How to Get Started,* Second Edition. Anderson Publishing Co., Cincinnati, OH, 1998.

Trojanowicz, R., Kappeler, V.E., Gaines, L.K., & Bucqueroux, B. *Community Policing: A Contemporary Perspective,* Second Edition. Anderson Publishing Co., Cincinnati, OH, 1998.

World List of Forensic Science Labs. Forensic Science Society, New Yorkshire, England, 1987.

Periodicals

American Journal of Criminal Justice
Official Publication of the Southern Criminal Justice Association
    University of Louisville, Urban Studies Institute, 426 W. Bloom Street, Louisville, KY 40208-5457

Correctional News
    California Probation, Parole and Correctional Assoc., Sacramento, CA 95815

Corrections Today
    American Correctional Association, 4321 Hartwick Rd., Suite LD208, College Park, MD 20740

Crime & Delinquency
    National Council on Crime and Delinquency, Sage Publications, Inc., Newbury Park, CA 91320

Criminology
    American Society of Criminology, 1314 Kinnear Rd., Suite 212, Columbus, OH 43212

The Criminologist
    American Society of Criminology, 1314 Kinnear Rd., Suite 212, Columbus, OH 43212

FBI Law Enforcement Bulletin
    FBI, U.S. Department of Justice, Washington, DC 20535

Journal of Crime & Justice
Sponsored by the Midwestern Criminal Justice Association
    Anderson Publishing Co., P.O. Box 1576, Cincinnati, OH 45201-1576

Journal of Criminal Justice
    Pergamon Press, Fairview Park, Elmsford, NY 10523

Journal of Criminal Justice Education
    Academy of Criminal Justice Sciences, Northern Kentucky University, 402 Nunn Hall, Highland Heights, KY 41076

Journal of Forensic Sciences
    American Academy of Forensic Sciences, 225 S. Academy Blvd., Colorado Springs, CO 80910

Journal of Police Science & Administration
    International Association of Chiefs of Police, 1110 Glebe Rd., Suite 200, Arlington, VA 22201

Justice Quarterly
    Academy of Criminal Justice Sciences, Northern Kentucky University, 402 Nunn Hall, Highland Heights, KY 41076

LAE Journal of American Criminal Justice Associations
    American Criminal Justice Association, Lambda Alpha Epsilon, Sacramento, CA 95860

Law Enforcement News
Criminal Justice Center, John Jay College of Criminal Justice, 899 10th Ave., Suite 438, New York, NY 10019

Police Career Digest and Express Job Newsletters
The Law Enforcement Co., P.O. Box 1672 Eastern Park, FL 33801

Police Chief
International Association of Chiefs of Police, 1110 Glebe Rd., Suite 200, Arlington, VA 22201

Police Times
American Federation of Police, 1100 N.E. 125th Street, Miami, FL 33161

Policing: An International Journal of Police Strategies and Management
MCB University Press, 60/62 Toller Lane, Bradford, West Yorkshire, England BD8 9BY

Security Management
American Society for Industrial Security, 1655 N. Fort Myers Dr., Suite 1200, Arlington, VA 22209

Security World
Cahners Publishing Co., P.O. Box 5510, Denver, CO 80217

Resources for Further
Career Information

The following sources of information are provided to help you in your career search. Certainly, they do not represent all the agencies, organizations, programs, or other sources of information available; however, they do provide a good starting point. Begin to write or call to collect information and applications. Keep records of where you have called, with whom you have spoken, and where you have sent résumés or applications.

We have also included, where possible, appropriate E-mail addresses and Web sites for you to utilize. Happy surfing!!

Law Enforcement

Federal Law Enforcement Agencies

Bureau of Alcohol, Tobacco, & Firearms
Personnel Division
650 Massachusetts Avenue, N.W., Room 4100
Washington, DC 20226
202-927-8423
http://www.atf.treas.gov/
PersDiv@atfhq.atf.treas.gov

U.S. Capitol Police
Public Information Office
119 D Street, N.E.
Washington, DC 20510

U.S. Department of Health and Human Services
Office of Inspector General
200 Independence Ave., S.W,
Room 5246 Cohen Building
Washington, DC 20201
202-619-0257
http://www.dhhs.gov/progorg/oig/
esec@os.dhhs.gov

Defense Security Service
400 Army Navy Drive, Room 901-E
Arlington, VA 22202
Army Liaison 410-865-2255
Navy Liaison 410-865-2246
http://www.dis.mil/
webmaster@www.dis.mil

U.S. Department of Justice
950 Pennsylvania Avenue, N.W.
Washington, DC 20530-0001
http://www.usdoj.gov
web@usdoj.gov
U.S. Department of State
Recruitment Division
P.O. Box 9317
Arlington, VA 22219
202-647-4000
http://www.state.gov/
publicaffairs@panet.us-state.gov

Department of Transportation
Office of Inspector General
400 7th Street, S.W., Room 2440
Washington, DC 20590
202-366-8734
http://www.dot.gov/oig/

Drug Enforcement Administration
Information Services Section (CPI)
700 Army-Navy Drive
Arlington, VA 22202
800-DEA-4288
http://www.usdoj.gov/dea/

Environmental Protection Agency
Office of the Inspector General
401 M Street, S.W.
Washington, DC 20460
202-260-7784
http://www.epa.gov/oigearth/
public-access@epamail.epa.gov

Federal Bureau of Investigation
(Special Agents)
J. Edgar Hoover Building
935 Pennsylvania Avenue, N.W.
Washington, DC 20535-0001
(202) 324-3000
http://www.fbi.gov/

Federal Trade Commission
6th St. and Pennsylvania Ave., N.W.
Washington, DC 20580
202-326-2020
http://www.ftc.gov/
consumerline@ftc.gov

Food and Drug Administration
Personnel Officer
Rockville, MD 20857
800-532-4440
http://www.fda.gov/
execsec@oc.fda.gov

General Services Administration
Office of Inspector General
18th and F Streets, N.W.
Washington, DC 20405
800-424-5210
http://www.gsa.gov/
public.affairs@gsa.gov

Immigration and Naturalization Service
Border Patrol Examining Unit
425 I Street N.W., 2nd floor
Washington, DC 20536-0001
205-514-4316
http://www.ins.usdoj.gov/

Internal Revenue Service
1111 Constitution Avenue, N.W., Room
    103
Washington, DC 20224
http://www.irs.ustreas.gov/

National Security Agency
9800 Savage Road
Fort George G. Meade, MD 20755-6000
301-688-6524
http://www.nsa.gov:8080/

U.S. Naval Investigative Service
Washington Navy Yard
Building 200
Washington, DC 20374
202-433-3858
http://www.ncis.navy.mil,

United States Civil Service Commission
Office of Personnel Management
1900 E Street, N.W.
Washington, DC 20415

United States Park Police
Personnel Office
1100 Ohio Drive, S.W.
Washington, DC 20242
202-619-7056
http://www.doi.gov/u.s.park.police/
park_police@ios.doi.gov

U.S. Air Force Security Service
    (Intelligence)
Building 626
Boiling AFB
Washington, DC 20332-6001

U.S. Customs Service
Office of Human Resources
1300 Pennsylvania Avenue, N.W.
Washington, DC 20229
202-927-1250
http://www.customs.ustreas.gov/

U.S. Department of Agriculture
Office of the Inspector General
P.O. Box 23399
Washington, DC 20026-3399
800-424-9121
http://www.usda.gov/oig/

U.S. Department of Commerce
Office of the Inspector General
14th St. and Constitution Ave., N.W.
Washington, DC 20230
202-482-4661
http://www.oig.doc.gov/

U.S. Department of the Interior
Bureau of Land Management
Office of Public Affairs
1849 C Street, Room 406-LS
Washington, DC 20240
202-452-5125
http://www.blm.gov/
woinfo@wo.blm.gov

U.S. Department of Labor
Office of Inspector General
200 Constitution Avenue, N.W.,
    Room S-5508
Washington, DC 20210
202-219-6730
http://gatekeeper.dol.gov/dol/oig/

U.S. Fish and Wildlife Service
Division of Law Enforcement
P.O. Box 3247
Arlington, VA 22203-3247
703 -358-1949
http://www.fws.gov/
r9le_www@mail.fws.gov

U.S. Marshals Service
Employment and Compensation Divi-
    sion
Field Staffing Branch
600 Army Navy Drive
Arlington, VA 22202-4210
202-307-9600
http://www.usdoj.gov/marshals/

U.S. Postal Inspection Service
P.O. Box 96096
Washington, DC 20066-6096
202-636-2300
http://www.usps.gov/websites/depart/
    inspect
incsc@email.usps.gov

U.S. Secret Service
1050 Constitution Avenue, N.W.
Washington, DC 20036-5303
202-435-5100
http://www.treas.gov/usss/

State Police-Highway Agencies

ALABAMA
Alabama Department of Public Safety
P.O. Box 1511
Montgomery, AL 36102
334-242-4394

ALASKA
Alask Dept. of Public Safety
State Trooper Division
5700 East Tudor Road
Anchorage, AK 99507
907-269-5722
http://www.dps.state.ak.us/ast/
pdtemple@psafety.state.ak.us

ARIZONA
Department of Public Safety
P.O. Box 6638
Phoenix, AZ 85005-6638
602-223-2290
http://www.dps.state.az.us/
arizdps@primenet.com

ARKANSAS
Arkansas State Police
1 State Police Plaza Drive
Little Rock, AR 72209
501-618-8200

CALIFORNIA
California Highway Patrol
Office of Public Affairs
P.O. Box 942898
Sacramento, CA 94298-0001
http://www.chp.ca.gov/
Publicaffairs@chp.ca.gov.

COLORADO
Colorado State Patrol
700 Kipling
Lakewood, CO 80215
303-239-4500
http://www.state.co.us/gov_dir/cdps/
csp.htm
goodwinj@safety.state.co.us

CONNECTICUT
Connecticut State Police
Commissioner
1111 Country Club Road
Middletown, CT 06457-9294
860-685-8000
http://www.state.ct.us/dps/CSP.htm
DPS.Feedback@po.state.ct.us

DELAWARE
Department of Public Safety
Division of State Police
P.O. Box 430
Dover, DE 19903-0430
302-739-5900
http://www.state.de.us/govern/agen-
cies/pubsafe/dsp/indxdsp.htm
kcaskey@state.de.us

FLORIDA
Florida Highway Patrol
State Police
Neil Kirkman Building
2900 Apalachee Parkway
Tallahassee, FL 32399
850-922-5319
http://www.fdle.state.fl.us/

GEORGIA
Georgia State Police
Department of Public Safety
P.O. Box 1456
Atlanta, GA 30371
404-624-7710

HAWAII
State Sheriffs Department
1111 Alakea St., 2nd Floor
Honolulu, HI 96813
808-538-5659

IDAHO
Idaho State Police
P.O. Box 700
Meridian, ID 83680
208-884-7003

ILLINOIS
Illinois State Police
Recruitment Unit
3001 Montvale Drive
Suite F
Springfield, Illinois 62704
217-785-0183
http://www.state.il.us/isp/isphpage.htm

INDIANA
Indiana State Police
Superintendent
100 N. Senate Avenue
Indianapolis, IN 46204
317-232-8241

IOWA
State Capitol Police
Chief
Wallace State Office Building
Des Moines, IA 50319
515-281-5824

KANSAS
Kansas Highway Patrol
Support Services Department
Odd Elks Building
122 S.W. 7th Street
Topeka, KS 66603-3847
785-296-6800
http://www.ink.org/public/khp/

KENTUCKY
Division of State Police
Commissioner
919 Versailles Road
Frankfort, KY 40601
502-695-6303

LOUISIANA
State Police Division
P.O. Box 66614
Baton Rouge, LA 70896
504-925-6117

MAINE
Maine State Police
36 Hospital Street
Augusta, ME 04333
207-624-7074

MARYLAND
Public Affairs Office
Maryland State Police
1201 Reisterstown Road
Pikesville, Maryland 21208
http://www.inform.umd.edu/UMS+State
    /MD_Resources/MDSP/index.html
pauinfo@qis.net

MASSACHUSETTS
Superintendent
470 Worcester Road
Framingham, 01702
508-820-2232
http://www.magnet.state.ma.us/msp/
troopers@tiac.net

MICHIGAN
Michigan Department of State Police
714 S. Harrison Road
East Lansing, MI 48823
517-336-6157
http://www.voyager.net/msp/

MINNESOTA
Minnesota State Police
444 Cedar Street, Suite 100-A
St. Paul, MN 55101
612-297-3935

MISSISSIPPI
Mississippi State Highway Patrol
P.O. Box 958
Jackson, MS 39205
601-987-1212

MISSOURI
State Highway Patrol
Superintendent
1510 East Elm Street
Jefferson City, MO 65102
573-751-3313
http://www.dps.state.mo.us/dps/mshp/
    hp.htm
mshppied@mail.state.mo.us

MONTANA
Montana Highway Patrol
2550 Prospect Avenue
Helena, MT 59620-1419
406-444-3780

NEBRASKA
Nebraska State Patrol
Troop Commander
3601 West Mathis, #1028
Lincoln, NE 68524
402-471-4680
http://www.nebraska-state-patrol.org/
sdanahy@mail.state.ne.us

NEVADA
Nevada State Highway Patrol
555 Wright Way
Carson City, NV 89711-0525
http://www.state.nv.us/dmv_ps/
    nhphome.htm

NEW HAMPSHIRE
New Hampshire State Police
10 Hazen Drive
Concord, NH 03305
603-271-3636

NEW JERSEY
State Police Division
P.O. Box 7068
West Trenton, NJ 08628
609-882-2000

NEW MEXICO
New Mexico State Police
P.O. Box 1628
Santa Fe, NM 87504
505-827-3370

NEW YORK
New York State Police
1220 Washington Avenue, Bldg. 22
Albany, NY 12226
518-457-6721
http://www.troopers.state.ny.us/
nyspmail@troopers.state.ny.us

NORTH CAROLINA
Division of State Highway Patrol
P.O. Box 29590
512 N. Salisbury Street
Raleigh, NC 27626-0590
919-733-7952
http://www.geocities.com/Capitol-
    Hill/4473/
webmaster@ncshp.org

NORTH DAKOTA
North Dakota State Highway Patrol
Superintendent
600 E. Boulevard Avenue
Bismarck, ND 58505-0241

OHIO
State Highway Patrol
Superintendent
660 East Main Street
Columbus, OH 43205
614-466-4991
http://www.odn.ohio.gov/ohp/
wwwohp@ohio.gov

OKLAHOMA
Oklahoma Department of Public Safety
Highway Patrol
Box 11415
Oklahoma City, OK 73136
405-425-2000
http://www.dps.state.ok.us/ohp/
smeyer@dps.state.ok.us

OREGON
Department of State Police
Superintendent
400 Public Service Building
Salem, OR 97310
503-378-3720
http://www.osp.state.or.us/
osp.webmaster@state.or.us

PENNSYLVANIA
Pennsylvania State Police
Department Headquarters
1800 Elmerton Avenue
Harrisburg, PA 17110
717-783-5599
http://www.state.pa.us/PA_Exec/
    State_Police/

RHODE ISLAND
Rhode Island State Police
Superintendent
311 Danielson Pike
North Scituate, RI 02857
401-444-1000

SOUTH CAROLINA
South Carolina State Highway Patrol
Law Enforcement Division
5400 Broad River Road
Columbia, SC 29210
803-896-7992

SOUTH DAKOTA
South Dakota Highway Patrol
Superintendent
500 East Capitol Avenue
Pierre, SD 57501
605-773-3105

TENNESSEE
Highway Patrol Division
Department of Safety
1150 Foster Avenue
Nashville, TN 37249
615-251-5166

TEXAS
Department of Public Safety
P.O. Box 4087
Austin, TX 78773
512-424-2000

UTAH
Highway Patrol
Superintendent
4501 South 2700 West
P.O. Box 141100
Salt Lake City, UT 84114
801-965-4518

VERMONT
Vermont State Police
Public Safety Department
Waterburg State Complex
103 South Main Street
Waterbury, VT 05671
802-244-8718

VIRGINIA
Department of State Police
Superintendent
P.O. Box 27472
Richmond, VA 23261-7472
804-674-2000
http://dit1.state.va.us/vsp/vsp.html
cvaughan.vsp@state.va.us

WASHINGTON
Washington State Patrol
P.O. Box 426000
Olympia, WA 98504
360-753-6545
http://www.wa.gov/wsp/wsphome.htm
webmaster@wsp.wa.gov

WEST VIRGINIA
West Virginia State Police
Superintendent
725 Jefferson Road
South Charleston, WV 25309
304-746-2111

WISCONSIN
Wisconsin State Patrol
P.O. Box 604
Tomah, Wisconsin 54660-0604
608-374-0513
http://www.geocities.com/Capitol-
    Hill/5952/
SRWilliams@Centuryinter.net

WYOMING
Wyoming Highway Patrol
Patrol Division
P.O. Box 1708
Cheyenne, WY 82003

For additional information concerning
state-level positions, contact the appropriate civil service commission.

Law Enforcement – Organizations

County/Local Law Enforcement Agencies

Students interested in possible hiring on the county and municipal level should contact the representative of the civil service commission and/or personnel officer of the county or municipal police departments. Also, consult the resources listed on pp. 197-201. Many of these resources provide listings of state and local agencies in the Criminal Justice system that employ personnel at this level.

Professional Organizations, Societies

Academy of Criminal Justice Sciences
Northern Kentucky University
402 Nunn Hall
Highland Heights, KY 41099-5998

American Federation of Police
3801 Biscayne Boulevard
Miami, FL 33137
http://www.aphf.org/p14_afop.html
policeinfo@aphf.org

Fraternal Order of Police
PO Box 17127
719 Lynn Street
Louisville, KY 40217
502-637-3371
http://www.kyfop25.org/
kyfop25@kyfop25.org

International Association of Chiefs
of Police
515 N. Washington Street
Alexandria, VA 22314-2357
800-THE IACP
http://www.theiacp.org/

National Association of Chiefs of Police
3801 Biscayne Boulevard
Miami, FL 33137
305-573-0070
http://www.aphf.org/p15_nacop.html
policeinfo@aphf.org

National Organization of Black
Law Enforcement Executives
NOBLE National Office
4609 Pinecrest Office Park Drive, Suite F
Alexandria, VA 22312-1442
703-658-1529
http://www.noblenatl.org/
noble@noblenatl.org

National Sheriffs' Association
1450 Duke Street
Alexandria, Virginia 22314-3490
703-836-7827
http://www.sheriffs.org/
nsamail@sheriffs.org?subject=nsa

The Police Foundation
1001 22nd Street, N.W., Suite 200
Washington, DC 20037

Courts

Federal Level

Administrative Office of the U.S. Courts
811 Vermont Avenue, N.W.
Washington, DC 20544

State and Local Levels

To secure information regarding employment on the state and local level, it is best advised to contact the administrative office of the state courts, usually located in the state capital or one of the state's major cities.

Professional Organizations, Societies

Academy of Criminal Justice Sciences
Northern Kentucky University
402 Nunn Hall
Highland Heights, KY 41099-5998

American Bar Association
750 North Lake Shore Drive
Chicago, IL 60611
312-988-5000
http://www.abanet.org/
info@abanet.org

The Federal Bar Association
1815 H Street N.W., Suite 408
Washington, DC 20006
202-638-0252
http://www.fedbar.org/
fba@fedbar.org

Institute of Judicial Administration
One Washington Square Village
New York, NY 10012

Association of Trial Lawyers of America
1050 31st Street, N.W.
Washington, DC 20007
800-424-2725
http://www.atlanet.org/public.ht
help@atlahq.org.

National Association of Criminal
    Defense Lawyers
1110 Vermont Avenue, N.W.
Washington, DC 20005

National Association of Women Lawyers
750 North Lake Shore Drive
Chicago, IL 60611

National Center for State Courts
300 Newport Avenue
Williamsburg, VA 23185
757-253-2000
http://www.ncsc.dni.us/
webmaster@ncsc.dni.us

National Criminal Justice
Reference Service (NCJRS)
16000 Research Boulevard
Rockville, MD 20850

National District Attorneys
Association (NDAA)
1033 North Fairfax Street
Alexandria, VA 23314

National Shorthand
Reporters Association
118 Park Street, S.E.
Vienna, VA 22180

Corrections

Federal Level

Federal Bureau of Prisons
Central Office
320 First Street, N.W.
Washington, DC 20534

South Central Regional Office
4211 Cedar Springs Road
Dallas, TX 75219

Southeast Regional Office
5213 McDonough Boulevard, S.E.
Atlanta, GA 30315

North Central Regional Office
Gateway Complex Tower II, 8th Floor
4th and State Avenue
Kansas City, KS 66101-2492

Northeast Regional Office
U.S. Customs House, 7th Floor
2nd and Chestnut Street
Philadelphia, PA 19106

Western Regional Office
7950 Dublin Boulevard
Dublin, CA 94568

State and Local Levels

If you are interested in working in a corrections occupation at the state or local level, contact the Department of Corrections in the state, county, or city in which you live or desire to be employed.

Departments of Corrections

Department of Corrections
P.O. Box 301501
101 S Union Square
Montgomery, AL 36130-1501

Department of Corrections
P.O. Box 112000
Juneau, AK 99811

Department of Corrections
1601 W Jefferson
Phoenix, AZ 85007

Department of Corrections
P.O. Box 8707
Pine Bluff, AR 71611

Department of Corrections
1515 S Street
P.O. Box 942883
Sacramento, CA 94283-0001

State Department of Corrections
2862 South Circle Drive, Suite 400
Colorado Springs, CO 80906-4195

Department of Corrections
24 Wolcott Hill Road
Wethersfield, CT 06109-1152

Department of Corrections
80 Monrovia Avenue
Smyrna, DE 19977-1597

Department of Corrections
1923 Vermont Avenue, N.W.
Washington, DC 20001

Department of Corrections
2691 Blair Stone Road
Tallahassee, FL 32301

Department of Corrections
2 Martin Luther King Drive
Atlanta, GA 30334

Department of Corrections
919 Ala Moana Boulevard
Honolulu, HI 96814

Department of Corrections
P.O. Box 83720
500 S. 10th
Statehouse Mail
Boise, ID 83709-0018

Department of Corrections
1301 Concordia Court
Springfield, IL 62794-9277

Department of Corrections
302 W. Washington Street
Indianapolis, IN 46204-2278

Division of Adult Corrections
Capitol Annex
Des Moines, IA 50319-0001

Department of Corrections
900 S.W. Jackson
Topeka, KS 66612-1284

Bureau of Corrections
State Office Building
Frankfort, KY 40601

Department of Corrections
Box 94304
Baton Rouge, LA 70804-9304

Department of Mental Health & Corrections
State House Station #111
Augusta, ME 04333

Division of Corrections
6776 Reisterstown Road
Suite 311
Baltimore, MD 21215

Department of Corrections
100 Cambridge Street
Boston, MA 02202

Department of Corrections
3rd Floor, Mason Building
P.O. Box 30003
Lansing, MI 48909

Department of Corrections
1450 Energy Park Drive
Suite 200
St. Paul, MN 55108-5219

Department of Corrections
723 North President Street
Jackson, MS 39202-3097

Division of Corrections
2729 Plaza Dr.
P.O. Box 236
Jefferson City, MO 65102-0236

Department of Institutions
1539 11th Avenue
Helena, MT 59620-1301

Department of Correctional Services
W. Van Dorn and Folsom Streets
P.O. Box 94661
Lincoln, NE 68509-4461

Department of Prisons
P.O. Box 7011
Carson City, NV 89702-7011

Department of Corrections
P.O. Box 1806
Concord, NH 03302-1806

Office of the Commissioner
Department of Corrections
CN 863
Trenton, NJ 08625-0863

Department of Corrections
P.O. Box 27116
Santa Fe, NM 87502-0116

Department of Correctional Services
1220 Washington Avenue
Building 2
Albany, NY 12226

Department of Corrections
214 W Jones Street
P.O. Box 29540
Raleigh, NC 27626-0540

Director of Institutions
State Penitentiary
P.O. Box 1898
Bismarck, ND 58502-1898

Department of Rehabilitation
& Corrections
1050 Freeway Drive North
Columbus, OH 43229

Department of Corrections
3400 Martin Luther King Avenue
Oklahoma City, OK 73136-0400

Department of Corrections
2575 Center Street, N.E.
Salem, OR 97310-0470

Department of Corrections
P.O. Box 598
Camp Hill, PA 17001-0598

Department of Corrections
40 Howard Avenue
Cranston, RI 02920

Department of Corrections
4444 Broad River Road
P.O. Box 21787
Columbia, SC 29221-1787

Department of Corrections
115 E Dakota Avenue
Pierre, SD 57501-3216

Department of Corrections
320 6th Avenue North
Nashville, TN 37243-0465

Department of Corrections
P.O. Box 99
Huntsville, TX 77342-0099

Department of Corrections
6100 S. South Fashion Blvd
Murray, UT 84107

Department of Corrections
103 S. Main Street
Waterbury, VT 05671-1001

State Department of Corrections
P.O. Box 26963
6900 Atmore Drive
Richmond, VA 23261-6963

Department of Corrections
P.O. Box 41101
Olympia, WA 98504-1100

Division of Corrections
112 California Avenue
Charleston, WV 25305

Division of Corrections
Health & Social Services Dept.
P.O. Box 7925
Madison, WI 53707-7925

Board of Charities & Reform
Herschler Building
Cheyenne, WY 82002

Academic Forensic Science Programs

Peterson's Guide to Four Year Colleges (1998) lists the following institutions as offering a major in Forensic Science.

Austin Peay State University
Clarksville, TN 37044-0002

California State University
Sacramento, CA 95819

Central State University
Edmond, OK 73034

Chaminade University of Honolulu
Honolulu, HI

College of the Ozarks
Point Lookout, MO 65726

Eastern Kentucky University
Richmond, KY 40475

Indiana University at Bloomington
Bloomington, IN 47405

Jacksonville State University
Jacksonville, AL 36265

John Jay College of Criminal Justice
445 West 59th Street
New York, NY 10019

Manhattan College
Riverdale, NY 10471

Ohio University
Athens, OH 45701

Point Park College
Pittsburgh, PA 15222-1984

St. John's University
Grand Central and Utopia Parkway
Queens, NY 11439

Southern Illinois University at Carbondale
Carbondale, IL 62901-4399

State University of New York
College at Buffalo
Buffalo, NY 14214

University of Central Florida
Orlando, FL 32816

University of Central Oklahoma
Edmond, OK 73034-0100

University of Mississippi
University, MS 38677

University of New Haven
West Haven, CT 06516

West Chester University of Pennsylvania
West Chester, PA 19383

U.S. Forensic Science Labs

Information regarding State Forensic Science Labs was edited from the World List of Forensic Science Labs, Forensic Science Society, New Yorkshire, England, 1997.

ALABAMA
Alabama Dept. of Forensic Sciences
P.O. Box 3510
Auburn, AL 36830-3510
33-887-3510
http://www.adfs.com

ARIZONA
Forensic Science Laboratory
3034 W. Kristal Way
Phoenix, AZ 85027
602-582-2063

Phoenix Crime Laboratory
620 W. Washington Avenue
Phoenix, AZ 85003
602-262-6197

ARKANSAS
Arkansas State Crime Laboratory
P.O. Box 8500
Little Rock, AK 72215
501-227-5747

CALIFORNIA
Kern County Regional Crime Laboratory
1431 L Street
Bakersfield, CA 93301
805-861-7656

Forensic Science Group
School of Public Health
University of California
Berkeley, CA 94720-7360
510-642-1271

California Department of Justice
Fresno Lab
6014 North Cedar Avenue
Fresno, CA 93710
209-278-2982

COLORADO
Colorado Bureau of Investigation
690 Kipling Street, Suite 4000
Denver, CO 80215
303-239-4303

Analytical Genetic Testing Center
7808 Cherry Creek South Drive, Apt. 201
Denver, CO 80231
303-750-2023
http://www.geneticid.com

CONNECTICUT
Department of Public Safety
State Police Forensic Science Labortory
278 Colony Street
Meriden, CT 06451
203-238-6324

Lifecodes Corporation
550 West Avenue
Stamford, CT 06902
203-328-9500
http://www.lifecodes.com

DISTRICT OF COLUMBIA
The George Washington University
2036 II Street N.W., Samson Hall 101
Washington, DC 20052
202-994-7319
http://www.gwu.edu/~fors

FLORIDA
University of Miami
Division Forensic Pathology
2221 S.W. 29th Avenue
Fort Lauderdale, FL 33312-4364
954-791-1917
http://pathology.miami.edu

DEA/SEL
5205 N.W. 8th Avenue
Miami, FL 33166
305-590-4830

GEORGIA
Hans Mayer Gidion
Forensic Examiner of Questioned Docs
218 Merrymont Drive
Augusta, GA 30907
706-860-4267

Carney & Hammond
Forensic Document Laboratory
4078 Biltmore Woods Court
Buford, GA 30519-6906
770-614-4440

HAWAII
Honolulu Police Department
Scientific Investigation Section
801 S. Beretania Street
Honolulu, HI 96813
808-529-3281

ILLINOIS
Illinois State Police
Southern Illinois Forensic Science
    Centre
606 E. College
Carbondale, IL 62901
618-457-6714

Hayes Forensic Document Laboratory
221 North LaSalle Street
Chicago, IL 60601-1206
312-236-5186

INDIANA
Department of Chemistry
Indiana-Purdue University
2101 Coliseum Boulevard
Fort Wayne, IN 46805
219-481-6289
http://cvax.ipfw.indiana.edu/chem-
    istry/kimble.htm

Indianapolis-Marion County
Forensic Services Agency
40 S Alabama Street
Indianapolis, IN 46204
317-327-3670

KANSAS
Wichita State University Biological
    Anthropology Laboratory
130 McKinley Hall
Wichita, KS 67260-0052
316-978-3195

KENTUCKY
Kentucky State Police Forensic
    Laboratory
100 Sower Boulevard, Suite 102
Louisville, KY 40601-8272
502-564-5230

LOUISIANA
William J. Farrell, Jr.
P.O. Box 6974
Metairie, LA 70009
504-469-0275

MARYLAND
Maryland State Police Crime Laboratory
1201 Reisterstown Road
Baltimore, MD 21208
410-653-4500

National Center for Forensic Science
3411 Philips Drive
Baltimore, MD 21208-1827
410-486-7486

U.S. Treasury, Bureau of Alcohol,
    Tobacco & Firearms,
ATF Forensic Science Laboratory
1401 Research Boulevard
Rockville, MD 20850
310-413-5227

MASSACHUSSETTS
Massachussetts State Police Crime Lab
59 Norse Pond Road
Sudbury, MA 01776
508-358-3104

MICHIGAN
Michigan State Police Crime Laboratory
720 Fuller Avenue, N.E.
Grand Rapid, MI 49503-1918

MINNESOTA
Forensic Nursing Services
Route 1, Box 171
Comfrey, MN 56019-9713
507-877-3663

MN BCA Forensic Science Laboratory
1246 University Avenue
Saint Paul, MN 55104
612-642-0700

MISSOURI
Independence Missouri Police Forensic
    Laboratory
223 North Memorial Drive
Independence, MO 64050
816-325-7325

MSSC Regional Crime Laboratory
3950 E. Newman Road
Joplin, MO 64801
417-625-9382

NEBRASKA
Nebraska State Patrol Criminalistics
    Laboratory
1600 Highway 2
Lincoln, NE 68502-5482
402-479-4941

Dr. John Vasiliades
Toxicology Labs Inc.
7701 Pacific Street, Suite 300
Omaha, NE 68114-5422
402-392-1086

NEVADA
Washoe County Sheriff's Department
Forensic Science Division
911 Parr Boulevard
Reno, NV 89512-1000
702-328-2800

NEW HAMPSHIRE
New Hampshire State Police Forensice
    Laboratory
Department of Safety
10 Hazen Drive
Concord, NH 03305
603-271-3573

NEW JERSEY
New Jersey State Police South Regional
    Laboratory
1101 South White Horse Pike
Hammonton, NJ 08037
609-561-2060

New Jersey State Police North Regional
    Laboratory
1755 Route 46 East
Little Falls, NJ 07424
201-256-7790

New Jersey State Police East Regional
    Laboratory
Sea Girt Avenue
Sea Girt, NJ 08750-2990
908-449-0303

NEW MEXICO
Albuquerque Police Crime Laboratory
400 Roma, N.W.
Albuquerque, NM 87120
505-768-2230

NEW YORK
Laboratory of Forensic Science
P.O. Box 1111
Corning, NY 14830
607-962-6581

Bender Hygienic Laboratory
9 Samaritan Drive
Albany, NY 12208
518-472-9124

Suffolk County Crime Laboratory
North County Complex, Bldg. 487
Hauppage, NY 11787-4311
516-853-5585

NORTH CAROLINA
Federal Forensic Associates Inc.
P.O. Box 31567
Raleigh, NC 27622-1567
919-848-3696

Maureen Casey Owens
153 Spring Creek Lane
Wilmington, NC 28405
910-686-9110

OHIO
Smithers Scientific Services Inc.
425 West Market Street
Akron, OH 44303-2099
330-762-7441
http://www.smithers-scientific.com

Tri-State Laboratories Inc
2870 Salt Springs Road
Youngstown, OH 44509
330-797-8844

OKLAHOMA
Toxicology & Accident Research
    Laboratory
AAM-610 Federal Aviation
    Administration
Civil Aeromedical Institute
P.O. Box 25082
Oklahoma City, OK 405-954-4866

Tulsa Police Department Forensic
    Laboratory
600 Civic Center
Tulsa, OK 74103-3822
918-596-9128

OREGON
National Fish & Wildlife Forensic
    Laboratory
1490 East Main Street
Ashland, OR 97520
541-482-4191
http://www.lab.fws.gov/labweb/for
    lab.htm

Richard Lazere PhD. PC
1130 S.W. Morrison Street, Suite 520
Portland, OR 97205-2216
503-223-3238
http://www.pacifier.com./~Hunter

PENNSYLVANIA
Analytic Bio-Chemistries Inc.
1680-D Loretta Avenue
Feasterville, PA 19053-7311
215-322-9210

National Medical Services
3701 Welsh Road
Willow Grove, PA 19090
215-657-4900
http://www.nmslab.com

PUERTO RICO
Institute of Forensic Sciences
P.O. Box 11878
Cappara Heights Station
San Juan, PR 00922
787-765-0615

TENNESSEE
University of Tennessee Chemical
Pathology and Toxicology Laboratory
3 N. Dunlap Street
Memphis, TN 38163
901-448-6355

TEXAS
South Central Laboratory (DEA)
1880 Regal Row
Dallas, TX 75235
214-640-0964

Texas Department of Public Safety
Crime Laboratory
1302 6th Street
Lubbock, TX 79401
806-747-4491

UTAH
Criminalistics Lab
Weber State University
1206 University Circle
Ogden, UT 84408-1206
801-626-6148

Utah Department of Public Safety
Box 148285
4501 South 2700 West
Salt Lake City, UT 84114-8285
801-965-4487

VIRGINIA
Criminal Justice/Public Safety
7525 Colshire Drive
McLean, VA 22102
703-610-1503

Naval Criminal Investigative Service
Regional Forensic Lab
9079 Hampton Boulevard, Suite 110
Norfolk, VA 23505-1098
757-444-8615

Virginia Division of Forensic Science
1 North 14th Street
Richmond, VA 23219
804-786-2281

WASHINGTON
Washington State Toxicology Laboratory
Department of Laboratory Medicine
University of Washington
2203 Airport Way S.
Seattle, WA 98134
206-343-5435

Washington State Patrol Crime
    Laboratory
2nd Floor Public Safety Building
Seattle, WA 98104
206-464-7074

WISCONSIN
State Crime Laboratory – Milwaukee
1578 South 11th Street
Milwaukee, WI 53204-2860
414-382-7500

WYOMING
Wyoming State Crime Laboratory
316 West 22nd Street
Cheyenne, WY 82002
307-777-7607

Professional Organizations, Societies

Academy of Criminal Justice Sciences
Northern Kentucky University
402 Nunn Hall
Highland Heights, KY 41099-5998

American Academy of Forensic
    Scientists
225 South Academy Boulevard
Suite 201
Colorado Springs, CO 80910

American Society of Questioned
Document Examiners, Inc.
1432 Esperson Building
Houston, TX 77002
http://www.asqde.org/
webeditor@asqde.org

The Forensic Sciences Foundation, Inc.
P.O. Box 669
Colorado Springs, CO 80901-0669
719-636-1100
http://www.aafs.org/career/Career
    Broch.html
membship@aafs.org

International Association for
    Identification
2535 Pilot Knob Road, Suite #117
Mendota Heights, MN 55120
http://206.241.48.46/
iaisecty@aol.com

International Narcotic Enforcement
    Officer's Association
112 State Street
Albany, NY 12207

Milton Helpern Institute of
    Forensic Medicine
520 First Avenue
New York, NY 10016

Security

Professional Organizations, Societies

Academy of Criminal Justice Sciences
Northern Kentucky University
402 Nunn Hall
Highland Heights, KY 41099-5998

Academy of Security Educators and
    Trainers (ASET)
Route 2
Box 3644
Berryville, VA 22611

American Society for Industrial Security
1625 Prince Street
Alexandria, VA 22314-2818
703-519-6200
http://www.asisonline.org/
news@infoinc.com

American Society of Safety Engineers
1800 E. Oakton Street
Des Plaines, IL 60018
847-699-2929
http://www.asse.org/
customerservice@asse.org

International Security Management
    Association (ISMA)
P.O. Box 623
Buffalo, IA 52728

National Fire Protection Association
1 Batterymarch Park
Quincy, MA 02269-9101
617-770-3000
http://www.nfpa.org/
library@nfpa.org

National Safety Council
1121 Spring Lake Drive
Itasca, IL 60143-3201
630-285-1121
http://www.nsc.org/

National Burglar and Fire Alarms
    Association
7101 Wisconsin Avenue, #901
Bethesda, MD 20814
301-907-3202
http://www.alarm.org/
staff@alarm.org

Federal Job Information Centers

For information about federal employment, contact the FJIC nearest you. For
career information call Career America
(912) 757-3000 (24 hours a day, 7 days a
week).

ALABAMA
520 Wynn Drive, N.W.
Huntsville, AL 35816-3426
205-837-0894

ALASKA
Federal Building
222 West 7th Avenue, #22, Rm. 156
Anchorage, AK 99513-7572

ARIZONA
VA Medical Center
650 E. Indian School Road, Building 21
Room 141
Phoenix, AZ 85012

ARKANSAS
(See listing for San Antonio, TX.)

CALIFORNIA
211 Main Street, 2nd Floor, #235
San Francisco, CA 94120
415-744-5627

COLORADO
12345 West Alameda Parkway
Lakewood, CO 80225
303-969-7050

CONNECTICUT
Federal Building #133
450 Main Street
Hartford, CT 06103
(For additional information services, see
Massachusetts)

DELAWARE
(See listing for Philadelphia, PA)

DISTRICT OF COLUMBIA
Theodore Roosevelt Federal Building
1900 E Street N.W., Room 1416
Washington, DC 20415
202-606-2700

FLORIDA
Downtown Jobs and Benefits Center
Florida Job Service Center
401 N.W. 2nd Avenue, Suite N-214
Miami, FL 33130
205-536-6738

GEORGIA
Richard B. Russell Federal Building
Main Lobby, #940A
75 Spring Street, S.W.
Atlanta, GA 30303
404-331-4315

HAWAII
Federal Building, Room #5316
300 Ala Moana Boulevard
Honolulu, HI 96850
808-541-2791

IDAHO
(See listing for Washington State)

ILLINOIS
77 W. Jackson Blvd., #530, First Floor
      Lobby
Chicago, IL 60604
312-353-6189

INDIANA
Minton-Capehart Federal Building, #339
575 N. Pennsylvania Street
Indianapolis, IN 46204
313-226-6950
(For additional information services, see
listing for Michigan. For Clark, Dearborn,
and Floyd Counties, see listing for Ohio.)

IOWA
(See listing for Kansas City, MO. For
Scott County, see listing for Illinois.)

KANSAS
(See listing for Kansas City, MO)

KENTUCKY
(See listing for Ohio. For Henderson
County, see listing for Michigan.)

LOUISIANA
Federal Building, First Floor Lobby
423 Canal Street
New Orleans, LA 70112
(For phone contact, see listing for San
Antonio, TX.)

MAINE
(See listing for Massachusetts.)

MARYLAND
George H. Fallon Building, Lobby
Lombard Street and Hopkins Plaza
Baltimore, MD 21201
(For phone contact, see lsiting for
Philadelphia, PA.)

MICHIGAN
477 Michigan Avenue, #565
Detroit, MI 48226
313-226-6950

MINNESOTA
Bishop Henry Whipple Federal Building
    #501
1 Federal Drive
Ft. Snelling, MN 55111
612-725-3430

MISSISSIPPI
(See listing for Alabama.)

MISSOURI
Federal Building #134
601 E. 12th Street
Kansas City, MO 64106
816-426-5702

MONTANA
(See listing for Colorado.)

NEBRASKA
(See listing for Kansas City, MO.)

NEW HAMPSHIRE
Thomas McIntyre Federal Building, First
    Floor Lobby
80 Daniel Street
Portsmouth, NH 03801
(For additional information services, see
    listing for Massachusetts.)

NEW JERSEY
Rodino Federal Building, Second Floor
970 Broad Street
Newark, NJ 07102

NEW MEXICO
New Mexico State Job Service
501 Mountain Road, N.E., Lobby
Albuquerque, NM 87102

NEW YORK
Jacob K. Javits Federal Building, Lobby
26 Federal Plaza
New York, NY 10278
or
James Hanley Federal Building
100 S. Clinton Street
Syracuse, NY 13261

NORTH CAROLINA
4407 Bland Road, #202
Raleigh, NC 27609
919-790-2822

NORTH DAKOTA
(See listing for Minnesota)

OHIO
Federal Building, #509
200 West Second Street
Dayton, OH 45402
513-225-2720

OKLAHOMA
(See listing for San Antonio, TX.)

OREGON
Federal Building, Room 376
1220 S.W. 3rd Avenue
Portland, OR 97204

PENNSYLVANIA
Federal Building, Room 168
228 Walnut Street
Harrisburg, PA 17108
717-782-4494
or
William J. Green, Jr., Federal Building
Second Floor
600 Arch Street
Philadelphia, PA 19106
215-596-7440

PUERTO RICO
U.S. Federal Building, #328
150 Carlos Chardon Avenue
San Juan, PR 00918
787-766-5242

RHODE ISLAND
(See listing for Massachusetts.)

SOUTH CAROLINA
(See listing for North Carolina.)

SOUTH DAKOTA
(See listing for Minnesota.)

TENNESSEE
Naval Air Station, Transition Assistance
    Center
7800 3rd Avenue, Building South 239
Memphis, TN
(For mail or telephone, see listing for
Alabama)

TEXAS
1100 Commerce Street
First Floor Lobby, #6B10
Dallas, TX 75242
or
Federal Building
First Floor Lobby
727 East Durango
San Antonio, TX 78217
210-805-2402

VERMONT
Federal Building
First Floor Lobby
11 Elmwood Avenue
Burlington, VT 05401
(For additional information services, see
Massachusetts.)

VIRGIN ISLANDS
(See listing for Puerto Rico.)

VIRGINIA
Federal Building %500
200 Granby Street
Norfolk, VA 23510
757-441-3355

WASHINGTON
Federal Building #110
915 Second Avenue
Seattle, WA 98174
206-553-0888

WASHINGTON, DC
(See listing for District of Columbia.)

WEST VIRGINIA
(See listing for Ohio)

WISCONSIN
(See listing for either Illinois or
Minnesota.)

WYOMING
(See listing for Colorado.)

About the Authors

Robert C. De Lucia, Ed.D., is Professor and Director of the Counseling Department at John Jay College of Criminal Justice in New York City. In addition to co-authoring *Career Planning in Criminal Justice*, De Lucia is editor and co-author of *Urban Learners: Serious about College Success* and has written numerous articles on college and career adjustment. He is a clinical member of the American Association of Marriage and Family Therapists and often collaborates in workshops and in private practice with his wife and co-therapist, Dr. Maria Grace La Russo. De Lucia is the father of two children, Benjamin and Matthew.

Thomas J. Doyle, M.S., is the Coordinating Director of Cooperative Education and Internships at John Jay College where he is liaison to the Drug Enforcement Administration, the U.S. Marshal's Service, U.S. Customs Service, and other agencies. Doyle has worked in the field of criminal justice career planning his entire working life. He holds a Bachelor's Degree in English and a Master's Degree in Criminal Justice. Doyle is the father of two children, Shayne Nicole and Thomas Jr.